Theorizing Patriarchy

Sylvia Walby

D1393796

BLACKWELL
Oxford UK & Cambridge USA

First published 1990
Reprinted 1991, 1992, 1993, 1994 (twice), 1995, 1997

Blackwell Publishers Ltd
108 Cowley Road
Oxford OX4 1JF, UK

Blackwell Publishers Inc
350 Main Street
Malden, Massachusetts 02148, USA

British Library Cataloguing in Publication Data
A CIP catalogue record for this book is available from the British Library

Library of Congress Catalog Card Number: 89–18057

ISBN 0–631–14769–1 (paperback)

Typeset in 10 on 12pt Sabon
by Wearside Tradespools, Fulwell, Sunderland
Printed and bound in Great Britain
by Athenæum Press Ltd, Gateshead, Tyne & Wear

This book is printed on acid-free paper

Contents

Acknowledgements

A lot of people over the last ten years have assisted in this book, whether knowingly or not, with comments on papers and talks which eventually became incorporated in the text. In particular I should like to thank the following for comments and for support: the Women's Studies Research Group at the University of Lancaster; Jackie Stacey, Celia Lury, John Urry, Paul Bagguley, Anne Witz, Lisa Adkins, Dan Shapiro, Alan Warde; all my students on the Women in Society course at the University of Lancaster over the last ten years for engaging in and debating the ideas behind the book; and Chris Quinn for expert assistance and support with the production of the manuscript.

List of tables

1

Introduction

Why are women disadvantaged compared to men? Has this inequality been reduced in recent years? What difference, if any, does the increase in women's employment make to other areas of women's lives? Is the sexual double standard a thing of the past? Are contemporary forms of femininity as restricting as those of the past? Is it useful to talk of 'femininity' as if it had one form? Is the increase in the divorce rate a sign of women's independence or of men's flight from family responsibilities?

This book aims to be, firstly, a comprehensive overview of the variety of ways of explaining women's subordination in contemporary society, and, secondly, an argument about why recent changes have occurred.

Answers to the questions posed above fall into four distinctive perspectives: Marxist feminism, radical feminism, liberalism, and dual-systems theory. This book will compare and evaluate the variety of frameworks against theoretical and empirical evidence. Other debates which cross-cut these divisions will be explored when they are particularly important, for instance, the new interest in post-structuralism and the critique of essentialism. The theoretical debates are the substance of the book, but up-to-date empirical evidence of the nature of gender inequality is used to assist in their assessment.

The second aim of the book is to argue for a particular approach to the analysis of recent changes in gender relations. It will ask about the relative importance of different sites of women's oppression and how this varies over time and between different social groups. Finally I will argue for a new way of theorizing patriarchy.

The six main chapters will have a different substantive focus: paid work, housework, culture, sexuality, violence, and the state. In each the first part will review the existing debates; the second will address recent developments.

During the course of the book I shall argue that the concept of 'patriarchy' is indispensable for an analysis of gender inequality and put forward a theory as to how its constituent elements articulate in contemporary Britain. Critics of the concept have argued that it necessarily invokes an essentialist, ahistoric analysis which is insensitive to the range of experiences of women of different cultures, classes and ethnicities (e.g., Barrett, 1980; Rowbotham, 1981). I shall argue that these criticisms are misplaced, relevant only to a few of the cruder early accounts. On the contrary, the concept and theory of patriarchy is essential to capture the depth, pervasiveness and interconnectedness of different aspects of women's subordination, and can be developed in such a way as to take account of the different forms of gender inequality over time, class and ethnic group.

The analysis of patriarchy in this book is most applicable to contemporary Western societies and their recent histories, in particular Britain. Since I am arguing that patriarchy can take different forms it would be inappropriate to assume that this model will necessarily apply elsewhere, though it may.

The book is structured by the cross-cutting of two questions: each chapter addresses the nature and significance of gender inequality in a different sphere as well as comparing different perspectives on that area. This introductory chapter will specify the different perspectives and some of the key debates. The conclusion draws together the argument as to the relative significance of different bases of women's oppression, by means of a historical analysis of the changing forms of patriarchy.

THEORETICAL PERSPECTIVES

In Britain the classic debate within feminist analysis has been between radical feminism and Marxist feminism; in the USA it has been between radical feminism and liberal feminism (Mitchell, 1971; Eisenstein, Z. R., 1981). More recently there has been an attempt to synthesize Marxist feminist and radical feminist analysis in dual-systems theory. In this book I shall deal with all four of these feminist perspectives and their sub-types. I shall start with a simple summary of the main theoretical features of the different perspectives and the main sites that they focus upon. These rather crude ideal types will be explored in much more detail in subsequent chapters.

While most of the interesting work on gender inequality has been done within feminist perspectives, this is sometimes in reaction to the 'malestream' orthodoxies. It is thus useful to give an account of these in order to understand not only errors of the conventional perspectives in the social sciences, but also the shape of the alternative feminist arguments. I shall thus give accounts of both functionalism and class analysis and their mistakes.

Radical feminism

Radical feminism is distinguished by its analysis of gender inequality in which men as a group dominate women as a group and are the main beneficiaries of the subordination of women. This system of domination, called patriarchy, does not derive from any other system of social inequality; for instance, it is not a by-product of capitalism. The relationship of patriarchy to class inequality and racism is addressed in different ways among radical writers.

Radical feminist writers introduce a range of issues into social science which have conventionally not been considered to be part of an analysis of social inequality. Even personal aspects of life are seen as part of this, as the slogan 'the personal is political' indicates. The question of who does the housework, or who interrupts whom in conversation, is seen as part of the system of male domination.

There are differences between radical feminists over the basis of male supremacy, but often this is considered to involve the appropriation of women's sexuality and bodies, while in some accounts male violence is seen as the root cause (e.g., Brownmiller, 1976; Firestone, 1974; Rich, 1980). Sexual practice is seen to be socially constructed around male notions of desire, not women's. Further, sexuality is seen as a major site of male domination over women, through which men impose their notion of femininity on women. Heterosexuality is socially institutionalized in contemporary society and organizes many other aspects of gender relations. Male violence against women is considered to be part of a system of controlling women, unlike the conventional view which holds that rape and battering are isolated instances caused by psychological problems in a few men.

The main problems that critics have raised about radical feminism are a tendency to essentialism, to an implicit or explicit biological reductionism, and to a false universalism which cannot understand historical change or take sufficient account of divisions between women based on ethnicity and class. This issue will be dealt with in detail within the examination of Firestone's account of reproduction in the chapter on the household.

Marxist feminism

Marxist feminist analysis differs from that of radical feminism especially in considering gender inequality to derive from capitalism, and not to be constituted as an independent system of patriarchy. Men's domination over women is a by-product of capital's domination over labour. Class relations and the economic exploitation of one class by another are the central features of social structure, and these determine the nature of gender relations.

The critical site of women's oppression also varies between Marxist feminists. Often it is the family which is seen as the basis as a consequence of the need of capital for women's domestic labour in the home (e.g., Seccombe, 1974). Others focus on the ideological rather than material level.

The family is considered to benefit capital by providing a cheap way of providing the day-to-day care of workers, such as food and clean clothes, and for producing the next generation of workers. It is cheap because women as housewives do this for no wage, merely receiving maintenance from their husbands. Thus capital benefits from the unequal sexual division of labour within the home.

Other Marxist feminists have argued for a less economistic analysis of both capitalism and gender relations (e.g., Barrett, 1980). Gender relations are seen as importantly constituted by discourses of masculinity and femininity which are not immediately reducible to the economic relations of capitalism.

Some Marxist feminists retain a materialist analysis of class relations and combine this with an analysis of gender relations in terms of ideology and culture.

The main problem raised by critics about Marxist feminism is that it is too narrowly focused on capitalism, being unable to deal with gender inequality in pre- and post-capitalist societies, and that it incorrectly reduces gender inequality to capitalism, rather than recognizing the independence of the gender dynamic.

Liberalism

Liberalism differs from both the above in not having an analysis of women's subordination in terms of such overarching social structures, but rather conceives this as the summation of numerous small-scale deprivations.

While there is no one basis of women's disadvantage, there are two major foci of analysis. Firstly, the denial of equal rights to women in education and in employment are often important concerns (e.g., Kanter, 1977). Women's disadvantaged position is related to specific details of prejudice against women. This is often combined with a second theme, that of sexist attitudes which act to sustain the situation. Attitudes are analysed as traditional and unresponsive to recent changes in real gender relations.

This approach has often generated empirical studies about gender relations which provide important information that can be analysed in a variety of ways. They provide extensive documentation of the lives of women. For instance, some of the major surveys of women's employment and the domestic division of labour might be considered to fall within this category (Martin and Roberts, 1984; Pahl, R. E., 1984).

Liberal feminism is often criticized for its failure to deal with the deep-rootedness of gender inequality and the interconnectedness between its different forms. For instance, the origin or reasons for persistence of patriarchal attitudes are not systematically addressed. In short the absence of an account of the overall social structuring of gender inequality gives rise to a series of partial accounts.

This does not exhaust the forms of feminist argument. For instance, there are attempts both to synthesize different forms of feminist analysis, and to synthesize feminist analysis with other mainstream frameworks.

Dual-systems theory

Dual-systems theory is a synthesis of Marxist and radical feminist theory. Rather than being an exclusive focus on either capitalism or patriarchy, this perspective argues that both systems are present and important in the structuring of contemporary gender relations. Contemporary gender inequality is analysed as a result of the structures of a capitalist and patriarchal or capitalist-patriarchal society.

Existing dual-systems theory considers the articulation of patriarchy and capitalism in a range of ways. They vary, for instance, as to whether they see patriarchy and capitalism as fused into one system of capitalist patriarchy, as does Zillah R. Eisenstein (1981), or whether they are conceptualized as two analytically distinct, if empirically interacting, systems, as does Hartmann (1979). Eisenstein (1981) considers that the two systems are so closely interrelated and symbiotic that they have become one. Patriarchy provides a system of control and law and order, while capitalism provides a system of economy, in the pursuit of profit. Changes in one part of this capitalist-patriarchal system will cause changes in another part, as when the increase in women's paid work, due to capitalist expansion, sets up a pressure for political change, as a result of the increasing contradictions in the position of women who are both housewives and wage labourers.

Other writers keep the systems analytically distinct (Hartmann, 1979; Mitchell, 1975). These writers themselves differ in their mode of separation of patriarchy and capitalism. Some allocate different levels of the social formation to the different systems, while others do not. For instance, Mitchell (1975) discusses gender in terms of a separation between the two systems, in which the economic level is ordered by capitalist relations, and the level of the unconscious by the law of patriarchy. It is in order to uncover the latter that she engages in her re-evaluation of the work of Freud. She rescues Freud's concept of the unconscious from the fierce criticism of his sexist interpretation of women's sexuality and desires, in order to argue for the significance of the level of the unconscious in understanding the perpetuation of patriarchal ideology, which would ostensibly appear to have no material basis in contemporary societies.

Hartmann's (1979) conception of the relation between capitalism and patriarchy is similar to that of Mitchell in that she wants to maintain the analytic separation of patriarchy and capitalism, while Eisenstein does not. But Hartmann is different in that she wishes to see patriarchal relations crucially operating at the level of the expropriation of women's labour by men, and not at the level of ideology and the unconscious. Hartmann argues that both housework and wage labour are important sites of women's exploitation by men. Within the field of paid work occupational segregation is used by organized men to keep access to the best paid jobs for themselves at the expense of women (Hartmann, 1979). Within the household women do more labour than men, even if they also have paid employment (Hartmann, 1981a). These two forms of expropriation also act to reinforce each other, since women's disadvantaged position in paid work makes them vulnerable in making marriage arrangements, and their position in the family disadvantages them in paid work. While capitalism changes the nature of employment to some extent, Hartmann argues that patriarchy pre-dates capitalism, and that this expropriation of women's labour is not new and distinctive to capitalist societies and hence cannot be reduced to it. Hartmann supports her argument with historical examples of how women have been excluded from the better jobs by organized male workers with, in some cases, the support of the state. It is a powerful and important contribution to the theoretical debate on gender relations.

One of the problems with 'dual-systems' analyses such as the three discussed here is whether they are able adequately to sustain the duality of capitalism and patriarchy. Young (1981) claims that this is an inherently impossible task. Dual-systems theorists usually sustain the distinction between capitalism and patriarchy by allocating them to different levels of society (in the way that Mitchell (1975) locates capitalism in the economy and patriarchy in the unconscious). If they do not do this, then, Young argues, they are not able to establish and sustain an analytic distinction between patriarchy and capitalism. If they make this distinction, then they are not able to account for patriarchal aspects in that level they have allocated to capital, or for capitalist elements in the level allocated to patriarchy.

Young has identified a key problem in existing dualist texts, but she overstates the strength of her argument when she declares this to be an inherent flaw in any future dualist analysis. The specification of the nature of the separation between patriarchy and capitalism is necessary and achievable. It is inappropriate to allocate different levels of the social formation to the different systems, in the manner of Mitchell, for the reasons noted by Young. However, Hartmann's analysis is problematic in that it both underestimates the tension between patriarchy and capitalism and insufficiently specifies the different structures of patriarchy.

A further limitation of existing forms of dual-systems theory is that they do not cover the full range of patriarchal structures. For instance, sexuality and violence are given very little analytic space in the work of Hartmann and Eisenstein. Most accounts suggest that either the material level (Hartmann, Eisenstein) or the cultural (Mitchell) is the significant basis of patriarchy. I think this is a mistake, and that a broader range of structures should be theorized as part of the patriarchal side of the dual systems. This is a flaw, but not an insuperable one. Radical feminists have contributed primarily analyses of sexuality, violence, culture and the state, socialist feminists those on housework, waged work, culture and the state. I think a proper synthesis includes: waged work, housework, sexuality, culture, violence and the state.

These four approaches – radical feminism, liberal feminism, Marxist feminism and dual-systems theory – are the main strands of analysis in the literature. However, I shall also examine various other minor strands as the occasion merits – for instance, materialist feminism and functionalism – together with two 'malestream' perspectives – class analysis and functionalism.

CLASS AND GENDER

Class is the main concept used within sociology to theorize social inequality. Hence it is appropriate to ask in a systematic fashion what is the relationship, if any, between class and gender. Class analysis has dealt with three main issues. Firstly, the determination of the distinction between class categories and the allocation of people to them. Secondly, the understanding of mobility between classes. Thirdly, the implications of class position and class mobility for political, or class, action and social consciousness – especially whether there is going to be revolution or not. I shall analyse the implications of different ways of dealing with the relationship of class and gender for each of these three aspects of class analysis.

Traditionally class analysis has ignored gender relations, only recently even attempting to justify this omission. Today there are several ways in which gender relations are fitted into the concerns of class theory. These will be scrutinized before moving on to more innovative ways of tackling the issue of class and gender. The second way of approaching the issue has been to liken gender relations to class relations and to mine the conceptual vocabulary of class analysis for tools with which to understand male domination. Thirdly, I shall examine the view that there is more than one system of class relations in contemporary Western societies, that there are class relations within both capitalism and patriarchy.

In this chapter I am taking class analysis to include both Marxist and Weberian accounts. While this may seem a little sweeping at first glance, there are in fact insufficient differences between them on the analysis of gender to warrant splitting them. Further, many modern British sociologists consider themselves to have integrated the positive features of each approach, so recent debates have seen some convergence of neo-Marxism and neo-Weberianism (Abercrombie and Urry, 1983).

In the 1960s, 1970s and early 1980s most writers on class ignored gender relations (Beteille, 1977; Lockwood, Goldthorpe et al, 1969; Blackburn and Mann, 1979; Stewart, Prandy and Blackburn, 1980; Goldthorpe, 1980). They rarely felt it necessary to establish the reasons for this, at best using resource constraints, in a footnote, to justify an all-male sample (e.g., Blackburn and Mann, 1979). The first full defence of this omission of gender was presented by Goldthorpe in 1983. This followed numerous criticisms of class theory for its sexist bias (e.g., Acker, 1973, 1980; Allen, 1982; Delphy, 1984; Garnsey, 1978; Murgatroyd, 1982; Newby, 1982; West, 1978).

Goldthorpe (1983) argues that women can be ignored for the purposes of class analysis because their position is determined by that of the man with whom they live, either husband or father. He argues that the family, not the individual, is the basic unit of social stratification. He suggests that in all important respects members of a family share the same life chances. He argues further that the position of the family is determined by that of the male breadwinner. He suggests that women do not bring resources of any significance to the family so do not need to be taken into account in determining the position of the family unit.

Goldthorpe attempts an empirical substantiation of these points using data from the Oxford Mobility Survey. Firstly, he argues that women's employment is too 'limited', 'intermittent' and 'conditioned' by that of their husbands, to affect the position of the family as a whole. Women, he suggests, move in and out of employment in relation to domestic events and their husband's jobs. She attempts to correlate the pattern of a women's movements in and out of paid work at the time of childbirth with that of the level of her husband's occupation.

This position has many serious flaws. Firstly, as many critics of class analysis have pointed out, significant numbers of people do not live in traditional nuclear families of the male breadwinner, wife and children model (Acker, 1973, 1980; Allen, 1982; Garnsey, 1978; Murgatroyd, 1982; Oakley, 1974; Stanworth, 1984). Other types of household composition include: single-parent households, usually headed by women; single-person households; unemployed households in which no one has paid work; married couples where the woman earns and, for reasons of ill-health, unemployment, etc., the man does not. Further the proportion of traditional households is steadily declining. The existence of these types of household causes two main problems for the conventional approach. Firstly, and most obviously, there is no male breadwinner to determine the position of the family. In order to overcome this difficulty in these circumstances the conventionalists usually accept the woman as head of household when there is no man. However, this gives rise to the second problem, as Delphy (1984) points out. It introduces a second method of classification of women, so that women can oscillate between having a class position in their own right determined by their employment and having their class position determined by their husband when they have one. This oscillation reduces the robustness of class analysis.

The second major flaw in the conventional approach is that women's employment is empirically more important than Goldthorpe suggests. Today women typically take one break of five years from paid employment while having children (Martin and Roberts, 1984). Such a short break does not constitute an 'intermittent' work history, but rather one of continuity. Women's employment also brings significant, not limited, income into the household. A wife's wage prevents many households falling into poverty. Indeed the affluent-worker study found that the greater income of the white-collar families in their sample was due to the earnings of the wives, not the men (Lockwood, Goldthorpe et al, 1969: 129a).

Britten and Heath (1983) argue that women's employment is sufficiently important to count as one of the determinants of a family's class position. They argue that households derive their class position from the employment of both husband and wife, not husband alone. This creates a new classification of households, since, while some will involve same-class spouses, some will not. Cross-class families exist where the spouses have jobs in different class categories. In Britain the commonest type is that in which male skilled manual workers, who are classified working class, are married to female routine white-collar workers, who are classified as middle class.

Britten and Heath go on to argue that this has implications for analysis of class action as well as class position. Cross-class families have distinctive voting patterns; that is, the classification of the wife's job affects both husband and wife's voting patterns. Britten and Heath demonstrate empirically the importance of women's employment in the link between class position and class action. However, it produces a very complicated set of methodological issues in researching class. Further, they do not escape from the problem that not everyone lives in a traditional family unit.

In order to overcome these problems some writers use the individual rather than the family as the unit of analysis. Class position is then derived from the occupational position of each person's job, without complicated references back to the employment of their spouse as well. Indeed this method has been used by several Marxists without reference to the debate above. For instance, Braverman (1974) discusses the class position of clerks without significant reference to the fact that they are female. He argued that they were proletarian on the basis of the deskilled nature of their work alone.

A further problem in conventional class analysis is that it fails to deal adequately with the inequality and the social division of labour within the household itself. If class analysis is supposed to theorize inequalities based upon a division of labour, then it ought, logically, to be applicable to inequalities based upon the domestic division of labour. There are serious inequalities within the household which theories of social inequality need to be able to articulate. For instance, women spend more hours on housework than men; have less access to household goods (e.g., men usually drive the 'family' car to their workplace); have less money and time for leisure; and so on. Further, if the link between material position and political action is the central question for class analysis, then we need to ask about the implications of changes in women's material position for gendered political action. These two points lead the analysis beyond conventional class theory. Theorization of relations within the household has not been part of the project of class analysis, neither has an investigation of political action beyond a narrowly defined class politics.

Some feminists have approached the issue of gender and class from a direction opposite to that discussed so far. Rather than asking how we can squeeze women into class analysis, they have asked how we can use the concept of class to theorize gender relations. This entails a reappraisal of the definition of class.

Definitions of class usually involve a notion of fundamental cleavage based upon different and economic position. Some add other levels to this, for instance, educational and other qualifications, common in neo-Weberian analysis; while others have a very tightly defined notion of economic difference, as in ownership or non-ownership of the means of production, in the manner of orthodox Marxist analysis. I shall examine attempts by two feminists to use the concept of class to capture the nature of inequalities between women and men: those of Delphy and Firestone.

Delphy argues that housewives constitute one class and husbands another. They have a relation of economic difference and of social inequality. She argues that housewives are the producing class, engaged in domestic labour, while husbands are the non-producing class, expropriating the labour of their wives. These classes exist within a patriarchal mode of production, in a manner similar to the classes in other modes of production identified by Marx. Delphy is thus arguing that housework is as much production as any other form of work. It is not a separate category, such as reproduction, consumption or an ideological activity. Women perform this work under patriarchal relations of production for the benefit of their husbands. Hence husbands are constituted as the expropriating class and housewives the direct producers.

Delphy has been criticized for stretching Marxist concepts of class and mode of production too far from their appropriate usage (Barrett and McIntosh, 1979; Molyneux, 1979). Her critics argue that there are too many differences between women for them to be appropriately placed in one class. Women married to middle-class men have a very different standard of living and way of life from those married to working-class men.

However, these are superficial differences which do not affect class position. A Marxist concept of class is based on relations of production, not lifestyle. Such contrasts in style of living are significant only if a Weberian definition of class is being utilized, which Delphy does not. All housewives gain their maintenance in the same way, even if they have different amounts. Since they have common relations of production, they are, in Marxist terms, within the same class.

Barrett and McIntosh (1979) and Molyneux (1979) argue further that Delphy uses the concept of mode of production incorrectly. They assert that within a Marxist system there can be only one mode of production within a social formation, while Delphy's account is based on there being both a patriarchal and a capitalist mode of production in the same formation.

However, this point is contentious within various Marxist debates and is not an established principal. Various Marxist writers, including John G. Taylor (1979), have argued that a capitalist and non-capitalist mode of production may articulate in a social formation, and that this characterizes many developing countries, although others, such as Wallerstein (1979), argue there is one capitalist world system. Thus there is no Marxist orthodoxy to refute Delphy, merely an existing lively debate within Marxism.

A further problem is that not all women are housewives, so Delphy provides only a partial theorization of women's position. Delphy tries to slide past this by suggesting that, since all women expect to be housewives, we can treat all women as if they are. However, we can hardly criticize Goldthorpe for this same problem and not Delphy as well. A theorization of gender must deal with the fact that some women are full-time housewives, and some are not. A final criticism of Delphy is that her account is economistic; that she neglects cultural, sexual and ideological aspects of gender inequality in her account. It is argued that gender inequality cannot be captured by such an economistic concept as class. This is the most serious of the criticisms.

Firestone (1974) also attempts to develop Marxist concepts and theory to build her analysis of women's oppression. She uses a broader concept of class than Delphy: all women are in one, all men in another. Sex is class. It is not restricted to housewives and husbands. Again the basis is a material one, although she conceptualizes this as reproduction, not production. Women are disadvantaged by their position in reproduction – pregnancy, childbirth, breast-feeding, child care and so on. Unlike Delphy, Firestone has a theory about non-material aspects of gender relations. She draws upon Marxist notions of the material base determining the political and ideological superstructure.

Firestone has been criticized for biological determinism. But while there is some truth in this it is overdrawn, since she does have a notion that struggle over the means of production will change women's subordination.

The question here, however, is whether the concept of class is useful for analysis of gender relations. Its strength is, firstly, that it powerfully captures social inequality and, secondly, that it captures the material aspect of this. Its weaknesses are, firstly, that it downplays the significance of non-economic aspects of women's subordination and, secondly, that it comes with a set of baggage that is difficult to drop about its relations to capitalist rather than patriarchal social relations.

While Delphy and Firestone have pointed to the centrality of material aspects of women's oppression, in particular those in the household, to the overall determination of gender inequality, many other analyses have not. For instance, violence is considered central by Brownmiller (1976), Hanmer (1978), Stanko (1985) and others. Institutional heterosexuality is considered central by Rich (1980) and MacKinnon (1982). Others, such as Hartmann (1979), in her analysis of segregation, consider paid work to be central.

Should the concept of class be expanded to cover gender inequality across all these areas? I think it should not be used to cover non-economic forms of inequality, since to do so would be to wrench the concept too far from its heritage. However, there are some major gendered economic cleavages to which it should be applied. So I would argue that housewives and husbands are classes, but that men and women are not. That is, certain aspects of patriarchal relations can be captured by the concept of class, but not all. Further, gender impacts upon class relations within capitalism. This means there are two class systems, one based around patriarchy, the other around capitalism.

RACE, ESSENTIALISM AND EPISTEMOLOGY

In addition to the debates between the perspectives discussed above there are a number of issues which cross-cut them. These are especially: the intersection of sexism and racism; essentialism and the sameness difference debate, as to whether there are essential differences between women and men; structure and agency; epistemology, especially whether feminist methods of enquiry are distinctive; and the nature and significance of anti-feminism.

Race and feminist analysis

The neglect of ethnic difference and inequality in many white feminist and non-feminist writings has come under intense scrutiny and critique in a number of recent texts (Amos and Parmar, 1984; Barrett and McIntosh, 1985; Brittan and Maynard, 1984; Carby, 1982; Davis, 1981; Hooks, 1982, 1984; Joseph, 1981; Lorde, 1981; Moraga and Anzaldua,

1981; Parmar, 1982). Analyses from the perspective of women of colour have raised a number of important issues for theories of gender relations.

Firstly, the labour market experience of women of colour is different from that of white women because of racist structures which disadvantage such women in paid work. This means that there are significant differences between women on the basis of ethnicity, which need to be taken into account.

Secondly, ethnic variation and racism mean that the chief sites of oppression of women of colour may be different from those of white women. This is not simply a statement that women of colour face racism which white women do not, but also a suggestion that this may change the basis of gender inequality itself. The best example of this is the debate on the family, which has traditionally been seen by white feminist analysis as a major, if not the major, site of women's oppression by men. Some women of colour, such as Hooks (1984), have argued that, since the family is a site of resistance and solidarity against racism for women of colour, it does not hold the central place in accounting for women's subordination that it does for white women. There is here a warning against generalizing from the experience of a limited section of women (white) to that of women as a whole.

A third issue is that the intersection of ethnicity and gender may alter ethnic and gender relations. Not only is there the question of recognizing ethnic inequality and the different sites of oppression for women of different ethnicities, but the particular ways in which ethnic and gender relations have interacted historically change the forms of ethnic and gender relations.

This critique is not specific to texts which use the concept of patriarchy, but is applied to most white feminist writings, including those of socialist feminists and liberal feminists. It is a serious criticism of existing texts. It will be further examined on specific topics in later chapters.

However, most of these writers do not deny that there is inequality between men and women. They are arguing that this takes varied forms, and that racism may be of overriding political concern to women of colour.

Essentialism and postmodernism

One of the issues in this debate on gender and ethnicity is whether existing feminist theory has a view of women as more uniform and undivided than is really the case. This question, of whether there is a unity among women and an essential difference between them and men, is part of a wider debate on essentialism in feminist theory.

On the one hand many feminists have assumed that it is legitimate to write of 'women' as a social category distinct from 'men' and have discussed the collective interest of women as opposed to that of men. Indeed this has been a fundamental part of early feminist theory. On the other hand post-structuralists and postmodernists, together with some Marxist feminists and some black feminists, argue that concepts such as 'patriarchy', which presume some coherence and stability over time and culture, suffer from essentialism. Segal (1987), for instance, criticizes radical feminists, such as Daly, for essentialism and reductionism and inability to analyse historical change. Some postmodernists have gone further and argued that not only is the concept of patriarchy essentialist but so also is that of 'women'. For instance, the project of the journal *m/f* was to argue that not only is there no unity to the category of 'woman', but that analyses based on a dichotomy between 'women' and 'men' necessarily suffer from the flaw of essentialism. Instead, there are considered to be a number of overlapping, cross-cutting discourses of femininities and masculinities which are historically and culturally variable. The notion of 'women' and 'men' is dissolved into shifting, variable social constructs which lack coherence and stability over time (Alcoff, 1988; Barrett, 1980, 1987; Coward, 1978; Fraser and Nicholson, 1988; Eisenstein and Jardine, 1980).

Flax (1987) argues that feminist theory is necessarily postmodern in its challenge of the notion that gender relations are fixed and natural. However, most feminist postmodernists attack forms of feminist theory which emphasize the commonalities shared by women. Indeed some postmodern theorists (e.g., Boudillard) may be considered anti-feminist.

The postmodern feminists draw theoretically upon the deconstructionism of Derrida (1976), the discourse analysis of Foucault (1981) and the postmodernism of Lyotard (1978) (who themselves do not seriously consider gender). A parallel, but theoretically unrelated, critique of the unity of 'women' has come from the writings of some black feminists. The deconstruction of categories within specific texts is a technique developed by Derrida and is advanced especially by feminist analysts within the field of cultural studies.

One of the limitations of the new post-structuralism and postmodernism is a neglect of the social context of power relations. Power is not neglected in the analyses of Foucault, since for him the knowledge at the base of each of his discourses is also power, but it is very dispersed. This dispersal together with de-emphasis of economic relations makes analyses of gender within a Foucauldian tradition overly free-floating.

I think that the postmodern critics have made some valuable points about the potential dangers in theorizing gender inequality at an abstract and general level. However, they go too far in denying the necessary impossibility and unproductive nature of such a project. While gender relations could potentially take an infinite number of forms, in actuality there are some widely repeated features. In addition the signifiers of 'woman' and 'man' have sufficient historical and cross-cultural continuity, despite some variations to warrant using such terms. It is a contingent question as to whether gender relations do have sufficient continuity of patterning to make generalizations about a century or two and a continent or so useful. While I agree that the answer to this cannot be given at a theoretical level, I shall argue in this book that in practice it is possible; that there are sufficient common features and sufficient routinized interconnections that it does make sense to talk of patriarchy in the West in the last 150 years at least.

However, many of the existing grand theories of patriachy do have problems in dealing with historical and cultural variation. I think this is due to a contingent feature in their analyses, that they utilize a simple base-superstructure model of causal relations. In a theory in which there is only one causal element it is not surprising that there are difficulties in understanding variation and change. This problem can be solved by theorizing more than one causal base. I am arguing that there are six main structures which make up a system of patriarchy: paid work, housework, sexuality, culture, violence and the state. The interrelationships between these create different forms of patriarchy.

Epistemology

Feminist challenges to mainstream social science have invoked a variety of approaches to knowledge. Some have argued that orthodox accounts are empirically incorrect on their own terms, while others have claimed that the very way that men have constructed what counts as authoritative knowledge is itself patriarchally constructed (Oakley, 1974; Smith, 1988; Stanley and Wise, 1983).

The more basic critique is that mainstream social science is simply empirically incorrect in relation to gender and those aspects of society that gender affects. For instance, conventional views that the source of the wages gap between men and women is largely due to women having less skill and experience than men can be shown to be untrue using econometric data (Treiman and Hartmann, 1981). Conventional views that there is little violence against women can be shown to be empirically untrue by new methods of collecting such information. That is, mainstream social science has a patriarchal bias which can be remedied by more accurate and thorough social research. Harding (1986) labels this approach to knowledge that of the feminist empiricists. They use established methods of research to argue that previous assumptions about women are unfounded, an approach which argues for a really scientific attitude to knowledge rather than relying on the existing patriarchally biased knowledge which falsely passes as science.

The limitations to this critique are that they assume that the methods of research and the way knowledge is put together are themselves scientifically neutral. A more far-reaching critique argues that the very way that men have typically constructed what counts as authoritative knowledge is itself patriarchal (Smith, D., 1988; Stanley and Wise, 1983). This second school, labelled the feminist standpoint epistemologists by Harding (1986), argues that the only basis of unbiased knowledge of the world is women's own direct experience. These writers contend that it is the standpoint of the oppressed woman which provides the clearest vision of social relations. The position was initially articulated via the slogan 'the personal is political' (see Millett, 1977), and is today developed into a critique of abstract theorizing because it is considered to be the form of knowledge that is furthest removed from women's experience. That is, the very way that mainstream science and social science construct knowledge is biased against women. Feminist standpoint epistemologists assert that we need a new feminist methodology which is closer to women's own experience. This is argued partly on the basis that abstraction itself is problematic, and partly that the social institutions within which abstraction takes place are run by men and reflect their interests. MacKinnon (1982) argues that currently men's thought is constituted as 'objective' and women's as 'subjective', with the former more authoritative than the latter. Men objectify women; this objectification is simultaneously both general and sexual. Women's resistance must be by embracing their 'subjective' experience. In this way women can resist their objectification.

Qualitative techniques which allow women to speak for themselves are considered to be more in keeping with a feminist methodology by reducing the amount of distortion that a patriarchally based science would introduce. In practice this means a methodological imperative to use qualitative rather than quantitative methods, to interview women and to report faithfully on their views. Oakley's research on women's views of childbirth is a classic example of this (Oakley, 1981). The introduction of the experiences of women into social science is considered an important corrective to distorted theories. This approach goes along with a distrust of meta-theorizing, since this is considered to be more affected by patriarchal bias than the words of women interviewees.

The limits of this approach to feminist methodology are the limits of the views of the women interviewed. Concepts and notions about structures outside their experience are ruled out. I think this is very problematic, since it is not clear why women's everyday experiences should be less contaminated by patriarchal notions than are theories. All knowledge is mediated via ideas and concepts, and those available are necessarily affected by patriarchal relations. Systematic enquiry and theoretical development are more likely to elucidate the nature of patriarchal relations.

Harding (1986) provides a clear and erudite account of the problematic debate between the feminist empiricist and feminist standpoint positions and treads a delicate balance between the two. The fragmentation of the scientific project which is a consequence of postmodernist thought is both a strength and a weakness. She argues that while the first group, the feminist empiricists, have made valuable contributions, their best work is in fact done when they make use of their standpoint as women to ask new questions, not merely the old; that is, when they adopt some aspects of the second school's approach. Harding maintains that the most important issue is the setting of the questions to be researched and the allocation of resources to do this, drawing upon a post-Kuhnian recognition of the central issue of the social construction of the research questions themselves. Science is a 'black box', crucially structured by the political context in which it operates. Women, and indeed different groups of women, need to be able to set their own research agendas.

Harding is ambivalent as to whether some methods of seeking knowledge are 'better' than others. Indeed her concept of science dissolves into a more general notion of knowledge as she refuses to privilege one form of knowledge creation over another. She slides towards a relativism in which each social group creates its own knowledge, a postmodernist, post-structuralist position, but draws back from its full implications.

The strength of Harding's work is her demonstration of the greater significance of the construction of the questions to be asked and how this has been patriarchally organized, rather than the narrower question of whether specific methods of investigation are more feminist than others. The position taken in this book is that the selection of questions and the resources devoted to their research is a social and political issue which is shaped by patriarchal institutions, but that the answer to any given question is not one which is socially and politically relative.

A weakness in Harding's work is her ambivalence to the point of abandoning that aspect of the project of science which is to create universalistically authoritative knowledge on the basis of systematic enquiry. In focusing on the social construction of science she denies the possibility of this project. In this I think she goes too far in that she tends to deny the utility and validity of each body of science within its own terms. There is one type of epistemology neglected by Harding in her otherwise excellent and thorough review of the literature which does retain the scientific project – that of realism. The realist approach maintains that there are deep structures, which can be discovered with systematic enquiry.

Realists such as Bhaskar (1979) argue that there are deep social structures, the discovery of which is key to our understanding of gender relations. These structures are not necessarily visible or immediately knowable. This approach contrasts with both positivist and standpoint epistemologies. Systematic study and scientific analysis are necessary to uncover these structures, which are emergent properties of social practices. They contain a duality of both structure and action (cf., Giddens, 1984). The theoretical project in this book is realist, in the sense that it is engaged in an identification of the underlying structures of social life. However, I do not think we need to make the distinction between necessary and contingent structures of a social system in the way that Sayer (1984) suggests, since patriarchy is an open social system which can take a variety of forms.

PATRIARCHY

The variety of definitions of patriarchy has been a problem in some early texts (see Barrett, 1980); however, it would be surprising if developing theories of patriarchy did not use the term in slightly different ways. Patriarchy as a concept has a history of usage among social scientists, such as Weber (1947), who used it to refer to a system of government in which men ruled societies through their position as heads of households (cf., Pateman, 1988). In this usage the domination of younger men who were not household heads was as important as, if not more important than, the element of men's domination over women via the household.

The meaning of the term has evolved since Weber, especially in the writings by radical feminists, who developed the element of the domination of women by men and who paid less attention to the issue of how men dominated each other, and by dual-systems theorists, who have sought to develop a concept and theory of patriarchy as a system which exists alongside capitalism (and sometimes racism too).

Yet the practice of incorporating a generational element into the definition of patriarchy has been continued by some of the major contemporary writers on this question, most importantly by Hartmann (1979, 1981b). I think that the incorporation of a generational element into the definition is a mistake. It implies a theory of gender inequality in which this aspect of men's domination over each other is central to men's domination over women. Yet in practice few contemporary theories of gender inequality establish that this is the case. For instance, while Hartmann uses a definition which incorporates generational hierarchy among men, this is not central to her theory of patriarchy, which focuses upon men's organizational ability to expropriate women's labour in paid work, and hence in the household. Thus inclusion of generation in the definition is confusing. It is a contingent element and best omitted.

Before developing the details of its forms, I shall define patriarchy as a system of social structures and practices in which men dominate, oppress and exploit women.

The use of the term social structure is important here, since it clearly implies rejection both of biological determinism, and the notion that every individual man is in a dominant position and every woman in a subordinate one.

Patriarchy needs to be conceptualized at different levels of abstraction. At the most abstract level it exists as a system of social relations. In contemporary Britain this is present in articulation with capitalism, and with racism. However, I do not wish to imply that it is homologous in internal structure with capitalism. At a less abstract level patriarchy is composed of six structures: the patriarchal mode of production, patriarchal relations in paid work, patriarchal relations in the state, male violence, patriarchal relations in sexuality, and patriarchal relations in cultural institutions. More concretely, in relation to each of the structures, it is possible to identify sets of patriarchal practices which are less deeply sedimented. Structures are emergent properties of practices. Any specific empirical instance will embody the effects, not only of patriarchal structures, but also of capitalism and racism.

The six structures have causal effects upon each other, both reinforcing and blocking, but are relatively autonomous. The specification of several rather than simply one base is necessary in order to avoid reductionism and essentialism. The presence of only one base, for instance, reproduction for Firestone (1974) and rape for Brownmiller (1976), is the reason for their difficulty with historical change and cultural variation. It is not necessary to go to the other extreme of denying significant social structures to overcome the charge of essentialism, as some of the postmodernist post-structuralists have done. The six identified are real, deep structures and necessary to capture the variation in gender relations in Westernized societies.

Patriarchal production relations in the household are my first structure. It is through these that women's household labour is expropriated by their husbands or cohabitees. The woman may receive her maintenance in exchange for her labour, especially when she is not also engaged in waged labour. Housewives are the producing class, while husbands are the expropriating class.

The second patriarchal structure within the economic level is that of patriarchal relations within paid work. A complex of forms of patriarchal closure within waged labour exclude women from the better forms of work and segregate them into the worse jobs which are deemed to be less skilled.

The state is patriarchal as well as being capitalist and racist. While being a site of struggle and not a monolithic entity, the state has a systematic bias towards patriarchal interests in its policies and actions.

Male violence constitutes a further structure, despite its apparently individualistic and diverse form. It is behaviour routinely experienced by women from men, with standard effects upon the actions of most women. Male violence against women is systematically condoned and legitimated by the state's refusal to intervene against it except in exceptional instances, though the practices of rape, wife beating, sexual harassment, etc., are too decentralized in their practice to be part of the state itself.

Patriarchal relations in sexuality constitute a fifth structure. Compulsory heterosexuality and the sexual double standard are two of the key forms of this structure.

Patriarchal cultural institutions completes the array of structures. These are significant for the generation of a variety of gender-differentiated forms of subjectivity. This structure is composed of a set of institutions which create the representation of women within a patriarchal gaze in a variety of arenas, such as religions, education and the media.

The chapters in the book will follow the main sites of the six structures, in order to be able to deal with the existing literature. However, as will be seen, my own argument focuses on structures, not sites. The argument as to the model of patriarchy, in the second half of each chapter, will follow the more theoretically adequate concepts of patriarchal structures.

CONTEMPORARY CHANGE

Are gender relations changing? Have women won their liberation? Or are recent changes superficial and insignificant? Have women lost in some areas as they have gained in others? What are the changes?

Women were 46 per cent of the paid workforce in 1988 as compared with 34 per cent in 1959 (*Employment Gazette*, Historical Supplement, Feb 1987, Table 1.1; May 1989, Table 1.1). They were paid 73.6 per cent of men's wages in 1986 as compared with 63.1 per cent in 1970, and 75.5 per cent in 1977 (Equal Opportunities Commission, 1988b: 45). Is this liberation in increasing numbers of women obtaining a wage for work, or entry to the most exploitative jobs?

More girls than boys have acquired 'O' levels since 1985, and the gap between male and female entrants to universities is closing steadily.

The illegitimacy rate, that is, the proportion of births outside of marriage as compared to inside, rose from 4.9 per cent in 1951 to 12.7 per cent in 1981 and 21.3 per cent in 1986 (Equal Opportunities Commission, 1988b: 8). The divorce rate rose from 5.9 per thousand marriages in 1971 to 12.9 in 1986 (Equal Opportunities Commission, 1988b: 5). Is this liberation from exploitative husbands or abandonment to poverty? The fertility rate in Great Britain fell from 2.86 per woman in 1965 to 1.78 in 1985 (Equal Opportunities Commission, 1988b: 9). Are women being liberated from child care; are they going on birth strike? Or is child rearing now a more intensive activity? Are men abandoning fatherhood?

Britain has the highest divorce rate in Europe. Britain has the joint lowest percentage of women elected to Parliament of any European country apart from Greece. Does this make Britain the most patriarchal country in Europe or the least?

Is the new reproductive technology progressive in its assistance to previously infertile women, or does it merely give men as experimental doctors a chance to gain control over women's power over reproduction?

Most of the theoretical perspectives described have implicit notions as to whether such changes constitute progress or stasis for women.

Most radical feminist writers see such changes as marginal, superficial modifications in the ways in which men exploit women. Only much more radical changes would count as real improvement in women's lives. Changes in household structure have meant that women shoulder the burdens of domestic labour increasingly by themselves, as men desert the responsibilities of fatherhood. The new reproductive technologies in practice help few infertile women and instead offer men power over reproductive material. As social relations change, men, as the dominant gender, remain in control over the new arena.

Liberal feminists typically view the changes optimistically, seeing the opening up of new fields for women, ranging from traditionally male jobs, to educational opportunities, to positions in formal politics, as advances for women. The public sphere, previously closed to women, is seen to be becoming accessible. This access will in itself bring increasing freedom to women.

Marxist feminists usually link the changing position of women with that of the working class. Thus in countries like Britain, which have witnessed a shift of power away from labour, women are seen to lose out. This is especially so in areas involving welfare provision, such as social security, nurseries and health. However, in countries where the labour movement is still making advances, women are typically seen as making progress as well.

Class theorists have a divided view on whether women are seen as making progress, insofar as they have commented on gender relations. On the one hand, those who note the increase in the number of women in paid occupations regard this as an improvement in the position of women. On the other hand, since these are usually seen as proletarian positions, it is not regarded as much of an advance.

Dual-systems theorists do not have a common view on the character of changing gender relations.

Few writers on gender consider issues of historical regress in the position of women (exceptions such as Koonz (1987) on Nazi Germany are few), or even the social forces which oppose advance (Harrison's (1978) account of opposition to the suffrage movement and Campbell (1987) and Dworkin (1983) on conservative women are unusual). I think this is a serious gap in feminist scholarship. Men and some women have actively and effectively opposed feminist demands.

In the last chapter I shall argue that we need to separate the notion of progress in the position of women from that of changes in the form of gender inequality. That is, to distinguish analytically between changes in the degree of patriarchy from changes in its form. There have been major alterations in the form of patriarchy as well as in its degree.

FORMS AND DEGREES OF PATRIARCHY

There have been changes in both the degree and form of patriarchy in Britain over the last century, but these changes are analytically distinct. Changes in degree include aspects of gender relations such as the slight reduction in the wages gap between men and women and the closing of the gap in educational qualifications of young men and women. These modifications in degree of patriarchy have led some commentators to suggest that patriarchy has been eliminated. However, other aspects of patriarchal relations have intensified. I want to argue that there have been changes not only in the degree of patriarchy but also in its form. Britain has seen a movement from a private to a public form of patriarchy over the last century.

I am distinguishing two main forms of patriarchy, private and public. Private patriarchy is based upon household production as the main site of women's oppression. Public patriarchy is based principally in public sites such as employment and the state. The household does not cease to be a patriarchal structure in the public form, but it is no longer the chief site. In private patriarchy the expropriation of women's labour takes place primarily by individual patriarchs within the household, while in the public form it is a more collective appropriation. In private patriarchy the principle patriarchal strategy is exclusionary; in the public it is segregationist and subordinating.

The change from private to public patriarchy involves a change both in the relations between the structures and within the structures. In the private form household production is the dominant structure; in the public form it is replaced by employment and the state. In each form all the remaining patriarchal structures are present – there is simply a change in which are dominant. There is also a change in the institutional forms of patriarchy, with the replacement of a primarily individual form of appropriation of women by a collective one. This takes place within each of the six patriarchal structures. (See Table 1.1.)

Table 1.1   Private and public patriarchy

Form of patriarchy	Private	Public
Dominant structure	Household production	Employment/State
Wider patriarchal structures	Employment State Sexuality Violence Culture	Household production Sexuality Violence Culture
Period	C19th	C20th
Mode of expropriation	Individual	Collective
Patriarchal strategy	Exclusionary	Segregationist

2

Paid Employment

INTRODUCTION

There are three main empirical features of gender relations in employ-ment that writers have addressed. Why do women typically earn less than men? Why do women engage in less paid work than men? Why do women do different jobs from men?

The chapter will begin by identifying some of the contemporary differences between men and women regarding pay and types and extent of work, move on to a consideration of the main perspectives on these issues, and finally suggest an alternative interpretation.

In 1986 women earned 74 per cent of men's hourly rates. The gap widens if we consider average gross weekly earnings, when women earn only 66 per cent of men's pay (New Earnings Survey, 1986). This increased gap reflects men's longer working hours and greater likelihood of shift and overtime premia. The disparity is even greater for part-time women workers, who earned only 76 per cent of full-time women's rates of pay in 1986 (New Earnings Survey, 1986).

In 1988 women constituted 46 per cent of the paid workforce (*Employment Gazette*, May 1989, Table 2.1). This percentage has been rising steadily since the Second World War. However, if we go back to the middle of the nineteenth century, we find that the female activity rate (the percentage of women employed or unemployed as a percentage of the total number of women) was as high in 1861 as it was in 1971, at 43 per cent (Hakim, 1980).

Unemployment rates among women are approximately the same as those of men, according to data from the Labour Force Survey. During 1984–6, 10 per cent of women and 11 per cent of men were unemployed (*Employment Gazette*, March 1988: 172). This is a higher rate for women than is shown in the official government statistics, since the latter include only unemployed people who are also claiming benefit; this excludes many married women, who are only allowed access to benefits via the claim of their husbands.

While male employment continues to fall from its high point in 1965, female employment, especially that of part-time women workers, continues to rise. Of the women in paid employment, 44 per cent were working part-time in 1986 (see table 2.1).

Table 2.1 Employment trends, Great Britain, 1961–88

Employees in employment	1961	1966	1971	1976	1981	1986	1988
All male	14,202	14,551	13,424	13,097	12,278	11,643	11,978
All female	7,586	8,236	8,224	8,951	9,108	9,462	10,096
% female	34.8	36.1	38.0	40.6	42.6	44.8	45.7
% full-time female			25.3	24.3	24.7	25.2	26.2
Part-time female as % of all female			33.5	40.1	41.9	43.8	42.8

Source: Calculated from *Employment Gazette*: Historical Supplement, Feb 1987, Table 1.1, for 1961–83; August 1987, Table 1.1 for 1986; May 1989, Table 1.1, for 1988. Each figure is for the month of June.

Men and women typically do not work in the same occupations or industries. The DE/OPCS (Department of Employment/Office of Population, Census and Surveys) survey in 1980 found that 63 per cent of women worked only with other women, and of the men they were married to 81 per cent worked only with other men (Martin and Roberts, 1984: 27–8). Women are not only concentrated in the lower grades of work (vertical segregation), but in different areas of work (horizontal segregation) (Hakim, 1979). Hakim (1979, 1981) showed that occupational segregation is an international phenomenon and that it is remarkably constant in Britain, showing only a very small decline during the period 1901 to 1977.

Hakim's index is based upon a study of occupations; however, the vertical and horizontal components of segregation may be separated by using Socio-Economic Groups (SEGs) to capture vertical segregation and the Standard Industrial Classification's Minimum List Headings (MLH), that is, an industrial classification, to capture the horizontal segregation. In the period 1971 to 1981 in Britain we find that there has been an increase in the proportion of women in the higher SEGs and a relative decline in their proportion in most of the lower SEGs, indicating a decline in vertical segregation (see Bagguley and Walby 1988, and tables 2.2 and 2.3). Horizontal segregation shows contrary trends for men and women in the same period. The percentage of men working in MLHs where the workforce was 90 per cent, 80 per cent, or 70 per cent male, decreased,

Table 2.2   Socio-economic groups by sex, 1981

	%	
SEG	Men	Women
Employers and managers	78	22
Professional	89	11
Ancillary	44	56
Supervisory non-manual	52	48
Junior non-manual	29	71
Personal service workers	13	87
Skilled manual	90	10
Semi-skilled manual	68	32
Unskilled manual	58	42
All employees	61	39

Source: Census of Population, 1981 (SEGs 16 and 17 have been excluded).

Table 2.3   Changes in vertical segregation by sex, Britain, 1971–81

	%	
SEG	Men	Women
1	41.88	101.98
2	10.08	35.10
3	2.78	22.99
4	6.33	12.59
5	28.21	40.45
6	−22.28	8.17
7	11.49	5.19
8	−0.75	19.85
9	−14.34	−28.58
10	3.63	−10.21
11	−25.87	−0.33
12	16.93	2.51
13	−13.68	−18.19
14	−21.04	−35.23
15	−20.26	−12.59
16	−1.71	50.04
17	98.21	9.46

Source: Bagguley and Walby, 1988.

while that of women in MLHs where the workforce was 70 per cent female, increased (see table 2.4). This apparent discrepancy shows the importance of differentiating the various dimensions of segregation.

Table 2.4   Horizontal segregation by sex, Britain, 1971–81

	100%		90+%		80+%		70+%	
	1971	1981	1971	1981	1971	1981	1971	1981
Men	0	0	20.61	7.41	42.64	35.71	60.32	54.6
Women	0	0	0	0	2.39	2.10	15.08	23.26

Source: Bagguley and Walby, 1988.

Thus during 1971–81 we have seen a decrease in vertical segregation, a lessening of the extreme horizontal segregation of men and an increase in extent of mild horizontal segregation of women.

There are significant divergencies between women by ethnicity in both economic activity and unemployment rates, which are explored more fully below. The pattern of gender relations in employment in Britain is quite distinctive. Women's economic activity rate in Britain is the second highest in the European Economic Community (EEC). Britain is the only EEC country which has a lower unemployment rate for women than for men. Britain has the second highest rate of part-time work among women in the EEC (see table 2.5).

The size of the wages gap between men and women varies between countries. Among Western nations it is least in the Scandinavian countries and greatest in the USA, with the rest of Western Europe, including Britain, in between.

There are, then, considerable inequalities between men and women in relation to access to paid work and the wages received. These are not uniform between all men and all women, since there are significant differences between women of different ethnic groups. There have been

Table 2.5   Women's Employment, EEC, 1984

EEC countries	West Germany	France	Italy	Belgium	Luxembourg	UK	Ireland	Denmark	Greece
Female activity rate	40.1	45.6	32.6	35.5	32.7	46.3	32.7	58.4	33.4
% female part-time	28.6	21.1	10.2	20.3	14.8	44.3	13.9	36.7	9.0
% unemployment	6.7	9.5	9.8	11.9	2.7	10.9	16.5	8.9	8.1
Ratio female/male unemployment rates	1.6	1.6	2.4	2.3	2.0	0.9	1.1	1.3	2.0

Source: Calculated from Tables T03, T18, T20, T36, EEC Labour Force Survey 1984. The Netherlands did not participate in the 1984 survey.

important changes in the position of women in paid employment, but the wages gap has remained tenaciously over the last decade.

Existing explanations of gender divisions in employment fall into four main schools of thought: economic and sociological functionalism; liberalism; Marxist and Marxist feminist analysis; and dual-systems theory. There is only a small amount of radical feminist literature on paid work, while there is a large amount of economic functionalism.

Economic and sociological functionalism

Functionalist analysis of paid work is strongly represented in the work of labour economists of the human capital school. These writers argue that women get paid less than men because they have less skill and labour market experience and fewer qualifications than men as a consequence of decisions as to the allocations of the time of men and women in households (see Becker, 1965; Mincer, 1962, 1966; Mincer and Polachek, 1974). A person's 'human capital' is the total of their abilities that they can sell to an employer. It is a concept similar to skill, but broader, since it includes not only training and qualifications, but job experience as well. This theory assumes that people get paid according to their value to their employer: the more human capital and the greater amount of time spent working, the higher the wage. It thus presumes a perfect labour market in which people are paid according to their value to their employer.

Human capital theorists argue that women have less human capital than men because of their position in the family. Women's work as carers of children (and also of husbands and elderly parents) precludes their acquisition of as many qualifications and as much labour force experience as men. This is partly because of the actual time spent in these tasks, which entails women leaving the labour market for several years. It is also because the expectation of performing such work means that women are less likely to spend time acquiring qualifications, since they expect to spend less time using them.

Human capital theorists suggest that labour market outcomes are the consequence of rational choices. It is further presumed that the household, not the individual, is the unit of decision making; that there is a household work strategy, not one of separate individuals who happen to live in households. Human capital theorists argue that it is in the interests of the household as a unit for one of its adult members to concentrate on domestic work and one on paid work. Household labour is seen as 'real work', and people decide which sort of work it is most effective to engage in. It is suggested that it must be more efficient to have this specialized division of labour than for both spouses to do some of each. Once the decision has been taken that a person is going to be a homemaker or a full-time waged worker it is difficult to reverse, because of the investments that are being made.

The theory predicts certain outcomes for differential wages for men and women, and for the extent of women's and men's comparative participation in paid work. Since women take the homemaker role, they acquire, on average, less human capital and hence less pay than men; further, they will spend less time in paid employment. The times at which women engage in paid employment is seen to be related to the level of wages; the higher the level of wages, the greater likelihood of women substituting paid work for household work. This means that in times of recession, when wage rates fall, women are likely to leave the labour force and revert to useful activity in the household, while in times of economic boom they would enter it.

Although human capital theory is drawn from modern neo-classical economics, it has striking parallels with the functionalist school of thought in sociology. While these arguments cross traditional disciplinary boundaries, the essential elements and structure of the argument are the same.

Parsonian functionalism (Parsons and Bales, 1956) also explains women's lesser involvement in paid work as a result of their primary position in the family. Parsons conceptualized women's position in the family as that of the 'expressive' role, while men took on the externally oriented 'instrumental' role. This division is likewise seen as differentiation in the interests of the family, and indeed society, as a whole, not one of power and inequality. Human capital theory and Parsonian functionalism have the same structure of argument in that they explain the position of women in paid work as a result of their position in the family, which is considered to be functional both for its members and for society as a whole. Further, the notion of a household rather than an individual work strategy is not confined to human capital and Parsonian theory; it is a common feature of many sociological analyses of gender and work (see, for instance, Pahl, R. E., 1984). There are two main levels of critique of human capital theory: firstly, whether it is consistent with data on women's employment; secondly, whether the assumptions are reasonable.

Human capital theory has been subject to extensive criticism, including, but not confined to, its analysis of gender relations in paid work. Treiman and Hartmann's (1981) authoritative study of the wages gap between men and women for the US National Research Council included a survey of the empirical evidence for the human capital explanation by leading econometricians. They found that in only two studies did worker characteristics account for more than one-fifth of the gap between men's and women's earnings, and in these instances (Mincer and Polackek, 1974, and Corcoran and Duncan, 1979) they amounted to less than half the difference (Treiman and Hartmann, 1981: 19).

The importance of this finding is difficult to overstate. It contradicts the economic and sociological orthodoxy that women's lower wages are a result of lesser skills and labour market experience. Treiman and Hartmann argue that the main source of wage differentials is job segregation by sex.

Polachek has tried to rescue human capital theory by arguing that it can explain occupational segregation. He suggests that women choose those occupations for which their lesser skills will give them the best rewards, and in which they are least penalized for their intermittent work patterns. Women's occupations are considered to require fewer skills than are men's and to attach fewer penalties to interrupted work histories.

However, England (1982, 1984) shows that the empirical evidence does not support Polachek's claims. The decline in women's earnings consequent upon a period out of the labour force was not significantly different between 'male' and 'female' occupations. That is, it could not be argued that women chose these occupations because it would penalize them less harshly for a period out of the labour market for child rearing.

A more theoretical problem for human capital theory is that it rests on the assumption of a perfect labour market in which employers pay employees according to their worth. This is parallel to the assumption in functionalist theories of social stratification that the best-paid jobs are the ones which require the greatest skills. This assumption has been challenged in a variety of ways. Whether a particular job requires that its workers are 'skilled' should be considered not only a technical issue, but also a social one. More powerful workers are more likely to be able to get their jobs designated as highly skilled than less powerful ones. For instance, Cockburn (1983) has shown how printers, because of the strength of their union, were able to maintain the status of their work despite the considerable reduction in the technically skilled part of it to little more than the work of a copy typist. As Phillips and Taylor (1980) have shown, this differential ability to call a job skilled has a gender aspect to it, since women workers are typically less powerful than male workers, and less likely than male workers to get a definition of their work as skilled to be accepted by an employer. That is, women may be skilled in the technical sense of the work requiring a lengthy period of training, but not in the social sense of getting this recognized in terms of grading and pay. Women's skill, or human capital, is more likely than men's to go unrecognized; thus there is not a direct relationship between human capital and pay, because of the different amounts of power of men and women workers.

Thus we see with this approach, both empirical problems, in that the evidence is not consistent with the theory, and theoretical problems, in the assumptions they make about the nature of the labour market and skill. Indeed the theoretical problems underlie the failure of human capital theory at the empirical level. The neglect of the institutionalized power relations which structure the labour market unequally for men and women lies at the heart of the failure of human capital theory and its related sociological equivalents.

Liberalism

Liberal approaches have focused on small-scale processes which differentiate women's position in work from those of men. Many of these, especially in role analysis, draw upon, and use as a backcloth, broader notions of cultural differentiation of men and women. Structural functionalist analysis of the family inspired some micro-level analyses of the dual roles played by men and women, and the relationship between paid work and the family. The analysis of the dual roles that women play both as mothers and paid workers illustrates the strength and weakness of this approach. Myrdal and Klein (1970) captured the detailed dilemmas and problems for women in this situation caught with conflicting demands on their time and labour, while drawing upon a Parsonian framework which provided the implicit understanding of the macro-structures which generated these roles. The availability of this wider framework, which was a strength of the approach insofar as it provided an explanation of the roles, was also a weakness in its stress upon values at the expense of the analysis of the material level, and upon function instead of power and conflict in the allocation of double work-loads on married women with paid employment.

Probably the most substantial recent text of this genre, which takes the sexual division of labour as its subject, is by Kanter (1977), who clearly documents the disadvantages that women face in corporations and describes the proximate mechanisms through which this takes place. She emphasizes the importance of cultural pressures and of organizational features which lead to less success among women than men in reaching the upper echelons of these institutions. The cultural and micro-structural features are convincingly documented; Kanter shows how the management ethic is primarily a masculine one, and how ideological notions attached to slots in the job hierarchy are gender specific and thus militate against a person of the other sex gaining access to such a position. She describes not merely general aspects of this culture, but also its day-to-day effects. For instance, she analyses the small groups in which male friendship and sponsorship networks act to exclude women from the knowledge and contact necessary for corporate success. She demonstrates how the structures of promotional ladders give advantages to the male majority in the workforce. She describes the debilitating affect upon the psyche of women in these corporations of the absence of successful female role models and of their consequent expectation of failure to gain a promotion in the corporation.

These are all pertinent and well-made points to produce in a detailed analysis of an organization; but this is not the same as constructing a theory of the gender division of labour, let alone one of gender relations overall. The analysis does not confront the basic causes of the unequal division of labour; of why there is a domestic division of labour in which women take the major burden of the work; of why men are the majority in the paid workforce in the first place; that there should be different cultures for men and women, such that we can talk of a masculine ethic among management; and so on. In short her analysis *presumes* a structure of gender inequality in the wider society. While she shows how this is played out in the structure of the business corporation, this is not an account of how it is caused. So, while it is a superb analysis in its own terms, it is not a total analysis of the sexual division of labour or of gender relations in general.

Kanter's work is a complex and sophisticated account of the construction of the cultural roles played by men and women within the workplace against a backdrop of a wider framework of society. However, its stress upon the norms, ideas and expectations is at the expense of an analysis of the macro-structures of power and of struggle.

Marxist and Marxist feminist analysis

Marxist and Marxist feminist writers explain the pattern of women's employment as determined by capitalist relations. Women's lower pay and lesser labour force participation are critically shaped by the capital–labour relation. Women are seen as a subordinate and marginal category of worker whose greater exploitation benefits employers, although a sub-group of this school sees women's position in the household, rather than paid labour, as an achievement rather than failure of the working class. There is great variation within class analysis as to the explanation of gender relations in paid employment and the significance of this for class relations. I shall identify four variants: firstly, that initiated by Braverman; secondly, the cyclical reserve army theory; thirdly, the family wage debate; fourthly, Marxist segmentation theory.

Braverman   Braverman (1974) has a general thesis on the development of capitalism into which he integrates an analysis of gender relations. There are two main parts to his argument: firstly, that there is a progressive deskilling of jobs in contemporary monopoly capitalism, and that women take most of these new less-skilled jobs; secondly, that household tasks shift to the factory, reducing the amount of labour to be done in the home and releasing women for waged labour.

Braverman has a model of structural conflict between capital and labour whereby deskilling occurs as a result of the attempt by employers to increase their profits at the expense of the workforce. Deskilling is designed to remove control over the labour process from skilled workers to the capitalist by splitting the conception of the task from its execution. It is also designed to reduce costs by decreasing the need for expensive labour and making it possible to employ cheaper labour on simpler tasks. This cheaper labour is female.

The second part of the argument concerns the changing relationship between the household and the market. Braverman argues that the amount of housework has decreased as a result of the household buying from the market goods it would previously have produced itself. Clothing and pre-prepared foods are examples of things which are cheaper to make under capitalist relations and forces of production than domestic ones. This is considered to release women for waged work.

As a consequence of these two parallel processes, women freed from domestic work are available to take up the new deskilled work in offices and factories. Thus their labour force participation rates rise. At the same time the labour force participation rates for men drop as they are expelled from skilled labour and become unemployed or retire early. Braverman forsees a convergence in the proportions of men and women in the paid workforce.

Both sides of Braverman's provocative and powerful argument have problems. Many have pointed out that the form of managerial control towards which Braverman sees all employers moving is in fact merely one among two or more (Elger, 1979; Friedman, 1977; Wood, 1982); thus there is not such an inevitable tendency to deskilling. Braverman's account of the reduction of the amount of time spent by housewives on housework is contradicted by evidence from time budgets taken over a number of years, which do not show such a decline among housewives (Bosé, 1979; Cowan, 1983; Vanek, 1980). However, it should be noted that the proportion of women who are full-time housewives is itself declining (see table 2.1 above) and women who also do paid work spend fewer hours on housework than their full-time counterparts (Pahl, R. E., 1984). The empirical questions appear unresolved in the literature and will be further addressed below.

Reserve army theory Braverman has a conception of women as a long-term reserve of labour which is now being brought into employment by the development of capitalism. Other Marxists, while also viewing women as a reserve army of labour, consider this to be as a short-term or cyclical phenomenon. Marx himself did not discuss the employment of women to any significant extent but he did identify different forms of industrial labour reserve, and argued that it was critical to capital accumulation. The function of a reserve, according to Marx, was to prevent workers being able to bargain up their wages and conditions of employment in times of increased demand for labour (Marx, 1954). This reserve could be of different types: floating, latent or stagnant. The floating was composed of people who had been employed in capitalist industry and been made unemployed. The latent comprised people who had not been employed by capitalist industry previously but who were available as a result of changes in that area of the economy, for instance, underemployed agricultural labourers. The stagnant consisted of those whose employment was at a very low level and intermittent. Later Marxists have argued that the notion of a latent reserve may be applied to married women.

Beechey (1977, 1978), in her early work, applies Marx's theory to women, arguing that they constitute a flexible reserve which can be brought into paid work when boom conditions increase the need for labour, and let go to return to the home in times of economic recession. Married women in particular can be used in this way because they have somewhere to go and something to do when employers no longer need their services.

they provide a flexible working population which can be brought into production and dispensed with as the conditions of production change . . .
. . . married women have a world of their very own, the family, into which they can disappear when discarded from production (Beechey, 1977: 57)

(However, more recently Beechey has changed her position on the usefulness of the reserve army concept (Beechey and Perkins, 1987).)

Bruegel (1979) has extended this analysis into a consideration of recent British experience, arguing that part-time workers in particular form a reserve army of labour. She shows how the number of women part-time workers in electrical engineering fluctuates more extensively with the trade cycle than does total employment in this industry.

There is some supporting evidence from the world wars, in which women were recruited to work, especially in the munitions factories, for the duration, and 'let go' at the end (Braybon, 1981). Further, some studies of job loss suggest that practices such as sacking part-timers first (until this was declared illegal discrimination in the late 1970s) and 'last in, first out' might contribute to the more tenuous hold of women on paid employment in times of economic retrenchment (Bruegel, 1979; MacKay et al, 1971).

However, there are some serious theoretical and empirical problems with this theory. Firstly, the theory has some internal contradictions. If capital is considered to be the determinant of the process in which women lose their jobs before men, then capital would be acting against its own interests if it were to let women go before men, since women can be employed at lower wages than men. The theory does not specify a mechanism by which women would be let go before men which is in the interests of the employer directly concerned.

Secondly, the empirical evidence does not support the theory. Women did not leave paid employment in greater numbers than men in the 1930s depression in the USA (Milkman, 1976) or in the mid-1970s recession across the Western world (OECD, 1976), neither have they in the recent British recession (Walby, 1989). Indeed in Britain in the 1980s the number of women in paid employment increased overall during the decade, despite a slight dip during the deep recession. Table 2.1 showed how, while men's employment opportunities have wilted since their mid-1960s peak, those for women have continued to increase.

There have been attempts to rescue the theory from these problems. Milkman (1976) argues that the reserve army effect is merely masked by the effects of job segregation by sex. She describes how the sector which was worst hit by job loss in the USA in the 1930s employed predominantly men, while women were to be found in those sectors which were least affected. The segregation of men from women in employment, with men concentrated in manufacturing and women in services, gave women relative protection from loss of employment.

The correlation identified by Milkman is undoubtedly important. However, as a response to the problems of reserve army theory it raises as many questions as it answers. Why are women concentrated in the most buoyant section of the economy? Why are men not substituted for women in the remaining jobs? In short, occupational segregation has become the central feature of the pattern of gender relations in employment and needs explanation. Yet this is not attempted by reserve army theorists. The relative position of women and men remains unexplained.

Family wage The first two versions of Marxist theory on gender relations in employment assume that women are a marginal and hence disadvantaged group within the labour market. In the third, a Marxist account of the family wage, Humphries (1977) argues that women's relative absence from the labour market is a result of the successful struggle of the working class for a family wage against the opposition of capital. In common with other Marxist writers on this topic she considers that women's employment is critically structured by the relationship between capital and labour. However, she considers women's place as full-time homemakers, and hence marginal position in paid employment, to be principally a victory for the working class, rather than a disadvantage for women. Humphries argues that the withdrawal of women from the labour market enables the family to raise its standard of living, ensuring the non-alienated care of the young, the sick and the old, to control the supply of labour to the labour market so as to raise the price of those who enter it, and to assist the solidarity of the working class. This situation is a result of a successful struggle by the organised working class for a family wage for men.

Humphries's argument has been criticized by writers such as Barrett and McIntosh (1980) for the lack of consideration it shows to the disadvantages faced by women in a gender-divided working class. Further, these writers show that, apart from in a minority of families, the family wage has never really existed, except as an idea. Many men who receive a so-called family wage do not support a wife or children; many women who do not receive a family wage do support children. The family wage is an ideology justifying higher wages for men, rather than a reality.

Marxist segmented labour market theory These three Marxist approaches have been criticized for paying insufficient attention to divisions within the labour market itself. Traditionally Marxist theory has focused on production rather than the market, the latter being associated with Weberian analyses. However, the significance of divisions by ethnicity and gender within the labour market itself have led to attempts at a Marxist theory of a segmented labour market. The various writings of Edwards, Gordon and Reich, collectively and individually, have argued that labour market segmentation can be understood as an outcome of the struggle between capital and labour (Edwards, Gordon and Reich, 1975; Edwards, R., 1979; Gordon, D. M., 1972). Essentially employers are seen to segment the labour market as a part of a divide-and-rule strategy. This prevents the homogenization of the proletariat and their ability collectively to resist the demands of capital. This segmentation is not an inevitable response of capital, but part of a historical development, in which employers try one strategy after another to control their workforce. Pre-existing divisions based on ethnicity as well as gender are utilized by employers in this segmentation strategy.

The problems with this analysis stem from two main sources: firstly, the key question of where these ethnic and gender divisions come from is not explained, leaving a large absence in the account; secondly, the periodization provided, which suggests that segmentation is specific to capitalism after the 1920s, is wrong, since ethnic and gender segregation existed long before this. Indeed segregation by gender pre-dates capitalism (Hartmann, 1979; Middleton, C., 1988), so capitalism cannot be considered its cause. So while the account is important in taking occupational segregation seriously in an analysis of social relations in employment, its explanation of why it takes a gendered form is incomplete.

Marxist accounts of gender relations in paid work are important in contextualizing these within the relations between capital and labour. However, they all ultimately fail for this same reason – the over-concentration on the capital–labour relation at the expense of a theorization of gender as an independent source of inequality.

Radical feminist

Radical feminists have written only a little on paid employment, the focus of their empirical work being sexuality and violence. When they have written on the topic it has often brought to bear their concern with men's power over women via violence and sexuality. Radical feminists have made some important contributions to the understanding of issues such as sexual harassment, but not much about the other aspects of the patterning of women's engagement in the labour market (see, for instance, MacKinnon, 1979).

Sexual harassment is variously defined, but usually includes unwanted sexual advances by a man to a woman. Among these are touching, suggestive comments, poking, leering, assault, attempted rape. Most feminist analyses take as central to the definition that women did not want these advances (see Stanko, 1985). Legal definitions of sexual harassment usually focus on the adverse affect that this behaviour may have on a woman's working conditions; it may constitute sexual discrimination, since a man would not have been treated in the same way. Indeed the focus of the writing of the radical feminist MacKinnon (1979) on sexual harassment is precisely on an argument that it constitutes sexual discrimination within the meaning of the law.

MacKinnon asserts elsewhere (1982) that sexuality is central to feminist analyses, to such an extent that women are defined by their sexuality for men. In her work on sexual harassment she manages to sustain this argument in the workplace. The problems with the analysis is that it does not, nor even attempts to, explain why women are in certain jobs not others, nor why women get paid less than men.

Stanko (1988) addresses the significance of sexual harassment for occupational segregation. Women in areas of work traditionally occupied by men are more likely to report sexual harassment than those in traditionally female areas of employment. I would interpret this to suggest that sexual harassment is utilized to maintain occupational closure against women, as well as a more generally pervasive form of control.

The contribution of an analysis of sexual violence by radical feminism is important, but is only a partial contribution to analysing women's position in employment.

Dual-systems theory

While analyses of employment using a class perspective do contribute significantly to our understanding of social relations at work, they are severely restricted by their lack of theorization of gender relations. Dual-systems theory attempts to combine class analysis with the theorization of patriarchy introduced by radical feminism. It posits two systems – patriarchy and capitalism – as analytically necessary to understanding gender relations (see Cockburn, 1983, 1985; Hartmann, 1979, 1981b; Walby, 1986, 1989; Witz, 1987).

Hartmann (1979) argues that patriarchal relations in employment cannot be understood in terms of capitalism alone because they pre-date the rise of this system. Central to her understanding of gender relations is job segregation by sex. She contends that this is central to men's control over women in all spheres of society. It is by excluding women from the better kinds of paid work that men are able to keep women at a disadvantage. Men are able to do this largely because they are better organized than women. Hartmann draws on examples of men organized in trade unions which excluded women, such as nineteenth-century craft unions, and the support of the state for the exclusion of women from certain forms of paid work. These practices are not new but existed in pre-capitalist times; for instance, the organization of men in guilds in medieval England. When men are in the better-paid jobs they are able to marry women on favourable terms, ensuring that wives do the majority of the housework and child care. Women, who need their husbands' financial support, are in no position to refuse. Men's access to the better jobs results in their earning the so-called family wage. Women's domestic work further hinders their ability to gain access to the better forms of work which require training. Thus we see a vicious circle in which women's forced absence from the best jobs leads to their disproportionate domestic burdens, which contributes to their lack of access to the best jobs.

Hartmann's powerful analysis lays out the main elements necessary for an examination of gender relations in paid work. However, in a few short articles many issues remain unclear or undeveloped. While I agree with a dual-systems approach, there are several ways in which I wish to go beyond the brilliant early formulation of Hartmann. Firstly, there is more tension between the two systems of capital and patriarchy than Hartmann suggests. Secondly, there is greater historical variation in the relations between the two systems – some periods being marked by greater tension, others by greater accommodation. Thirdly, ethnic variation and inequality needs to be taken more fully into account. (Westwood (1984) provides a dual-systems account which explores the intersection of gender and race in factory work.) Fourthly, there are important effects of different forms of capital restructuring on the articulation between the two systems, especially those which have a spatial dimension. Fifthly, we need to differentiate between patriarchal strategies in the workplace, for instance, between exclusion and segregation and also between sub-types of the latter. Sixthly, the role of the state needs specifying and discriminating between different conjunctures. Seventhly, the role of further structures, such as those in sexuality and in violence, needs greater development. Eighthly, the concept of patriarchy needs development.

TOWARDS A NEW APPROACH TO PAID WORK

These eight points may be summarized as four ways in which I wish to develop the analysis of a dual-systems approach to gender and employment. Firstly, the articulation of patriarchy with both capitalism and racism needs further explication, especially in relation to the importance of the internal dynamics of these other systems. Secondly, the different internal structures of patriarchy need systematic exploration in respect of their impact upon employment. Thirdly, different patriarchal strategies relating to employment need to be distinguished. Fourthly, these articulations will vary across time and space.

Tension between patriarchy and capitalism, and historical variation in the relations between the two systems

While Hartmann does note that there is some tension between capitalist and patriarchal relations, she primarily presents a picture of harmony between the two systems. This is the case especially in her analysis of the family wage system from which both employers and husbands are seen to benefit, the former from the lower wages they can pay women, the latter because of the greater control that it gives them over their wives.

However, as we saw above in the discussion of the third version of Marxist theory on women and work, the theory of the family wage has been shown to be an ideology rather than a reality, in that many people do not live within such a practice.

Further, as I have argued elsewhere (Walby, 1983b, 1986), there is even more tension and struggle between patriarchy and capitalism than Hartmann suggests. Indeed this is the logical result of the rival interests of the dominant groups of each system in the exploitation of women's labour. This is because the utilization of women's labour by one system is at the expense of the other; if women are working for capitalists they have less time to work for their husbands. While compromises may be struck, this does not vitiate the basic principle of conflict. Indeed the history of women's labour since the development of capitalism may be read in this light as one in which there is endemic conflict, but in which there are historic political compromises hammered out after moments of crisis.

Periods of heightened struggle include: firstly, the entry of women in greater numbers than men to the first factories in the early and mid-nineteenth century, which led to a cross-class patriarchal alliance opposition that sought to utilize the state to control women's work via the Factory Acts (Walby, 1986); secondly, there were conflicts during the world wars over the recruitment of women to the munitions factories between the all-male engineering unions, such as the Amalgamated Society of Engineers, and the engineering employers (Braybon, 1981; Summerfield, 1984). The war-time conflicts were again resolved by state action; in this instance it was legislation to secure the removal of women from 'men's' work at the end of the war. In both these instances, conflicts based in particular industries, cotton textiles and engineering, became constructed as issues of national significance in which the state intervened as a matter of general importance. In a third example, the entry of women into clerical work, the state became involved around the employment of women only in its own bureaucracies. After the First World War numerous government committees debated the issue[1] and, not surprisingly, resolved the matter in the interests of the employer (themselves), to ensure access to cheap female labour. Not all conflicts over the introduction of women into paid employment reached the national political arena, of course. Others, for instance over clerical work where the government was not the employer, did not lead to state intervention.

The first two instances became issues of national political importance and the disagreement was resolved only after government action. These contests were followed by periods of accommodation between the rival forces. We have a picture of sequential conflict and compromise, rather than one of uniform conflict or harmony. It should also be noted that there was a *political* solution to material conflicts on both these occasions. However, I do not mean to imply a cyclical variation between conflict and accommodation. There are also historical developments in the relationship between patriarchy and capitalism which mean that the following round of strife is always on a different base or balance of forces from the previous one. In relation to disagreements over employment a key change has been in women's gain of political citizenship, and hence greater representation of their interests at the level of the state.

Ethnicity and racism

Many analyses of gender and paid employment treat women as if they were a unitary category in a way which seriously neglects divisions based on ethnicity and racism (Carby, 1982; Hooks, 1984). This general problem of assuming that the experience of white women speaks for the experience of all women has been discussed in general in the first chapter; the analysis here builds specifically on the issue of paid work.

While the economic activity rate[2] of white women was 67 per cent in 1984–6,[3] that for women of West Indian origin was higher at 71 per cent, that for women of Indian origin lower at 56 per cent and that for women of Pakistani or Bangladeshi origin lower still at 18 per cent (*Employment Gazette*, March 1988: 165–6).[4] The variation between men by ethnicity is much smaller, with rates from 88 per cent to 72 per cent.

Part-time working is more common among white women than ethnic minority women. While 43 per cent of white women employees worked part-time in 1984–6, only 28 per cent of ethnic minority women did so.[5]

Generalizations about the distinctive pattern of British women as compared to those of European women in the extent of part-time working need to be tempered by recognition of this ethnic variation.

While unemployment rates do not show much variation by sex in the Labour Force Survey, there is considerable variation by ethnicity. Minorities have on average double the white rates of unemployment, 21 per cent for black men and 19 per cent for black women; indeed the unemployment rate for women of Pakistani and Bangladeshi origin is 38 per cent (*Employment Gazette*, March 1988: 172).[6]

There are differences in wage rates which are controversial because of differing interpretations of the reliability of the data and the variety of factors which affect it. At first glance it appears, using data from the PSI survey (Brown, Colin, 1984), that, while minority men earn significantly less than white men, minority women earn more than white women. When Asian women are differentiated from West Indian women it appears that Asian women earn less than white women, while West Indians earn more. However, if only the age range 25–54 is considered, this gap is reversed to a very slightly higher rate for white women. Women in the older age-band earn less, and this group is larger among native white women than among West Indian women because of the timing of immigration into Britain. Thus the surprisingly higher rates of pay among this latter group are partly an age effect, reflecting the disadvantages of older women. There is also the effect of the part-time–full-time division; white women are more likely to be in part-time work than black women, with consequent depressing effects on their average wage level given the lower hourly rates of part-timers. Bruegel (1988) argues that there are further reasons for the unexpected figures. More black women live in London, and London wage rates are higher than those in the rest of the country; so it is partly a locality effect which, she adds, has little meaning, since prices are higher in London. Further, the poorest households are the ones least likely to be picked up in a survey. A further factor accounting for these differences is that Afro-Caribbean women were often recruited into Britain for specific jobs, such as in the National Health Service, which were coincidentally highly unionized areas in the public sector.

It is now generally accepted that ethnic inequality in the labour market is significantly the result of direct and indirect racial discrimination. The existence of such discrimination in general is now well documented (see, for instance, Bergmann 1980a, 1980b; Dex, 1983; Mana, 1984; Miles and Phizacklea, 1980; Phizacklea, 1983, 1988; Rex and Moore, 1967; Rex and Tomlinson, 1979; Wallace, 1982). This discrimination shows up particularly clearly in the unemployment rates, which are twice as high for ethnic minorities as they are for white people. It is interesting here to note that there is no significant gender gap in unemployment rates. This is an instance in which disadvantage by gender and by ethnicity do not have the same effects in the labour market.

The data on wage rates is initially surprising because it appears to run counter to the usual explanation of the different experiences of white and minority women in the labour market as a result of racial discrimination. As I have shown, however, this is largely a statistical artefact.

An understanding of racist structures must then be considered an essential part of the explanation of gender relations in paid employment.

There are two further points that I want to make. Firstly, some of the institutions which act as foci of racial practices act simultaneously as foci of sexist practices. In particular historically, though less so today, many trade unions have acted in the defence of existing white male members at the expense of both blacks and women (Miles and Phizacklea, 1987; Cockburn, 1983). This may be part of the explanation of why ethnic inequality seems to be greater among men than women. That is, white men have organized in the labour market to protect their interests at the expense of all other groups, whether white female, black female or black male. There are fewer institutional factors to create racist divisions between black and white women in the labour market than for black and white men. White women have not had the equivalent of trade unions with which to institutionalize their advantage over black women (although there are other institutions).

Secondly, ethnicity and racism do not only create differences and inequalities between women; they also affect the nature of gender relations themselves. That is, the intersection of sex and race in the labour market may affect the form of gendered patterns of employment. A striking example of this is the changing gender composition of the textile industry in post-war Britain, which cannot be explained in terms of gender and class alone, but which requires an account of racial inequality and the new international division of labour.

The industry in this period was undergoing serious decline as a result of the new international division of labour in which textiles were increasingly being made in the Third World rather than in Britain or the other industrialized nations (Froebel, Heinreichs and Kreye, 1980). This led to severe downward pressure on wages in Britain in order to attempt to compensate for the increased competition. In such circumstances it would have been usual to predict that any shift in the gender composition of the workforce would be towards an increase in the proportion of women, who can generally be paid less. However, the figures indicate the opposite trend. Between 1970 and 1982 the percentage of the workforce that was female declined from 51 per cent to 42 per cent (*Department of Employment Gazette*, 1970–9, and *Employment Gazette*, 1980–2, Tables 4.1).[7] This appears to be the result of the hiring of black male workers to work a night shift in order to utilize the capital machinery on a more intensive basis. A similar process has been identified by Fevre (1984) on woollen textiles. Only men could work the night shift, because women were barred from doing so as a consequence of the nineteenth-century factory legislation. Only black men would take jobs at the wage rates on offer, because racial discrimination in the labour market closed the more lucrative forms of employment to them.

The change in the gender composition of the textile workforce is then directly related to the changing racial composition, with an increase in the employment of black men and a decrease in the employment of white women. This change in the gender composition of cotton textiles, then, can be explained only in the context of the intersection of racist structures with those of patriarchy and capitalism.

Capital restructuring and spatial variation

My account of the significance of historical variation has already indicated that I do not think that it is possible to explain concrete forms of gender inequality by theorizing from macro-systems of patriarchy and capitalism alone. There are different forms of both patriarchy and capitalism. Further, there are complex historically specific ways in which the structures and practices which make up those systems intersect. Time is one way in which instances of interconnection are separated from each other; space is another. The specific forms of gender inequality in different spatial locations may vary as a result of the detailed differences in patriarchal and capitalist structures. Indeed some of the new forms of capital restructuring have been notable for their new use of space.

Regional issues Women's employment rates differ markedly between individual regions in Britain. The highest rates on the British mainland have historically been found in the North-West of England and the lowest in Wales (31.5 per cent and 18.5 per cent respectively in 1951) (Walby, 1985: 172). This is significantly an industry effect, in that cotton textiles, which employed a high proportion of women in its workforce, was located in the North-West, and coal mining, which employed no women underground after the 1842 Mines Act, was a major form of work in Wales (Walby, 1985). Indeed Bowers (1970) shows that almost all regional variations in women's employment rates in 1961 and regional changes between 1954 and 1964 could be accounted for by regional variations in industrial structure.

The importance of the regional variation in women's employment rates has been declining in the post-war period, largely as a result of the increasing rates in those regions in which they were previously least employed for pay (Walby, 1985: 173), though also partially due to a decline in such sex-typed industries as cotton textiles and coal mining.

Current rounds of economic restructuring may be thought of as built upon previous rounds (see Massey and Meegan, 1982). The conceptual work done on this geological metaphor of restructuring by Massey (1984) can usefully be developed for application to reorganization of gender relations. A new round of industrial restructuring with its new compromises between capital, labour and patriarchy builds upon the gender relations in employment left by previous compromises between patriarchal and capitalist relations and embodied in the division of labour in those industries. Hence it is not surprising that the regions with the fastest growth rates today, when patriarchal closure against women's employment is weaker than before, are those which had the lowest rates of female employment as a product of previous intense patriarchal closure (Walby, 1985). For instance, East Anglia, which had a female employment rate second lowest only to Wales in 1951, had the fastest employment growth rate of any British region between 1952 and 1979, while the region with the highest female employment rate in 1951, the North-West, was the only region to suffer a decline in total employment between 1952 and 1979 (Fothergill and Gudgin, 1982: Table 2.1; Walby, 1985: 172–3).

International The most profound differences emerge between those countries known variously as the First World, the developed nations or the overdeveloped nations on the one hand and the Third World, developing or underdeveloped nations on the other (see Boserup, 1970; Leacock and Safia, 1986; Mies, 1986; Rogers, 1981). The conventional account is that the West brings enlightenment to the underdeveloped world and assists the liberation of women. The examples, relating to employment, which best fit this notion are those in which women are enabled to leave seclusion behind, and enter the world of paid work with the associated privileges of citizenship of the public sphere and decreased control over them by fathers and husbands. However, this view is now widely contested on two main grounds. Firstly, it underestimates the extent to which women engaged in and had control over forms of labour before colonization and/or industrialization, for instance, in the extent to which women worked the land and had rights over their produce. Secondly, it underestimates the extent to which Westernization meant the importation of the model of the domesticated housewife and its imposition on working women. For instance, Rogers (1981) argues that aid agencies misunderstand the actual gender relations of production in Third-World countries and encourage inappropriate forms of land reform which remove customary rights, and hence incentives, from women farmers, while providing new technology which assists men but not women in their labour. Blinded by Western notions of femininity, they do not recognize the full extent of women's work.

The international dimension is also of importance, not only as a form of variation in gender relations in employment, but also for its effect on gendered employment relations in Britain (Mies, 1986; Elson and Pearson, 1981; Mitter, 1986; Schreiner, 1918). Most basically, the standard of living in nations such as Britain depends upon the labour of those in the Third World, through unequal exchange relations (Frank, 1967; Wallerstein, 1979). Further, the specific forms of industrial restructuring, which have had different effects upon male and female workers in the metropoles such as Britain, the USA and West Germany, have depended upon new international forms of capital (Froebel, Heinreichs and Kreye, 1980; Massey, 1984; Mitter, 1986). The new international division of labour has an intensely gendered form, although this is not often recognized (Mitter, 1986). A strong case for the interconnectedness of the exploitation of First- and Third-World women by patriarchal capitalism is made by Mies (1986).

Mies argues that the dependency of women in the industrialized countries is possible only because of the exploitation of women in non-industrialized countries:

> It is my thesis that these two processes of colonization and housewifization are closely and causally interlinked. Without the ongoing exploitation of external colonies – formerly as direct colonies, today within the new international division of labour – the establishment of the 'internal colony', that is, a nuclear family and a woman maintained by a male 'breadwinner', would not have been possible. (p. 110)

Mies argues that the domestication or, as she calls it, the housewifization of women in the metropolitan capitalist nations is dependent upon the exploitation of the Third World. She argues that the development of this family form was historically specific and was restricted to the rise of imperialism during the nineteenth century. It started with the bourgeoisie and was spread to the working classes. The first stage is the process of imperialism, conquest and the development of the luxury trade. The second stage is the development of an internal colony in which women are colonized by men in Europe. The relations within the industrialized countries is only half the account, the other is that in the Third World.

Mies argues that there has been a shift in the international division of labour from the old one in which raw materials were exported from the colonies for processing in the industrialized world and then marketed world wide, to a new international division of labour. In the new division industrial production is transferred to the developing countries, producing unemployment in the industrialized countries. It is women who are the new industrial producers in the Third World, and it is women who are the consumers of these items in the First World. Women are the optimal labour force in the Third World since their designation as dependent housewives enables them to be paid low wages. Women in the First World, fired from their jobs as a result of the transfer of industry, are the consumers. Mies's account also manages to integrate a concern with issues as wide-ranging as violence against women to movements for national liberation. She argues that violence against women is used to ensure their subordination. She goes on to assert that patriarchy is not distinct from capitalism, and that capitalism is merely the latest form of patriarchy.

Mies has provided a far-reaching, provocative account of the interconnections between the First and Third Worlds. Its strengths are its view of the international linkages at the economic level, the powerful account of developments over time, and sensitivity to the different ways in which women can be oppressed and exploited. Its weaknesses stem from problems in some of the supporting evidence and theoretical silences, not unexpectedly, given the scope of the project. Firstly, her argument that women in the First World are currently subject to housewifization following the transfer of industry to the Third World is empirically incorrect. Women are entering paid employment in greater proportions than ever before, despite having higher unemployment rates than men in almost all Western countries bar Britain. To be fair, one should note that this process is not complete, but nevertheless the direction of change is the opposite from that which Mies argues is the case. Secondly, the nuclear family form was not unique to modern capitalism. Laslett (1977) and MacFarland (1978) have shown that it is not unique and that it pre-dated the rise of capitalism, so could not have been caused by it. Even the more intensely domesticated version in which the woman is not allowed to take outside employment is not unique to the Victorian middle classes, since it can be found among Islamic cultures, especially among their urban middle and upper classes. In short Mies places too much explanatory emphasis upon changes in capitalism, despite her interest in a world system of patriarchy. Thirdly, in practice she does distinguish between patriarchy and capitalism at some points, which contradicts her claim that they are one system. Nevertheless the international interconnectedness of patriarchal relations is firmly established.

When the focus is returned to Britain it appears that the new forms of capital restructuring have sometimes involved the movement of capital from old industries in Britain and other countries of the First World to the Third World, where labour is much cheaper to employ (Froebel, Heinreichs and Kreye, 1980; Massey, 1984). However, this was the case in some industries more than others and the argument should not be generalized too far (Gordon, 1988). The industries in Britain which have suffered most employment decline as a consequence of the movement of capital are in the manufacturing rather than the service sector (Blackaby, 1978). While cotton textiles, which employs a high proportion of women, has been very significantly changed by the process, most of the other industries affected by the new international division of labour employed a high proportion of men. Many of the newly employed workers in the Third World are women. In these countries, as in Britain, women are cheaper to employ than men (Elson and Pearson, 1981; Mies, 1986; Mitter, 1986). Gender relations have been a very important issue in recent political upheavals in many Third-World countries. For instance, as patriarchal politics they are central to the resurgence of Islamic fundamentalism (Kandyoti, 1987) as well as feminist politics in the Third World (Jayawardena, 1986). These changes in the sexual division of labour are, then, highly contested.

Space is thus important, not only as a source of variation in gender relations in employment, but also because it is implicated in forms of power of one social group over another. It would be a serious mistake to attempt to explain gender relations in employment in Britain without such a consideration of the international dimension.

Capital restructuring makes changing demands upon workers differentiated by gender and location. Analyses of the gender division of labour must be careful not to treat capital as a homogenous entity.

Flexibility: a new form of capital restructuring? Not all forms of capital restructuring have a spatial dimension. Recent debates have suggested that 'flexibilization' is the latest form of capital restructuring. In Atkinson's account, firms, under renewed pressure from competition and in a strengthened position in relation to their workers because of the recession, are implementing a series of labour market decisions which together amount to the development of the flexible firm (NEDO, 1986). The key features of this are the development of functional flexibility among the 'core' workforce and numerical flexibility among the peripheral workers. Functional flexibility means the multi-skilling of workers so that they can easily be transferred between tasks according to the day-to-day needs of the firm. Numerical flexibility means that those workers who do not have special, firm-specific skills are employed in such ways that the hours of labour they provide can be varied according to the day-to-day needs of the firm. This includes the development of sub-contracting, part-time work, overtime, temporary contracts and other processes which casualize the workforce.

The thesis is controversial, especially as to the extent to which it is actually happening, and the extent to which it is new (Pollert, 1987). Further, there are different versions of the thesis. For instance, Piore and Sable (1984) stress the potential for human development in the new forms of production which might supersede the mass assembly line with custom-oriented products and enriched labour processes.

The most important aspect of the thesis for an analysis of gender relations is what it might contribute to the explanation of the growth of part-time working among women. According to Atkinson this is a result of the drive of numerical flexibility. However, the rise of part-time working in Britain started in the Second World War and continued steadily ever since, so the timing is inconsistent with his model of flexibility as he presents it (Walby, 1989).

Significance of the state

I have suggested above that the state has been central to the resolution of certain key conflicts between patriarchal and capitalist forces over the utilization of women's labour. However, the mode of intervention of the state has not always been the same. The critical change is primarily a result of the winning of political citizenship for women during first-wave feminism. This change within the state is explored further in the chapter on the state; here I am going to examine the changing role of the state in the regulation of women's employment.

During the nineteenth- and early twentieth-century campaigns to restrict women's work, such as in the cotton industry and the munitions, women did not have the vote and were thus without direct representation in Parliament. Neither was there any other way in which women's interests were represented at the level of the state to any significant degree.

In the first major conflict over women's right to work after their winning of the franchise, women won. This was during the 1930s depression in which there were fierce arguments over women having paid jobs when men did not. Despite the political pressure, no marriage bar was brought in by the state, notwithstanding the widespread use of and some evidence of an increase in this practice in individual industries (Lewis, 1980: 214; Lewenhak, 1977: 215; *The Vote*, 1932: 52, 129).[8] However, there women did lose some rights to welfare payments: married women's access was denied under the 'not genuinely seeking working' clause of the Anomalies Act, and was compounded by denial of benefit to women who would not take work as domestic servants, even if they were skilled textile workers (Bagguley, 1989).

However, in the next major conflict, over women as munitions workers in the Second World War, women did lose the argument at the level of the state, in that legislation (the Restoration of the Pre-War Practices Act 1942) was passed supporting the all-male unions' demands that if they allowed women in for the duration of the war they would be expelled at the end of it (Soldon, 1978; Summerfield, 1984). But, interestingly, this legislation was never fully implemented after the war (Summerfield, 1984; Walby, 1986).

The next major intervention of the state into regulating women's employment was in the opposite direction. That is, the state shifted from restricting women's employment to assisting it and the conditions under which it was performed. In 1970 the Equal Pay Act was passed (to be implemented in 1975), and was followed by the Sex Discrimination Act in 1975. The origins of this change and analysis of reasons for its effects are discussed in the chapter on the state; it is the actual effects which are of concern here. The legislation is widely believed to be relatively ineffective (see Gregory, 1982, 1987); however, it does appear to have led to a closing of the wages gap by 10 per cent from 63.1 per cent of men's hourly rates in 1970 to 75.5 per cent in 1977 and back to 74.3 per cent in 1986 (or 54.5 per cent of men's gross weekly earnings in 1970 to 64.9 per cent in 1977 and 66.3 per cent in 1986) (Equal Opportunities Commission, 1987: 38–9). While some have implied that closing the gap was an artefact of the incomes policy of the period (Campbell and Charlton, 1978), Weir and McIntosh (1982) demonstrate that the effect is in fact due to the legislation.

In addition, never again has the state introduced legislation restricting women's access to employment. The debate has shifted onto the question of how effective it is in opening up further avenues of employment.

I have argued that the state is an important factor in the determination of women's employment; that this is not a result merely of economic or economic and familial reasons. Further, that the role of the state is not uniform but has changed radically as a result of women gaining political citizenship.

Other structures

My system of patriarchy has two further structures: patriarchal relations in sexuality and male violence. It is important to consider what impact these could have on gender patterns in employment.

Sexuality   It is conventionally thought that sexuality has little to do with paid work. indeed such a dichotomy is fundamental to Mitchell's (1975) version of the dual-system approach, in that, while sexuality is a province of patriarchal relations, the economy is determined by only capitalist relations. However, there are ways in which patriarchal sexual practices do have an effect on gender patterns of employment. The most important of these is sexual harassment. This was discussed above under the heading of the radical feminist contribution to the analysis of paid employment (especially via MacKinnon, 1979), but work from a variety of perspectives has in fact been done in this area (e.g., Hadjifotiou, 1983; Hearn and Parkin, 1987; Stanko, 1988).

Sexual harassment acts both to control women with work and to exclude women from certain types of work. The exclusionary effect is possibly the most dramatic. This is when sexual harassment is used by men to prevent women from entering a field of employment which has previously been all male. A survey in Leeds found that 96 per cent of women in non-traditional areas of employment had experienced forms of sexual harassment at work (Leeds, 1983). The most publicized recent event of this order was in the London Fire Brigade in the mid-1980s, when women, testing their new rights of entry under the equal opportunity legislation, were subject to gross physical and sexual attacks to discourage them.

Sexual harassment is not, however, confined to women working in traditionally male areas of work, although it is reported less often in the surveys. The same Leeds survey cited above found that 48 per cent of women in traditional spheres of employment for women had experienced sexual harassment. Indeed Stanko (1988) thinks the difference in reporting rates may be due merely to women in traditional areas having less power to make complaints.

Violence   Sexual harassment is a continuum of behaviours which may extend to the use of physical force. The threat of physical force may also be relevant, in that fear of it often prevents women walking in public spaces after dark, with consequent effects of access to jobs which require this, such as shift working.

However, the main relevance of violence in relation to gender and paid work is when it is legitimate violence carried out by the state to police industrial relations disputes and employment law.

Differentiation of patriarchal strategies in employment

Hartmann's analysis of job segregation by sex was a critical advance in theorizing gender relations in employment. However, there is more than one form of closure. The first critical distinction I would like to make is between segregation and exclusion as two distinct patriarchal strategies in paid work. The exclusion strategy is aimed at totally preventing women's access to an area of employment, or indeed to all paid employment; the segregation is a weaker strategy aimed at separating women's from men's work and at grading the former beneath the latter for purposes of remuneration and status. This distinction is illuminated by a comparison between engineering and clerical work. Unions of skilled manual engineering workers succeeded in their strategy of excluding women from skilled manual work from their foundation to the middle of the twentieth century. Even as late as 1940 we find Tanner, the President of the Amalgamated Engineering Union (AEU), declaring that 'We, as an organisation are opposed to the introduction of women as a general principle' (Engineering and Allied Employers' National Federation, Central and Special Conference Shorthand Minutes, 8 April 1940, p. 430). The critical turning point was in the middle of the Second World War. In 1943 the AEU admitted women as members for the first time (Jeffreys, 1970). At this time they changed to a segregation strategy; women were to be admitted but confined to certain areas of work and separate sections of the union. This alteration was as a result of the failure of the exclusionary strategy. Employers had long fought the engineering union's ability to control the labour supply; indeed a long and bitter series of strikes and a lock-out in 1897 was over this issue (*The Engineer*, 1897; Jeffreys, J. B., 1945: 143–8). Women were being admitted to engineering work under the pressure of the war-time shortage of male workers, and other, general, unions were beginning to recruit them (Walby, 1986).

In clerical work the men were never able to establish an exclusionary strategy, despite efforts to do so. It was attempted at the turn of the century while the occupation was developing its modern form, but they did not have the power to enforce this strategy (Holcombe, 1973; Humphreys, 1958; Martindale, 1938). For instance, the General Secretary of the National Union of Clerks, Mr Elvin, declared in his union's journal that there would be problems in the office 'until that ideal time arrives when female labour will not be known in factory workshop or office' (*The Clerk*, 1908: 131). However, they never had the strength to see this strategy through, and turned instead to one of segregation. The separation of men and women was then a consequence of the struggle between men workers, women workers and employers. Segregation was a strategy to minimize direct competition between men and women by preventing women from working in those areas of clerical work where men remained, while still allowing women to be a source of cheap labour for employers in other grades (Holcombe, 1973; Humphreys, 1958; Martindale, 1938; Walby, 1986).

The exclusionary strategy was predominant among the craft unions of nineteenth- and early twentieth-century Britain, while general unions, and unions which developed later in the period, were more likely to follow a segregation strategy (Walby, 1986). This change in union approach to the issue of women is due to three main factors. Firstly, it was a consequence of a losing battle against the entry of women by specific unions (e.g., AEU); that is, a failure of the exclusionary strategy. Secondly, it was due to the greater growth of the general unions which recruited semi- and unskilled workers, whose strategy was one of segregation almost from the start. Thirdly, it was due to the shift in state policy from one which would respond to pleas by organized male workers for assistance through legislative means of closure against women, to one, after women won the vote, in which women's rights of entry were supported.

The segregation strategy itself is composed of several historically and spatially specific sub-types. The most important new form of labour market segmentation in Britain since the 1940s is that of the division between part-time and full-time work, the former being performed almost exclusively by married women. The conditions of work are different between part-time and full-time in two main respects: part-time jobs pay less than full-time ones on average; part-timers have less secure contracts of employment, making them more vulnerable to dismissal (Robinson, 1988).

Full-time women earned 66 per cent of men's weekly earnings, and 74 per cent of their hourly wages, while part-time women earned only 56 per cent of men's hourly rates in 1986. Part-time women earned 76 per cent of full-time women's hourly rates (New Earnings Survey).

Part-time workers who are employed for less than eight hours a week do not gain any of the advantages of the right to claim unfair dismissal, maternity benefits, redundancy payments. Those who work between eight and 16 hours can claim these rights only if they have been with an employer more than five years (Robinson, 1988).

Britain has a more extreme differentiation between the rights of part-time and full-time workers than many other countries (Manley and Sawbridge, 1980). This may at least partially account for the higher proportion of part-time women workers in Britain than in any other EEC country bar Denmark (Walby, 1983a). That is, they are more attractive to British employers than others because they do not come with the employment rights which they have in other European countries. This is not to say that women who work part-time do not wish to do so. Results from the Women in Employment survey clearly indicate that these hours are largely a preference of the women themselves so that they can more easily combine this work with their domestic work (Martin and Roberts, 1984). But employers' decisions to create particular sorts of jobs are rarely considered to be more than partially influenced by the preferences of their employees.

The existence of part-time work has facilitated the large post-war rise in female activity rates. Indeed Britain still has one of the highest rates of female employment in the EEC, despite the greater depths of the British recession. Women's employment continues to grow, as table 2.1 above showed.

A further way of differentiating forms of segregation are those proposed by Witz (1987, 1988), who considers the appropriation of sets of skills by specific groups of workers and the fighting over the boundaries of occupational competence, as well as the exclusion or inclusion of women in a pre-defined occupation. She introduces the notion of demarcationary closure to describe this.

Thus I am proposing to go beyond Hartmann's introduction of the concept of segregation to the analysis of patriarchal relations in paid work. The major distinction is that between exclusion and segregation. Segregation itself can be found in different forms. One type here is the distinction between full-time and part-time. A second distinction is between individual exclusionary closure and demarcationary closure. The effects have both horizontal and vertical forms, as we saw at the beginning of this chapter, where it was noted that recently in Britain there has been a decline in vertical segregation simultaneous with an increase in horizontal segregation.

The most important distinction, however, is that between exclusion on the one hand and segregation with inclusion on the other. Indeed these two forms of patriarchal strategy can be found in other arenas than paid work. In particular they can be seen in both the state and in sexuality (see the chapters below). I shall argue at the end of the book that these two forms of patriarchal strategy underlie two historically distinct forms of patriarchy.

CONCLUSION

While the review of theories of gender and employment has so far been conducted in terms of four main perspectives, there are some central issues which cross-cut these perspectives. These are important for my argument as to the interrelationship of the different patriarchal structures. Thus in the first part of the conclusion to this chapter I would draw out the following three points:

1   The labour market is more important and the family less important as the determinant of women's labour force participation than is conventionally assumed.
2   Women's lesser participation in paid work is a result of material constraints rather than a matter of 'choice' or of cultural values, as is frequently argued.
3   Politics and the state are much more important in the structuring of the sexual division of labour than is often recognized; we need an analysis in terms not merely of economy, but of *political* economy.

Labour market versus family

The conventional view has been to argue that women's position in employment (and indeed in most aspects of society) is determined by their position in the family. This is very clear in the analyses of neo-classical economists such as Mincer (1962, 1966), in functionalist sociologists such as Parsons and Bales (1956), and in Marxist writers such as (early) Beechey (1977, 1978). I think that this is wrong, except in the weak sense in which individual women faced with decisions will take their immediate domestic circumstances into account. It is doubtless true that a woman today considering employment decisions will be constrained by her domestic circumstances. A married woman is likely to be faced with expectations for domestic services from her husband and other 'dependents', combined with the likelihood that her husband's greater earning power will give him considerable influence over her decisions and, most importantly, her expectation of psychic and financial gains if she embraces the role of wife and mother enthusiastically. If our analysis is restricted to the current moment then it will look, superficially, as if the family significantly structures a woman's employment decisions. However, while this may be critical for an understanding of immediate decision making, it does not provide an explanation of the structures which constrain a woman's 'choice'. It does not explain why women do not have the same access as men to the better jobs. It is an explanation of these circumstances that I seek, not a description of how women negotiate them.

It has been shown that women's lower pay cannot be explained in terms of their lower skill and qualifications, that is, as a result of their position in the family. It has been further demonstrated that women's labour force participation is not explicable in terms of their being used as a reserve army of labour, that is, in terms of their position in the family.

Rather, the structuring of the labour market, in particular, occupational segregation by sex, emerges as critical to the explanation at every turn. It is because women are concentrated in low-paying industries and occupations that they get paid less than men, not primarily due to human capital deficiencies. It is because women are to be found in the growing sectors of the economy, the service sector, rather than in the declining manufacturing sector, that they have not lost employment as much as men in times of recession such as the 1980s. The explanation of occupational segregation is critical to the explanation of gender inequality in paid work.

The causal link between labour market and family goes largely (but not exclusively) in the reverse direction from that conventionally assumed; it goes from the labour market to family, not vice versa, when we ask questions about causation at a structural level.

Materialist versus culturalist

A further conventional view is that women's patterns of employment are determined by cultural and ideological factors rather than material ones; this is related to the notion that the gender division of labour is consensual rather than conflictual. For instance, it is assumed that women voluntarily left paid work at the end of the world wars, that women voluntarily gave up paid work on marriage, that women choose light rather than heavy work, and that they choose not to gain training. These assumptions are not borne out by the evidence. Women left paid employment at the end of the First World War because they were forced to by agreements between employers and male unions, backed by state legislation. Women used to give up paid work on marriage because they were forced to by the marriage bar, which forbade married women from remaining in most forms of formal employment; their preferences were irrelevant to employers. After the removal of the marriage bar during the Second World War, the growth in married women's paid employment was enormous. Many women have been engaged in work as heavy and dirty as that of men, although this is often not recognized. Women's access to training, such as the universities, has had to be fought for; initial entry was won by first-wave feminism, but struggles continue. In short I am arguing that women's access to forms of paid employment is an issue of conflict as much as consensus; about issues of material power as well as normative values.

The level of the analysis is again important as it was for the discussion of the relative importance of the labour market as against the family in shaping women's patterns of employment. If we look at women's own expressed beliefs of the reasons they do certain things, not others, it appears as if cultural values are of riding significance; however, the deeper question is what creates the structures that lead to these beliefs.

Politics These issues relate to a further conventional view: that women's employment is not significantly affected by political processes. I am arguing that politics both in the sense of state action and organized collective behaviour not at the level of the state have been important in shaping women's employment (and hence men's).

The state was called upon by organized male workers in the nineteenth century to support their demands to exclude women from the best jobs. Feminist struggle has made a major change in the conduct of the state towards women workers since women gained political citizenship. Overt attempts to bar women have occurred much less frequently, while today the state ostensibly supports women's equal rights in employment through the Equal Pay and Sex Discrimination Acts (although this is not a policy pursued with vigour).

Gender relations in employment are critically affected by political struggle; women have not acquiesced in their exclusion from the best jobs.

Contemporary changes

Women have increasingly been entering paid employment in the post-war period, especially married women (since single women have usually taken paid work (see table 2.1)). This entry into such an important aspect of the 'public' sphere has traditionally been seen as a sign of the emancipation of women. Women's labour is less available for exploitation by husbands within the household. Exclusionary practices against women in the labour market are less frequent than before, either by organized male workers or the state.

In the light of such evidence one might write of the lessening of gender inequality. However, the degree of inequality between men and women in terms of pay, conditions, and access to well-rewarded occupations has declined only very slightly. That is, there has been only a slight qualitative change in the position of women within employment, despite the considerable quantitative increase in their participation rates. The wages gap has declined only slightly, from women earning 63 per cent of men's earnings in 1970 to 74 per cent in 1986, while the expanding sector of part-time workers earn only 76 per cent of full-time women's pay (New Earnings Survey, 1986). The extent of vertical segregation is still extensive, despite some decreases in the decade 1971 to 1981, as shown in tables 2.2 and 2.3 above. While horizontal segregation by industries has declined for men, it has increased for women between 1971 and 1981, as shown in table 2.4 above.

So while the absolute exclusion of women from paid work is diminishing, their segregation into low-paying industries and occupations and part-time work has declined only a little. Women are gaining access to the public sphere of paid employment, but are subordinated to men within it.

This process of change from private to public form of patriarchal exploitation of women is a product of two main forces for change. Firstly, there is the demand for cheaper labour by employers within a capitalist labour market. This produces a continuing pull towards the entry of women into paid employment because patriarchal production relations constitute women as a cheaper labour force than men on average. As we have seen, however, this process is complicated by the differing forms of capital restructuring and of racism. Secondly, feminist struggle has helped undermine patriarchal exclusionary strategies. This has occurred on a number of sites, but those of the state and the trade unions are of particular importance here. The winning of the suffrage has enabled women to block exclusionary strategies being supported by the state. Trade unions themselves have been changed by women's entry to membership, and by increasing organization within them, from vehicles for patriarchal exclusionary strategies to at worst vehicles for segregation strategies.

The combined result of capitalist forces and feminist struggle have been primarily responsible for the change from private towards public patriarchal exploitation of women's labour.

NOTES

1 These committees included: The Machinery of Government Committee, the Committee on the Organization and Staffing of Government Offices, the

Gladstone Committee, the War Cabinet Committee on Women in Industry, the Women's Advisory Committee of the Ministry of Reconstruction, and the Treasury Committee on Civil Service Recruitment After the War (Walby, 1986).

2   Percentage of people of working age – 16 to retirement age – who are either employed or seeking employment, divided by total number of people of working age.

3   Average for 1984, 1985 and 1986 from the Labour Force Survey, *Employment Gazette*, March 1988: 165. This three-yearly average is presented by the *Employment Gazette* to overcome the problems of sampling error due to the small numbers of ethnic minority people in the survey.

4   However, these figures may underestimate the amount of economic activity among Pakistani and Bangladeshi women by not picking up the extent of homeworking.

5   Calculated from Labour Force Survey data presented as a three-year average by *Employment Gazette*, March 1988, Table 3. The calculation is to turn the figures into percentages of employees who are classified as full-time and part-time, and omit the self-employed and those on schemes for whom such a distinction is not given.

6   Although the *Employment Gazette* states that the last figure should be treated with caution, given the small numbers involved.

7   Since the figures for cotton are not always given separately, these are the sum of SIC MLH (Standard Industrial Classification, Minimum List Heading number) 412, 'spinning and doubling on the cotton and flax systems', and SIC MLH 413, 'weaving of cotton, linen and man-made fibres'.

8   However, while the national state did not introduce a marriage bar, some local authorities did, in their capacity as employers. The extent of women's political activity seems to have been a major factor in determining the outcome: for instance, there was no bar in Nelson, where women were organized, but there was in Lancaster and Preston, where women were not (Mark-Lawson, Savage and Warde, 1985).

3

Household Production

The family is conventionally considered to be central to women's lives and to the determination of gender inequality. Perspectives as different as Marxist feminism and Parsonian functionalism agree on this. The family is seen as a pillar of stability and as fundamental to social order, whether these things are admired or detested.

However, I shall show in a whole variety of ways that, while the family is important in many women's and men's every-day experiences, it is less important than is usually thought. As a site of production relations its significance is declining, as women increasingly spend more time under capitalist relations of production rather than privatized patriarchal production relations in the household. Further, it is changing under the impact of developments elsewhere and does not have such reciprocal causal effect on these. Production carried out in the household is continuing to undergo significant restructuring, partly as a result of the expansion of capitalist production, and partly because of changes in the state under pressure from feminist and other gendered forces.

The definitions of 'family' and 'household' are problematic. The two concepts differ, since not all members of a 'family' share a common household, and not all members of a household are members of the same family. Thus the common interchangeability of the terms is a mistake. Further, the significance of the family, as conventionally defined as composed of husband-breadwinner, wife-homemaker and dependent children, is being challenged by the fact that the number of people who live in such families is small. One solution to these problems is to reinterpret the notion of 'family' as a discourse, and to explore its varying and multiple meanings in contemporary society (Bernardes, 1986); to explore the 'project' of the mobilization of the discourse of the family (Gubrium, 1988).

In this chapter I shall address the household rather than the family, and, more specifically, production relations within the household. The family will be considered insofar as it bears upon gender relations of production and the structures through which women's labour is expropriated in the household. Sexuality, male violence to women, and culture are examined in separate chapters and will only be touched on here. While these structures are important for the conduct of relations between men and women in the home, they span a wider range of institutional spaces than just the household. For instance, sexuality is not confined to marriage. Hence it is inappropriate to consider them in this location alone.

I am focusing primarily on production relations here, though I am defining the area usually described as 'reproduction' as production, since it is work. There has often been a conceptual split between 'reproduction' and 'production'. Engels's definition of reproduction as a set of specific tasks associated with the birth and care of children and with food and shelter is not uncommon. This practice is hopelessly flawed as an analytic device, however, since all the tasks typically designated as 'reproduction' can be performed in a way conventionally recognizable as 'production' – from food provision in the commercial baking of bread, restaurants and wet nursing, to child care in the running of boarding schools and factory creches, to cleaning by laundries and agency cleaners, to sexual and emotional servicing in brothels and private psychotherapy. As Delphy (1984) has noted, the issue is not the distinction between tasks, but rather between the social relations under which these forms of work are performed.

In addition to the perspectives of radical feminism, Marxist feminism, liberal feminism and dual-systems theory, there has been a historically significant contribution to the analysis of the family by functionalism, which will be considered as well.

Parsonian functionalism

While functionalist accounts of the family, classically developed by Parsons and Bales (1956) and developed by Goode (1963) and Smelser (1959), are usually considered totally discredited in modern sociology, nevertheless this perspective frequently reappears with newer labels. For instance, Althusser's ostensibly Marxist account of the family as an ideological state apparatus has strong affinities with Parsonian accounts. Hence it is worth-while briefly examining the traditional writers and their critics to explore the basic issues and to prevent needless future repetition of past mistakes.

Parsons conceptualized gender relations in terms of sex roles; men in the family performed the instrumental role and women the expressive one. The family itself existed as a social institution because it performed essential functions for society: those of the socialization of children and of the stabilization of adult personalities. The relations between men and women was considered basically to be one of being different but equal. Men have the task of being oriented to the external world, women of looking after the internal needs of the family members. These roles must be kept separate, according to Parsons, otherwise there would be conflict and tension between the occupational structure and the kinship system.

Functionalism has often been criticized for being unable to deal with social change but, since it did address the issue of change and the family (see Goode, 1963), this is not an adequate criticism. Parsons suggested that with the development of a more complex society there was a differentiation of functions between institutions. As society industrialized, the production function of the family was split off into other institutions. Hence there have been real changes in the form and function of the family. However, Parsons was insistent that more recent changes such as the post-war rise in the divorce rate, change in sexual morality and decline in the birth rate did not mean the collapse of the family as an institution. Rather, he said, the rise in the divorce rate would be checked and divorcees would remarry and return to the institution of the family, while the decline in the birth rate was merely a temporary phenomenon.

Some of the more sophisticated functionalist writers, such as Goode (1963) and Smelser (1959), have tried to grapple with long-run historical change and the family. Goode argued, on the basis of a survey of family forms across the world and several centuries, that there was a functional fit between the family and industrialization. Smelser examined the conflicts in the process of the form of the family adjusting to the new industrialized environment. In both cases they agreed with Parsons that the small nuclear family of husband, wife and dependent children was functionally suited to industrialized societies, but added analyses of conflict and change to this process of adaptation.

However, historical evidence does not support their contentions. Laslett (1977) shows that the nuclear family in England long pre-dated industrialization, while Anderson (1971) documents how the family grew, rather than shrank, in size during early industrialization. Industrialization and the form of the family do not have a simple relationship.

A more serious problem in Parsons's account of the family is its failure to deal with social inequalities. Rather than different but equal, the position of men and women is one of dominance and subordination. For instance, time-budget studies show that the leisure time of women, after the performance of work and essential activities, is less than that of men. Even when both men and women have full-time jobs women have less free time, 24.6 hours per week, as compared with 33.5 hours per week for men. Women who have part-time jobs and those who are full-time housewives have more free time, but not as much as men who work either full-time or part-time (Equal Opportunities Commission, 1987: 50).

A second major problem is that of Parsons's characterization of the task of women in the expressive role as an ideological activity, rather than as work. Oakley (1974) has soundly demonstrated that housework is work like any other, even if it is not rewarded by money. This tendency to view housework as a cultural activity is not confined to Parsonian functionalism, but is to be found in Althusser's Marxist functionalism as well. Althusser regarded the family as an ideological state apparatus, disregarding the economic and material significance of women's labour, and his argument is thus similarly flawed.

A third problem is that Parsons's account of the family is descriptively inaccurate insofar as it is intended as a general account of the post-war Western family. Rather this small nuclear family, with its wage-earning husband, full-time housewife and dependent children, is confined to the middle classes of white ethnic groups in the Western world of the 1950s. In other classes and ethnic groups more or fewer people are attached to the household group, while the 1950s were historically exceptional in the low rate of women's waged work.

Despite these problems with Parsonian functionalism, which have led, properly, to its overt dismissal by serious social scientists, some of the central features of the argument are retained implicitly within other texts, merely with new labels. I have already referred to the similarity with Althusserian Marxism; there are some further examples.

The functionalist heritage: household work strategies and the family

One important part of functionalist thinking which is still commonplace in modern social science, despite the apparent rejection of functionalism, is that of the household as a consensual unit with a fair division of duties. This arises in particular in the notion of a household work strategy in which the sexual division of labour between husbands and wives is considered to be part of a collective decision by the household, in the light of their joint interests. That is, a conception of the household as a unit in which decisions are taken in an egalitarian way in the interests of all members. This is a notion of the genders as different but equal.

This model is perhaps clearest in the work of economists, such as Mincer (1962, 1966), who considered that women did not take up as much paid work as men as a result of a household work strategy. This account, described and criticized in more detail in the previous chapter on paid work, also has an account of the smooth fit between this household structure, the market and other economic institutions.

The model is also to be found, more implicitly and with less adjacent baggage, in the work of Ray E. Pahl (1984). Pahl considers the division of labour in the household to be the result of a household work strategy, collectively agreed upon, in the interests of the household as a whole. While his overall conception of society is not a functionalist one, his account of the household is strikingly similar. Again we have no account of power and conflict in the family, though Pahl does detail an inequitable division of labour between spouses.

The underlying feature of these accounts which causes the problem is the preservation of the functionalist's conception of the family, a unit of consensus, as the main concept to deal with gender. In this usage there is a refusal to allow conceptual space to theorize gender inequality. If the fundamental unit locks men and women in one consensual unit, then there is no conceptual space to theorize the inequality between men and women.

Of course, the use of the family as the central link between gender and society, with its attendant problems, is not confined to functionalism. It can also be found in conventional class analysis, where women are tucked into the class of their husband or father. Again the result is identical – inequality between men and women is conceptually eradicated.

In all instances the necessary alternative is to theorize gender, not the family, as the central concept.

Radical feminism

Radical feminist accounts of gender and production in the household stress the exploitation of wives by husbands and do not suffer from assumptions of consensus. They vary as to the conceptualization of the link between the household and other aspects of gender inequality from those writers, such as Firestone (1974), who see reproduction and hence the household as central to women's subordination, to those who see other sites as much more important, for instance Brownmiller (1976), who sees rape as central, and to those who argue that institutionalized heterosexuality is the basis, for instance, Rich (1980). Within this latter view, perhaps the most common among radical feminists, material aspects of the household are subsumed into the institution of heterosexuality. It is the sexual relations which organize the material relations. Since the main issue in these accounts is sexuality I shall review these writers in the later chapter on sexuality, and shall focus in this chapter on those radical feminists who have had most to say about the specifically material aspects of the household.

Firestone's argument about the central role of reproduction in women's subordination is perhaps the classic account. She argues that reproduction is the basis of women's subordination by men. The biological hazards surrounding reproduction, such as pregnancy, menstruation, childbirth, breast-feeding, and child rearing, make women vulnerable and dependent on men. This creates two classes based on sex, men and women. Firestone draws on and develops many Marxian concepts in her analysis.

Firestone considers reproduction to be the real material base of human society, more basic than production. The organization of the rest of the social superstructure is determined by the forms of reproduction, albeit in a complex and mediated way. For instance, the forms of love, which can be so destructive in an unequal society, are structured, ultimately by reproduction. Firestone argues that when women are dependent on men, as they must be given their vulnerability due to reproduction, the love experience is corrupted by power play. This is both because women are trying to catch the best husband, and because men's emotional development has been stunted by their upbringing in a patriarchal family.

Firestone sees the only solution to lie in the eradication of the basic problem: women's vulnerability in reproduction. Developing forms of technology provide the possibility that human society may escape the limitations of biology, but only if the means of reproduction can be seized and controlled in the interests of women.

Firestone has been criticized for a having a reductionist and biologistic analysis, which is necessarily universalistic and ahistoric (Barrett, 1980). Indeed she is classically taken to epitomize radical feminist thought and its failings. Barrett and others (e.g., Segal, 1987; Rowbotham, 1981) argue that, by setting up all men as exploiters of all women, radical feminists are necessarily biologically reductionist, as these can only be biological categories. These falsely generate a static account, since, by definition, biology cannot change.

Further, Firestone has been criticized for a naive view of scientific progress by those who think technology is more likely to be used against women, since it is controlled by patriarchal interests (Rose and Hanmer, 1976). However, while it is fair to criticize theories of patriarchy, such as that of Firestone, for not having an adequate theory of change, it is not appropriate to suggest that all their proponents think that change does not take place (although some do take this position). For instance, Firestone has a well-developed model of change in patriarchy, despite having set up reproduction as its sole basis. She does this by considering both technology and political struggle to be further causal entities, although these are not integrated with her initially stated theoretical position. Firestone argues that changes in technology produce the capacity for change in the mode of reproduction, in much the same way that Marx argued that changes in the forces of production created the possibility for the emergence of the next mode of production. Firestone contended that women have to seize the means of reproduction in order to achieve this transformation (a part of her argument often glossed over by those who criticize her for naively optimistic technological determinism). This is parallel to Marx's reasoning that the proletariat has to seize the means of production in order to move to the next mode of production. Thus in practice Firestone introduces into her argument both technology and political struggle as causal entities. However, she fails to integrate these into her theoretical discussion, leaving it as a loose empirical end. In practice she has a model of change involving three causal entities – reproduction, technology and political struggle; in theory she has one – reproduction. The major logical flaw in her argument is the failure to elevate these empirically based notions of technological change and political struggle into theoretical constructs. It might still be the case that we disagree with her synopsis, but she should not be dismissed at such a superficial level for theoretical inadequacy.

One of the remaining and serious problems with Firestone's account of reproduction, however, is that it conflates the social aspects of child rearing into the biological aspects of pregnancy and childbirth. There are a vast variety of ways in which child-care has been socially organized, and Firestone's notion of a 'biological nuclear family' is misplaced. Indeed an alternative feminist future is one in which child care is socialized and shared, despite women's role, for a few months, in pregnancy and childbirth.

Not all radical feminists see reproduction and children as the major source of women's oppression as does Firestone. For instance, Rich (1977) considers children to be a major source of joy to women and motherhood to be a potentially blissful experience. Motherhood as an institution under patriarchy does give women a lot of problems, but this is due to patriarchy, not to motherhood itself. There is nothing essentially oppressive about children.

Indeed Rich's embrace of motherhood as a valuable and central experience for women has attracted critical attention from some writers for being a eulogy to an essential feminine experience. Hester Eisenstein (1984) divides feminist theory into two schools in a sameness/difference debate and argues that writers such as Rich adopt a woman-centred analysis in which traditional womanly characteristics are fêted. Some critics have gone as far as suggesting that radical feminist woman-centred analysis is necessarily essentialist (Segal, 1987). That is, it adopts an unvarying conception of what it is to be a woman and is contaminated with biologism.

This criticism goes too far in relation to Rich as well as in relation to Firestone. Rich's conception of the social constructedness of the institution of motherhood and her plea for new variations on its form under a non-patriarchal society at least qualifies any assertion that she has a notion of a universal essential conception of mothering and womanliness.

Radical feminist analyses of the household introduce important notions of power and inequality between the sexes which are necessary to any adequate analysis. While many of the critics of radical feminist approaches to the family focus on supposed essentialism or biologism, I have argued that this feature of their analyses is unduly exaggerated. While it is a danger in certain texts, it is not a necessary feature of radical feminist analysis. However, the conditions under which the form of the family and its production relations are constructed, and how it changes, are insufficiently specified in most radical feminist accounts; in particular, they deal inadequately with variation across time and ethnicity and with the intersection with class relations.

Liberalism

Many writers on the division of labour within the household do not explain their findings in terms of an overarching system of social inequality, but nevertheless produce important research findings. The following writers, who I am loosely grouping together under the heading of liberalism, have tended to emphasize the diversity of arrangements between men and women in the household. A further common feature is their focus on the importance of ideology, of norms and values, in the determination of gendered patterns in the sexual division of labour.

Young and Willmott (1975) argued that the family was becoming more symmetrical as a result of several factors. They asserted that sex roles within the family were becoming less segregated, with men taking on more domestic tasks and women more likely to go out into paid work. The trend to smaller families and a declining birth rate assisted this process, as did the increase in married women's paid employment and changes in attitudes.

However, as Oakley (1974) points out, Young and Willmott have very flimsy evidence for their contention that men are doing more housework, since in their study 'helping' with one item a week counted as doing housework.

A more recent example of the genre is by Ray E. Pahl (1984), whose thoroughly documented study of the divisions of labour within the household and between paid, unpaid and informal work is a classic of its kind. Pahl's main focus is the division between the market and household economies, together with all the sub-types in between. Indeed his main argument is that the informal economy which fits between the household and market economy is much more important than previously assumed. However, his work found that, while the informal economy has grown over the last decade or so, it is not more important in the lives of the unemployed than those of the employed, as his early speculation had suggested, since the former lack access to the necessary goods and contacts. The division between different parts of the economy has very important implications for gender divisions, given women's traditional concentration in the unpaid sector. Pahl's emphasis on the informal sector points up the previously neglected contribution of men to the unwaged economy, since while men do not do much routine housework, they are major actors in the informal economy.

However, Pahl is somewhat inconsistent on the nature of the sexual division of labour. On the one hand he stresses the vast and complex variety of sexual divisions of labour: 'The household strategies of ordinary working people in the nineteenth century were, inevitably, very varied' (p. 65), while, on the other, his study documents the extremely rigid allocation of many specific household tasks to women: 'Clearly, it is overwhelmingly obvious that women do most of the work in the household' (p. 270). Pahl suggests that ideology is very important in determining the sexual division of labour: 'Although I recognize that this must be a partial view, I think it is important to emphasize the role of ideology in constraining the work practices and divisions of labour of women both inside and outside the household' (p. 63). His explanation of why nineteenth-century employment of women as servants grew more rapidly than that in the factories was in terms of their 'preference' and orientation to giving up paid work on marriage (p. 67).

I think this underestimates the active opposition of men to women taking paid work, and overemphasises women's acquiescence to this (as I have argued more fully elsewhere (Walby, 1986; Chapter 2)).

The biggest problem in Pahl's work stems from his inadequate theorization of the gender relations involved in the division of labour. He suggests that there is a household work strategy and that the household can be taken as the unit in much of the analysis. However, this prevents him from theorizing the gender relations involved, since the genders are conflated into one consensual unit – the household. This has serious implications for his explanation of changes in the sexual division of labour, since he has no theoretical space to analyse the shifting balance of power between the sexes. For example, important changes which impact on the sexual divisions of labour in all three sectors of the economy, such as the reduction of patriarchal closure in the labour market, cannot theoretically be built into the account, because he has no conceptual space for a conflict of interest between the genders. Hence his version remains one of rich description, and valuable for that, but it is not a theoretically adequate explanation.

Marxism and Marxist feminism

Marxist feminist analyses start from the significance of class relations and the exploitative economic relations between classes for the under-standing of gender relations. These are seen to be importantly implicated in the oppression of women, sufficiently so that women's liberation from the family would not be achievable outside a socialist society. There is no one Marxist feminist approach to the household, but many varied ones, and indeed some Marxist writers have said next to nothing about gender and the household. Approaches range from those which see gender and the family determined principally at an ideological level, to those which view it primarily at an economic one; from those which see the family as neutral in the oppression of women which stems from capitalism, to those which view it as the critical site of women's oppression.

Following Marx's almost total neglect of the topic, Engels (1940) produced an early attempt by a Marxist to take feminist issues seriously. He considered that the basis of women's oppression was to be found in the family. He produced an analysis which grounded gender inequality both in a material division of labour between the sexes and in its significance for class relations. Engels argued within a base–superstructure model of society in which the material base determined the political and ideological superstructure. The material base was composed of two parts: production and reproduction. Production was the production of tools, food and other commodities. Reproduction was the reproduction of the species through biological processes of birth and also the rearing of children. The balance of power between the sexes was dependent upon the relative importance of these two spheres for society. In early human history women were in the ascendancy; later this matriarchy was overthrown. This world historic defeat of the female sex was a result of the growth of class society. With developing productivity in the sphere of production larger surpluses were generated, the control over which became the source of division and conflict between the class which controlled them and the class which generated them. The class which controlled the surpluses sought to impose sexual monogamy on their wives in order to ensure that the heirs were their own biological sons. Hence the development of the monogamous family with male control over women was seen by Engels as part of the strategy of the ruling class to maintain control over the economic surpluses.

Engels's account has been subject to much criticism. In his history of the family and its passage from matriarchy to patriarchy, he appears to have confused matrilineal societies, in which descent is traced through women but in which men still have control, with matriarchal societies, in which women have control (Delmar, 1976). Most scholars do not think matriarchal societies have ever existed, although not all would agree (Stone, 1977). Further, Engels's assumption that proletarian families would not involve the subordination of women, since only bourgeois ones had property to pass to heirs, is clearly empirically incorrect. Another problem is his biologism in the account of why men undertook production and women reproduction, a consequence of conflating the social aspects of child care into the biological aspects of pregnancy and birth.

Despite these serious flaws, Engels's account does provide the basis of a materialist account of women's subordination in his recognition of the material nature of the work that women do. This insight was lost to many subsequent generations of Marxist theorists, for instance Althusser, and has only recently been regained.

Althusser (1971) had a theoretical view of the family as an ideological state apparatus whose function was to socialize children for the capitalist system. The parallels of this Marxist functionalism with the Parsonian functionalism are striking, and the same range of criticisms apply.

The 'domestic labour debate' took place in reaction to this tendency to see women's work in the family as an ideological rather than an economic activity and vigorously asserted the material significance of women's domestic labour for capital. In this debate the relationship between housework, or domestic labour, and capital was systematically examined. The central question was just how central or peripheral domestic labour was for capital, and hence for the determination of the structure of society. The more central it was to capital, the more important were women as political actors. The debate was implicitly about the significance of the feminism of the 1970s. The argument proceeded via a series of technical arguments about 'value', the Marxist unit of economic worth. If domestic labour created this directly, then it was more important than if it did not.

James and Dalla Costa (1973) argued that housework created both value and surplus value, that women's work was central to capitalism, and that women were politically central to a socialist movement. They contended that the work that women did in the household was necessary for workers to be able to go and do their jobs in the factories and offices, and so was essential to the workings of the economy. Capitalism could not function without women cooking, cleaning and keeping house. Hence domestic labour must create value, women must be central to capitalism, and feminism must be central to socialist strategy.

Such writings were accused of sloppy use of Marxist concepts by those who had a more traditional interpretation of Marxism. Indeed one of the themes of the debate was the extent to which Marxist concepts could be developed to take account of gender relations, and to what extent they must retain a narrower usage.

Seccombe (1974) argued that domestic labour created value but not surplus value. He agreed that housework was embodied in the husbands who sold their labour to a capitalist, thus transferring value from the housewife to the capitalist via the husband. However, domestic labourers could not be considered to create surplus value, since housewives did not have a direct relationship with the capitalist, which, Seccombe argued, was theoretically necessary for the creation of value. The implication of this was that there was an equal exchange between husband and wife of housework for maintenance (since no surplus was extracted). This notion was criticized by Gardiner (1975), who pointed out the obvious inequality between spouses and the benefit to the husband of the arrangement.

The debate dealt with a very narrow range of issues related to the household, and an even smaller range of those associated with gender inequality. It did not really address the issue of whether you could read off political implications from degree of exploitation (see Coulson, Magas and Wainwright, 1975) or the non-economic issues within the household (see Molyneux, 1979). Nevertheless, its significance was in unequivocally demonstrating that women's domestic labour should be analysed as work within a Marxist perspective.

The criticism of Marxism in general and Marxist analyses of gender in particular as economistic led to the demise of this debate. Later writers such as Barrett (1980) stressed the importance of a non-economistic analysis. Barrett argued for the importance of ideology in the construction of gender. These ideologies were critically generated around the institution of the family: 'it is within the family that masculine and feminine people are constructed and it is through the family that the categories of gender are reproduced' (p. 77). More precisely Barrett argues that gender is socially constructed 'within an ideology of familialism' (p. 206), in order to take account of those who are not reared in conventional families. The significance that Barrett attaches to ideology is not considered to peripheralize the importance of gender. Rather she argues within a post-Althusserian Marxism which gives greater theoretical weight to ideology than do earlier forms of Marxism, although she does not go so far as to describe ideology as material. This ideology is centrally rooted in the family, making the family the central institution for the oppression of women.

In explaining the existence and form of the family Barrett is ambivalent. Women, she declares, do not benefit, while working-class men and the bourgeoisie may. The answer can only be found in a historical as well as theoretical analysis (p. 223). Through a sophisticated and erudite Marxist feminist analysis Barrett effectively argues that there is no logic of capitalism behind the oppression of women, though capitalist developments are implicated. But the cessation of the analysis at a point at which a historical analysis is demanded means that a final resolution of the theoretical dilemmas for Marxist feminism which she has presented is absent.

This shift away from an economic analysis of women's oppression was reflected in a growing interest in psychoanalytic theory. One of the most influential of these was Mitchell (1975), in her attempt to rehabilitate Freud for feminism. Mitchell's willingness to consider causes of women's oppression other than class and capitalism develops her analysis way beyond the limits of conventional Marxist feminism. I shall consider her work later alongside that of other dual-systems theorists who attempt to combine an analysis of capitalism and patriarchy, and in the chapter on sexuality, since this is her main focus.

The strength of Marxist feminist analysis of gender and production in the household is its exploration of the link with capitalism. Its weakness is the overstating of this at the expense of gender inequality itself. Its strengths and weaknesses are thus the mirror image of those of radical feminism.

Dual-systems theory

Dual-systems analyses of gender and production in the household are an attempt to combine the strengths of Marxist feminist and radical feminist work. Delphy, for instance, retains both the materialism of Marxist analysis and the focus on men's oppression of women of radical feminist analysis.

Delphy (1984) has produced a striking materialist feminist analysis of the expropriation of women's labour by their husbands in the household. She argues that the exploitation of women's labour in the home is the cornerstone of their oppression by men. Unlike the Marxist feminist analysis in the domestic labour debate, Delphy conceptualizes this as patriarchal exploitation, since men, not capital, are seen to be the beneficiaries. This exploitative system is characterized as a domestic mode of production which is parallel to, but separate from, the capitalist mode of production which exists simultaneously. Following the Marxist concept of mode of production, Delphy identifies two classes: the producing class – housewives – and the expropriating class – husbands. She argues for the distinctiveness of the relations of production in the domestic mode, showing how different are the social relations through which men expropriate the labour of their wives. Unlike Engels, who made a distinction between the work of men and women on the grounds of different tasks, Delphy differentiates on the basis of relations of production. That is, domestic work is not defined in terms of a set of tasks (e.g., cooking, cleaning, birthing), but in terms of the social relations under which it is performed. Delphy uses food production and preparation in French peasant households as an illustration of this distinctive conceptualization.

Delphy's account is limited by the perfunctory treatment of capitalist relations. Most of her analysis is about patriarchal domination, and only a small part about the intersection with capitalism. Indeed had she not made clear, if limited, reference to a capitalist as well as patriarchal mode of production it might have been more appropriate to categorize her a sub-type of radical feminism. The articulation of the domestic mode of production with that of capitalism is an area where Delphy's thesis is seriously limited and needs extensive development.

Delphy's theoretically innovative and insightful account can be criticized for its rather sloppy use of Marxist terms and for stretching Marxist concepts to purposes for which they were unintended and, according to her severest critics, not suited (Barrett and McIntosh, 1979; Molyneux, 1979). However, while some refinement of the concepts is certainly needed, I think this should be regarded more as a project for development than for rejection (see Walby, 1986: 37–42, 51–5). Prior narrow usage of a term is not a sufficient argument against conceptual development.

Hartmann's (1981b) dual-systems theory (already referred to in relation to her analysis of paid work) incorporates a hypothesis of the household which involves capitalist relations to a much greater extent than that of Delphy. She argues that women are forced to marry on bad terms because of their weak position in the labour market, as a result of patriarchal closure in employment.

Hartmann uses time-budget studies to show that husbands were a net drain on the time of a woman, not sharers of domestic burdens (1981a). She compares households with children and mothers in which there is a husband present with those in which there is no husband. Women in the former do more housework than those in the latter. Hartmann's analysis is that women are caught between the patriarchal exploitation of husbands in the home and that of capitalist employers in the labour market.

As already noted, Hartmann produces a powerful account, but one which is rather lacking in historical and cultural specificity.

Carol Brown (1981), in reply to Hartmann's article on 'The unhappy marriage of Marxism and Feminism', attempts to supply some historical specificity to the analysis of the household by dual-systems theory. She examines the change in the relation of children to mothers and to fathers over the last century. At the beginning of this period fathers had, and practised, the right to the custody of the children if the marriage ended. Today the assumption is that mothers have custody on divorce unless there are extraordinary circumstances.

Brown explains the shift in terms of the changing value of children at the intersection of patriarchal and capitalist relations. In the nineteenth century children had an economic worth to the family as a result of the wages they brought into the household between childhood and marriage. Today they are an economic drain until they leave, because of the extension of education and delayed entry to the labour market. The expansion of the formal education and training of young people is considered to be caused by the need of monopoly capital for better-trained workers. Private patriarchs in the family, no longer economically benefiting from children, are happy to let the custody of children on divorce go to the mother.

Brown's analysis of the different forms of patriarchy and the historical changes between them is a significant development in theory of patriarchy. However, there are problems in the explanation of the change from one to the other. The motor of the change between them is inappropriately seen as the development of monopoly capital with needs for certain types of worker training. This explanation is in terms of the functional logic of capitalism and seriously underestimates the role of social struggle both by feminists and by the labour movement for these services. First-wave and inter-wave feminism in alliance with the labour movement played a very significant role in the winning of these demands (see Banks, 1981; Mark-Lawson, Savage and Warde, 1985; Middleton, L.,

1978). Brown's dual-systems theory is too heavily weighted to the role of capitalism as the motor of change, and insufficiently to that of patriarchy and women's resistance to this.

Black feminism

Many of these accounts have presumed that it is possible to write of 'the' family, or at least 'the family in contemporary Western nations'. Most of them have also argued that the family is a, if not the most, central institution in the oppression of women. Both these propositions are incorrect, as has been pointed out by a number of black feminist writers (Carby, 1982; Hooks, 1982, 1984; Parmar, 1982). They contend both that there are significant differences in family forms between ethnic groups and that the family is less a source of oppression for women of colour than it is for white women. Hence previous feminist theory has made a serious error in attempting to develop a general theory of women's oppression on the basis of white women's experience alone.

The form of the household in contemporary Britain varies between different ethnic groups, not only between white and black, but between ethnic minorities as well. In Afro-Caribbean households the notion of the dependent full-time housewife is even less likely to be true than in native white families. The Policy Studies Institute survey showed that 31 per cent of West Indian households with children under 16 were single-parent households as compared with 10 per cent among whites and 8 per cent among Asians (Brown, 1984: 49). West Indian women have the rate of highest economic activity, 74 per cent, as compared with 46 per cent among whites and 39 per cent among Asians (dropping to 18 per cent among Muslim Asians) (Brown, Colin, 1984: 186).

Hooks (1984) argues that the family is less significant in the oppression of black American women (here referring to Afro-Americans) than for white American women. This is partly because the family is a basis of solidarity and resistance to white racism – it is a haven from a racist society – and partly because the comparison between waged work and housework is less favourable to waged labour for women of colour than for white women, because racist structures mean that they get worse jobs. While white women can regard paid work as a source of positive identity and material independence, for women of colour the waged work available to them is drudgery. Hooks is thus very critical of liberal feminists, such as Friedan (1965), who advocate paid work as a solution to the boredom, isolation and powerlessness of housewives.

These points of Hooks are strongly and effectively made, and clearly the household has a different place in the experience of women of different ethnic groups in a racially divided society. However, it is not clear that Hooks has also refuted the notion that the family is simultaneously a source of oppression of women. For instance, she does not argue that women do not undertake disproportionate amounts of labour in households of any ethnic group.

Most of these arguments I have addressed so far have engaged with general issues about the structure of the household. In this second part of the chapter I will address some of the most significant of the current changes in the patriarchal relations of production in the household, with a view to identifying the causes of these changes and an overall intention of specifying the relationship between the different patriarchal structures. This will be organized under three headings: reproductive technologies, the domestic division of labour, and the changing household structure.

Reproductive technologies

Since Firestone argued that reproduction was the basis of men's control over women and that modern technological developments could, if used appropriately, eventually solve this problem for women, it is important to examine recent innovations in reproductive technology to see if this is indeed happening. Indeed Shorter (1984) argues that modern medicine has already rescued women from their biology. Some other writers (e.g., Corea, 1985) have in fact argued the opposite, that the development of the new reproductive technology is increasing rather than decreasing patriarchal power. They contend that we are witnessing a shift in power over the process of reproduction away from women towards a male controlled medical profession.

Technological assistance in the control of fertility is sometimes thought of as a recent advance. For example, the pill is considered by Young and Willmott (1975) to have helped moves to women's emancipation in the 1960s, while Shorter (1975) suggests that modern gynaecology is the saviour of women. However, human intervention into reproduction is not new. Some forms of contraception have been found in most cultures (Gordon, L., 1977, 1979). The pill is merely a current Western form; its development does not mark the invention of birth control. Abortion also has been widely practised to limit the number of births in pre-capitalist, as well as capitalist, countries (McLaren, 1978; Donnison, 1977).

The application of modern medicine to childbirth has been interpreted by Shorter (1984) as liberating for women, and by Ehrenreich and English (1979) as an increase in patriarchal control over women. Shorter argues, like Firestone, that childbearing has been one of the great scourges of life for women. Childbearing is difficult, painful and dangerous. However, he argues that this has been alleviated by the development of modern obstetrics; modern medicine with its drugs and techniques has removed the threat of death and injury which were previously commonplace results of childbirth.

In a contrary view Ehrenreich and English argue that the development of medical intervention into childbirth should be interpreted as an increase in male control over women's bodies and reproduction. The medical takeover of assistance to birthing women from midwives is a move to male from female control over the process. Ehrenreich and English argue that this was a deliberate extension of patriarchal control. Birthing women have often received assistance from 'wise women' and midwives as well as doctors (Donnison, 1977), and indeed those attended by early doctors had a higher mortality rate than those assisted by midwives (Ehrenreich and English, 1979). Attempts to control the process of reproduction were not new, since the licensing of midwives was controlled by the Church in medieval England, precisely because of their powers of intervention to limit as well as to assist fertility (Donnison, 1977). But Ehrenreich and English argue that the development of male medical intervention was a major shift in control.

There are two parts to the argument. Firstly, whether the medical intervention was an improvement in the conditions of childbirth for women. Secondly, whether control passed out of women's hands into those of men. Firestone thought that technology would improve the position of women in reproduction, as does Shorter. However, Ehrenreich and English suggest that it did not, and that women were better off under the care of midwives. This latter is also the argument of Rothman (1982), who asserts that many aspects of the 'high-tech' deliveries of today – fitting women into a hospital schedule using drugs, inducement of birth, forceps, episiotomies (cutting) and other forms of intervention – are medically suspect, and not advances. I think this argument about disadvantages of certain aspects of medical intervention is important, but is sometimes overstated. Childbirth under modern medical conditions is safer for women and their babies than previous forms of care, but some forms of intervention are more for the convenience of doctors than their patients. The second part of the issue is whether this is a movement into male control. This is true. Hospital-based medicine is controlled by a medical profession which is male dominated not only in terms of its personnel, but in terms of its priorities and practices. Home-based forms of delivery with greater female control have been replaced by hospital-based forms with greater male control. Safer childbirth is at the expense of male control.

However, the conflicts over reproduction have been not only between women and men, but with medical professionals, the Church, eugenicists and others (Gordon, L., 1977, 1979; Witz, 1987). Doctors supported women's claims to have access to contraception and abortion under their control, thus expanding their sphere of competence. In the early and mid-twentieth century women won access to contraception in an alliance with doctors and eugenicists. The eugenicist argument was that women who would not make good mothers should not do so, for the good of the race or nation. In 1967 a similar alliance won access to abortion for women under similar circumstances, essentially that if the mother was medically or socially unfit, broadly defined, to be a mother, then she should be allowed to abort (Greenwood and Young, 1976; Gittins, 1982; Gordon, L., 1977, 1979; Stopes, 1981).

The new reproductive technologies have been the subject of recent controversy among the New Right as well as among feminists. The techniques involved include especially the treatment of infertile women by in vitro fertilization. This process involves: giving drugs to a woman to make her super-ovulate, that is, produce a lot of ripe eggs; performing minor abdominal surgery to remove the eggs; getting a man to produce some sperm; mixing the eggs and sperm together, 'in vitro' (a glass receptacle), and watching for fertilization; placing these embryos into the woman's womb; hoping that they attach themselves to the womb and grow. The success rates of the treatment are extremely low and the anxiety and distress of the infertile woman are exacerbated by repeated attempts to conceive. 'Spare' reproductive material is used for experimentation. The legal limit in Britain at the moment is on embryos up to 14 days since fertilization (Arditti, 1984; Stanworth, 1987).

How are we to understand such developments? On the one hand, they might be part of the technological fix to women's reproductive dilemmas that the radical feminist Firestone sought. On the other, radical feminists involved with FINRRAGE (Feminist International Network of Resistance to Reproductive and Genetic Engineering) have argued that few women have benefited by these processes, and that their real purpose is medical and scientific experimentation (Arditti, 1984; Corea, 1985). In this latter view male doctors are seen to be seeking power over the process of reproduction which previously lay within women's control. These forms of intervention give a male-dominated medical profession the basis to remove one of women's few bases of power, that is, the power to create children. It might also be considered that the processes are cruel to the women because the rate of success is so low and the raising of expectations so unwarranted.

However, as new medical procedures often have high failure rates, this is not specific to the reproductive technologies and thus should not be described as woman-torture. Nevertheless a focus on the view of infertile women, through whose eyes these techniques might be considered progress, is too narrow a perspective (Lorber, 1987). It is the wider social context which means that involuntary childlessness contradicts many women's conception of their own womanhood. The social processes which construct infertility as an awful negation of a woman's life meaning are a more important focus for analysis. However, this again is not sufficient by itself (Stanworth, 1987).

The political battles around these new methods of intervention into reproduction are similar to struggles around more established forms of reproductive control, such as abortion and contraception. As Linda Gordon (1977, 1979) has demonstrated, struggles for reproductive freedom in the West since the nineteenth century have always involved not only feminists, seeking access to these techniques for all women as part of a campaign for women to control their own bodies, but also doctors and eugenicists, pursuing the introduction of these techniques to further their own agendas of professional expansion and population control. Gordon documents how, at certain historical moments, medical professionals and eugenicists supported the legalization of contraception and abortion – doctors to enlarge the scope of their professional ambit, eugenicists to shape the racial composition of the population.

While struggles between men and women are determinant of reproductive control, they are not the whole matter. Other, both specific, professional constituencies, largely doctors, and also nationalist and racist interests, are significant also. In short, reproductive control cannot be understood outside the intersection of class and race groupings as well as patriarchal ones.

Domestic division of labour

A second major substantive question is whether the domestic division of labour between men and women is becoming more equal. Braverman (1974) assumed that women spend less time on housework as a consequence of many goods previously produced in the home, such as clothing and bread, now being purchased on the capitalist market. Young and Wilmott (1975) argued that the family was becoming more symmetrical, with greater participation of husbands in housework and greater participation of women in paid employment. They conducted a survey which purported to document this trend, especially among younger families in which the husband held a job that was skilled, clerical, professional or managerial. However, as Oakley (1974) notes, the argument was based upon husbands 'helping' their wives with tasks at least, but not necessarily more than, once a week. That is, the amount of domestic labour which Willmott and Young found.might have been negligible, and is insufficient empirically to ground their argument.

Vanek (1980), using time-budget data, found that housewives spent as long, if not longer, doing housework in the 1960s as they did in 1924. Time-budget studies are a more substantial way of assessing who spends how much time on housework, since they involve detailed diary keeping of activities over a specified period. In 1924, American housewives spent 52 hours per week on housework, while in the 1960s it had risen to 55 hours per week. This lack of decline might appear unlikely given the introduction of so many household aids during the period. However, some of these inventions add to a housewife's labour because they are associated with rising standards. For instance, in the case of washing machines, Cowan finds that clothes are washed more often, thus the overall time on cleaning clothes is not reduced (Cowan, 1983). It is necessary to distinguish between different aspects of housework, some of which have decreased and some of which have increased in the time taken to do them. Many household gadgets do not reduce work, suggest both Bose (1979) and Cowan (1983). We expect carpets to be vacuumed at least weekly, instead of being once a year. Other gadgets need time to be cleaned and repaired, eliminating any savings in time. However, Bose suggests that utilities, such as running water, gas and electricity, have reduced the time a housewife spends on related work. The biggest increase in time comes from child care, household management and shopping. New theories of child psychology push mothers into spending more time socializing their children than before. Overall, then, these writers argue, housewives have as much to do as before, although it is different work. Indeed there are other ways in which the work of women has been expanding in recent years. In particular there are a growing number of elderly people and an increase in the amount of time that women spend in caring for them (Finch and Groves, 1983). This situation would appear to support the position of the Parsonians, the Marxist functionalists, and the radical feminists who see women's domestic position as necessary for the present constitution of society and essentially unchanging.

However, there are some serious problems with these accounts. Firstly, they focus only on the role of full-time housewives. Women who do paid work as well as housework spend significantly less time on the latter than

do full-time housewives (as in fact Vanek does note). Since the proportion of women who are full-time housewives has fallen dramatically over
recent decades, as the proportion of women in paid work has increased,
the overall figures for women, as opposed to full-time housewives, show
a reduction in the time spent on housework. A smaller proportion of
women at any one time are doing the job of full-time housewife which
requires the long hours of domestic work.

However, the main reason that women in paid work do less housework than full-time housewives is not the optimistic one given by
Willmott and Young, that husbands are doing a greater share. Husbands
do very little more, as figures by Gershuny et al (1986) demonstrate. This
is confirmed by Morris (1984), who shows that, even when men were
unemployed and their wives employed, this did not lead to any significant
increase in housework by the men.

The main reason is that women who are full-time housewives do more
housework than women who also have paid jobs is that the former are
much more likely to have small children. In fact this is really a phase of
the modern life-cycle for British women. Many women, on childbirth,
leave paid work, and re-enter the labour market when their children go
to school at five years old. This is the most intensive period of domestic
labour, and it is not surprising that women are most likely to be full-time
housewives during this period. Ray E. Pahl's (1984) work confirms that
households in which there are young children are more likely to have the
woman doing even more of the domestic labour than those where there
are no small children. Unfortunately the nature of Pahl's index of the
division of domestic labour (DOMDIV) precludes the possibility of
asking whether husbands do more housework when their wives are
employed, or simply that their wives do less.

One of the most important reasons for the changes over time is that a
larger proportion of married women are not engaged in looking after
small children and are entering paid work. As the amount of housework
declines for this category, so they having been engaging in paid work.
Any marginal increase in symmetricality in the family is due to women
moving towards a male pattern of engagement with paid work and less
housework, not, to any significant extent, to men moving towards a
female one and doing housework.

An important qualification to the interpretation of the time-series data
is that there are substantial differences between women of different social
classes. The trajectory of change of working-class housewives was in a
consistent downward direction between 1937 and 1974/5, while that for
middle-class housewives shows an increase between 1937 and 1961, only
falling between 1961 and 1974/5 (Gershuny, 1983b: 38–9). It appears

that the main cause of the different directions of change is that between 1937 and 1961 the amount of housework done by middle-class house-wives increased as they were losing the assistance of servants in house-work, not a form of assistance working-class women ever had.

Today the social class of the husband's job makes no significant difference to the unevenness of the domestic division of labour: middle-class husbands contribute no more than working-class men. However, a woman's class does make a difference. If the husband's class is held constant, then we find that, the higher the class of the woman's job, the less uneven is the domestic division of labour (Pahl, R. E., 1984: 272). This would suggest that a better job can improve a woman's bargaining position over the domestic division of labour.

I have argued, then, that there have been significant changes in the amount of housework done by women, but not by full-time housewives, nor, to any ·significant extent, by husbands. Women overall do less housework, though full-time housewives do as much as decades before. The causes of these changes are partly demographic, in that women have a longer period of their lives not looking after children, and partly as a result of tasks previously done as housework, under patriarchal relations of production, now being increasingly performed outside the household, either under capitalist relations of production or by the state. The expansion of capitalist production into such commodities as clothing and food preparation, the extension of utilities such as running water, electricity and gas by a combination of local and central state and private capital, have reduced the amount of time spent on these activities. Women now spend less of their lives engaged in privatized patriarchal production relations in the household and more under capitalist produc-tion relations, which are patriarchal in a different way.

Changing household composition

The internal structure and composition of a typical British household has been undergoing massive changes in the last couple of decades.

Fewer people are living in marriages today than 15 years ago, a reversal of the trend from 1901 to 1971. People are marrying later, the mean age of first marriage for women in England and Wales rising from 22 in 1971 to 24 in 1986 (Equal Opportunities Commission, 1988b: 5). This is a reversal of the trend between 1931 and 1971, during which the age at first marriage fell (Abercrombie et al., 1988: 277). The divorce rate is rising from 5.9 per thousand marriages in 1971 to 12.9 in 1986 (*Population Trends*, 50, Winter 1987, Table 14). Britain had the highest divorce rate in Europe in 1985 (*Social Trends*, 18, 1988, p. 43). The rate of remarriage of divorcees is declining. This decline in the rate of marriage is only partially compensated for by the increase in cohabiting couples, which have a significantly different legal and practical status.

The proportion of single-parent families has increased, from 8 per cent of families with children to 14 per cent in 1985. In 1985, 86 per cent of one-parent families with dependent children were headed by women (*General Household Survey*, 1985: Table 3.4). More children are being born out of wedlock. The illegitimacy rate, that is, proportion of births outside marriage as compared to inside, rose from 4.9 per cent in 1951 to 12.7 per cent in 1981 and 21.3 per cent in 1986 (Equal Opportunities Commission, 1988b: 8). That is over one-fifth of children are today born outside a married-couple household. Given the increase in the illegitimacy rate and the rising divorce rate, we should expect that the number of female-headed households with dependent children will continue to rise above its current level of one in seven.

Fewer marriages are composed of a male breadwinner and female full-time housewife because of the increase in the rate of paid employment among married women during the post-war period, although this has not increased in the last decade. The fertility rate in Great Britain is declining, falling from 2.86 per woman in 1965 to 1.78 in 1985 (Equal Opportunities Commission, 1988b: 9).

How are we to understand these changes? Is this liberation from exploitative husbands or abandonment to poverty? Are women being liberated from child care; are they going on birth strike? Are men abandoning fatherhood?

The notion that the household is essentially unchanging in capitalist or patriarchal societies is quite simply shown to be wrong in the face of such evidence. Both Parsonian and Marxist functionalism, which considered the nuclear family to be necessary for the functioning of either society or capitalism, are contradicted by such changes.

I would argue that these alterations in the family are the outcome of structural changes in the relationship between men and women outside the family – in particular, the increase in the paid employment of women. Given my argument that women get a raw deal in marriage, we would expect the propensity of women to live in marriages to decline the more that they have other alternatives. This theory is supported by the fact that the higher the social class of a woman the less likely she is to marry. That is, women with alternative forms of economic support are less likely to enter a dependent relationship on a man. They are also more likely to leave husbands when they have access to alternative forms of support. The less men have to offer women economically, the less likely women are to marry them. Unlike women, it is men of the lowest social classes who are least likely to marry. The less a husband earns, the more it is in a woman's interest to leave him. The data on divorce supports this, since divorce rates in 1979 in England and Wales were highest among marriages where the husband was unemployed, 34 per thousand, or an unskilled manual worker, 30 per thousand, and lowest where the husband was a professional, 7 per thousand (Haskey, 1984).

Thus we should expect that, as women gain increasing access to paid employment, they will be less likely to live in marriage relations. While the jobs that women have are not as good as the ones that men have, the increase in women's employment still represents an improvement in the position of women.

A further reason for women's flight from marriage is that, even if paid employment is not effectively available, the level of state benefits to lone mothers sometimes provides a better material basis than many women obtain in marriage. Jan Pahl (1985) suggests that women leaving violent men are likely to note an increase in their living standards when they receive social security, rather than maintenance from their husbands. Gail Wilson (1987) shows that the material benefit or disadvantage to women of marriage varies by life-cycle stage and husbands' income. Women in low-income households with pre-school age children are materially better off when supported by the state than by their husbands. Women with high-income husbands have materially more to lose if their marriages break up.

So far I have looked at women's changing economic interests in marriage. Men too have changing interests. Indeed the figures also show a male flight from fatherhood. Ehrenreich (1983) suggests that it is this male abandonment of fatherhood which is the real cause of the decline in nuclear families, not women's abandonment of the family.

Central to this issue is that of why people have children. The significant decline in the birth rate in Western countries suggests that it is much less attractive than it once was. While once children were an economic asset, in that they would bring in a wage to the household for several years between childhood and their own marriage, this is no longer the case. Today children are usually a financial drain on the household during their entire time in residence, and some, who go on to higher education, remain so for several years after leaving home. Thus there are sound economic reasons for the decline in the birth rate.

A further factor is the change in the divorce law. Divorce and legal separation have been made progressively easier during the last hundred years, since civil divorce first became a legal possibility in 1857. The Act of 1923 allowed divorce to women on the same terms as men, while that of 1969 made the grounds for divorce much easier (Smart, 1984); these laws were further 'liberalized' in 1984 (see chapter on the state for further details). The increase in the rate of divorce in 1971 when the 1969 Act came into force (*Social Trends*, 1988: 43) suggests that such legislation does have measurable consequences. However, the legal changes are not the main, only a contributory, factor to the decline in the family. They affect only the rate of divorce and separation pending divorce, not that of other causes, such as the increase in single mother-hood, later age of marriage, lower rate of remarriage, and declining birth rate.

Thus we see several important economic reasons why both women and men are disadvantaged by marriage. The major causes of changes in the household and reproduction are the increasing proportion of women in paid work, and the extension of welfare benefits to independent women. The reasons for those changes are discussed in the chapters on paid work and on the state and politics.

Having established that there are significant changes in the patriarchal production relations in the household, the next question is that of the significance of these changes for patriarchy. The conventional debate is between those who argue that there is no fundamental change – the Marxist and Parsonian functionalists – and those who maintain that there is progress towards a more symmetrical family – usually, but not necessarily, the liberals.

Instead I think we are experiencing a simultaneous change in both the degree and the form of patriarchy which is producing these changes in the household. There is a significant decline in the patriarchal control over women in the household. Their labour is not expropriated to the same extent by their husbands. The individual personal control over women by husbands is reduced, since women can leave any specific husband, but they do not escape the wider patriarchal relations by doing this. For instance, they are still responsible for children. Further, there is an increase in the direct capitalist expropriation of women's labour.

CONCLUSIONS

Is the household, then, a major site of the oppression of women? If so, why do women marry and enter into such exploitative relations?

The answering of the question of the significance of household production relations is complicated by the different levels at which that question has meaning. Firstly, there are the immediate situations and choices facing each woman. Usually it is the evaluation of these costs and benefits that is central to the significance of marriage as an oppressive institution. The answer is complicated by the significant differences in the placing of women in relation to the household not only by class and ethnicity but also by age, marital status and position in the labour market.

The conventional feminist answer is that 'it is difficult to argue that the present structure of the family-household is anything other than oppressive for women' (Barrett, 1980: 214). This position is contested, firstly, in some of the writings of women of colour; secondly, in some about the new divorce laws; and, thirdly, by some dual-systems theorists.

Hooks, as we saw earlier, argued that the family was a site of resistance to racism and that household labour was less alienating than waged work to those, such as women of colour, who had access only to the worst jobs. However, while both these things may be true, this does not mean that the household is not also a site in which men oppress women, in that men benefit from women's domestic labour.

The second objection is similar insofar as it suggests that there are worse things than marriage for a specific sub-set of women. Weitzman (1985), analysing changes in the divorce law in California, implies that being divorced if you are a middle-aged, middle-class homemaker with little labour market experience is worse than staying married. Women in such situations suffer a massive drop in their living standards. This is a consequence of losing a high-earning husband, having no access to good jobs, and being left with little or no income support from their husbands as a result of the changes in divorce law.

These arguments highlight the need to distinguish between different groups of women when assessing whether marriage is in their immediate interests or not. Two groups have been identified as having an interest in marriage, both as a result of the labour market offering less advantage than homemaking. Women who have committed themselves to the role of homemaker, to such an extent that they have no alternative way of gaining a good livelihood, have a real material interest in staying married to their husbands. Indeed these material interests can be politically mobilized to resist changes which might be considered to threaten marriage. The successful opposition to the ratification of the Equal Rights Amendment in the USA and (unsuccessful) opposition to the availability of abortion and contraception may be interpreted in this light.

A more fundamental materialist analysis is that marriage is in the immediate material interests of most women, not merely specific minorities, and that the lack of alternatives is common to the majority. When job opportunities are not available to women because of patriarchal closure in the labour market, marriage remains the best material option for many. Those who marry are not suffering from false consciousness and an ignorance of their real interests, but are acting in their own best interests, given restricted options.

Are women, then, passive victims, forced into marriage? I think that this is an inappropriate way of viewing the situation, since women are embracing their real options. Indeed women struggle to improve their lot within marriage, even when this appears to mean digging themselves deeper into the marriage option. For instance, if a woman is going to marry and give up an independent stake in the labour market, then it is in her interests to ensure that her husband does not leave her.

Is, then, a feminist critique of marriage misplaced? I think not, because of the significance of the restriction of alternatives in all these analyses. Marriage and homemaking is only alright for women because the alternatives are worse. None of the points made in this section contradict the analysis of the exploitation of women's labour in the home by her husband, with all the attendant restrictions on a woman's autonomous development, and, as we shall see in other chapters, restrictions on a woman's sexuality and vulnerability to male violence. The household is important in all these dimensions of women's oppression. The fact that there is not a better option for most women does not contradict this.

However, it does make an analysis in terms of 'women's interests' immeasurably more problematic. We need to distinguish a woman's immediate interest in personal survival, which is often bound up with the family-household, from her long-term interest in the eradication of the oppression which exists within the family and hence in this institution as it currently exists. Any discussion of whether the family-household is oppressive for women should make this distinction between immediate and long-run interests.

There is a further level which must be separated in this analysis. So far it has dealt with individual women's interests within the existing social structure, merely separating the short-run from the long-run. The really important question is that of explaining the family-household form and the social structuring of patriarchy within which women make their choices.

Conventionally, the family is seen as central to the determination of other social structures which shape gender relations. For instance, it is argued that the family determines women's participation in the labour market, not vice versa. I have already argued that at an individual level we cannot understand women's commitment to the family-household unless we understand the restricted options elsewhere, that the other structures are fundamental to explaining women's typical decision to marry. At the level of social structural change I also want to argue that the family is as determined as it is determining.

This analysis of the household has argued that there are sufficient material reasons for women's engagement in marriage to obviate the need for an analysis in terms of false consciousness. However, this is not to argue that popular cultural forms which represent a very restricted range of possibilities are irrelevant in women's decision making. On the contrary, most women will not experience the tensions around marriage and household in terms of such materialist issues, but more often in terms of the issues of popular culture.

Gender relations in the household have changed significantly both over the last hundred years and especially over the last couple of decades. Women are no longer necessarily bound to an individual husband who expropriates their labour till death does them part. Instead, increasing numbers of women change husbands, have children without husbands and engage in work for an employer other than their husband. Women spend a smaller proportion of their life-time's labour under patriarchal relations of production, although while they are full-time housewives they spend as many hours on this labour as did women many decades earlier. Women from different ethnic groups vary as to the extent to which they are engaged in these patriarchal production relations.

Many of these changes have been struggled for by feminists for many years. The freedom to dissolve marriages and to work outside the home have been important feminist demands. However, these changes have also brought some problems for women. In a patriarchally structured labour market, women, if they have children, are rarely able to earn sufficient to keep themselves above the poverty line. 'Liberation' from marriage is then usually a movement into poverty.

These changes are another instance of a movement from a private towards a public form of patriarchy. Women are still usually engaged in the labour of rearing children, but not as often for the benefit of an individual patriarch.

4

Culture

Ideas about masculinity and femininity are to be found in all areas of social relations; they are part of the actions which go to make up the patriarchal structures. This chapter is concerned primarily with the representation of gender, which is part of the process that makes up cultural notions of femininities and masculinities. It will also address the questions of how individuals come to adopt personal identities as masculine or feminine, and how the content of these are determined.

The most traditional approach to sexual difference is to see masculine and feminine identities as reflecting biological structure, of bodies, hormones, muscles and genes. Such biological theories have been widely criticized (c.f., Oakley, 1972). However, the social significance of biological attributes remains as one of the issues that social theories of gender identity must deal with.

The chapter will examine three main approaches to gendered subjectivity: firstly, socialization theory; secondly, neo-Freudian, psychoanalytic theory; thirdly, discourse analysis. The perspectives I have been using in earlier chapters do not neatly divide between these approaches to culture and subjectivity. Liberals have typically adopted socialization theory, though might also be considered to have a position in discourse analysis. Marxists have typically used either psychoanalysis or discourse analysis. Radical feminists are typically represented in either socialization or discourse analysis.

There are three main issues within the debates: firstly, whether there is a dominant ideology which is significant for gender inequality; secondly, whether there are essential differences between masculinity and femininity; and, thirdly, the tension between individual autonomy and unity of a person on the one hand, and structural determination on the other.

The first issue is whether there is a hegemonic, or dominant, ideology (cf., Abercrombie et al, 1980, on this issue for class relations) which is important in the maintenance of gender relations. Are women brain-washed into passivity and acquiescence by their socialization into femininity (Comer, 1974), or by an overarching patriarchal world religion (Daly, 1978)? In short, do women suffer from false consciousness? Or, are women's direct experiences a true form of knowledge of the world, and their subordination due to real material circumstances?

The second issue picks up the problem of essentialism in feminist thought: whether, in efforts to explain gender difference, theorists treat this in an over-rigid, timeless way, which is contradicted by history and the variety of forms of femininity and masculinity between classes and ethnic groups.

The third issue is an argument between liberal humanism's conception of the individual as a unified self-motivating being, and the post-structuralist analysis of meaning within discourses which decentres this rational, self-present subject (Weedon, 1987).

Traditionally ideology and culture have been considered to be best understood as a set of beliefs which are related in some way to other social phenomena. More recently writers in this field have argued that it is inappropriate to theorize ideology outside the material relations in which it is embedded.

SOCIALIZATION THEORY

The conventional position, at least till recently, has been to see masculine and feminine identities as a result of a process of socialization (Belotti, 1975; Comer, 1974; Parsons and Bales, 1956; Sharpe, 1976). Socialization is considered to take place primarily during childhood, during which boys and girls learn the appropriate behaviour for their sex. Writers proposing this theory have clear notions of what distinguishes masculinity and femininity, usually conceived of as mirror opposites. Masculinity entails assertiveness, being active, lively, and quick to take the initiative. Femininity entails cooperativeness, passivity, gentleness and emotionality.

Training in one or the other set of gender attributes is considered to start from birth in every aspect of their lives, as when babies are dressed in different colours, pink and blue, and encouraged or discouraged from greedy feeding (Belotti, 1975). Socialization proceeds with a set of rewards and punishments, ranging from changes in tone of voice to physical chastisement. Thus little girls are more likely to be told to be quiet and not to make a noise in circumstances where little boys would be expected to be boisterous.

The toys and games of childhood are also gendered. For instance, little girls are likely to be given dolls while boys get train sets and lego. Little girls are expected to play at ironing daddy's hanky, while little boys play soldiers. These games differ both in terms of the level of activity – boys having more active games – but also in the orientation of the object of play to adult roles – dolls are a preparation for childcare, soldiers for warfare.

The books and magazines that children and adolescents read are considered to differentiate gender identities further. In these, girls will be portrayed helping mummy with domestic chores, while boys are engaged helping daddy in manly ones or engaging in adventures. They show stereotyped images of the activities of both children and adults, contributing to expectations of both present and future gender roles.

Television and other media carry this process further (Tuchman, 1978). Advertising usually shows women as either sexually glamorous or as wives and mothers, while men occupy positions of power. Women are even shown less often than men (Tuchman, 1978). Not only are the overt images problematic for women, but there are a series of techniques, such as the 'authoritative' voice-over being more often male (87 per cent), which further contributes to the subordinate conception of women on television (Tuchman, 1978). Finally there are the story-lines themselves, which suggest restrictive feminine conduct as more appropriate for women. For instance, single working women are more often portrayed as the victim of violence than are married women (Tuchman, 1978). Indeed the plot of many Hollywood movies is one in which the narrative starts when a woman steps out of line and ends when she is restored to proper feminine subjection (Kuhn, 1982).

Education is considered to continue the process, both in terms of the formal curriculum, since boys and girls usually study different subjects, and of the hidden curriculum, in what they pick up informally. Boys are more successful at the upper reaches of the educational system. Even the dynamics of classroom interaction is set against the girls, who tend to be more reticent (Stanworth, 1983). Boys are more likely to take science and craft subjects, while girls take arts and domestic subjects. In this way they are prepared for their adult roles in the sexual division of labour (Deem, 1978, 1980; Sharpe, 1976).

While many of the early studies on gender socialization centred on femininity, an increasing number of studies have taken masculinity as their focus (Brod, 1987; Kimmel, 1987; Hearn, 1987; Fasteau, 1975; Tolson, 1977). These tend to concentrate on the unproductive aspects of masculinity for men, such as the stunting of the ability to express emotions, rather than masculinity as a route to privilege and power.

In short, socialization is considered to cause the differentiation of the genders into masculine and feminine subjects. Institutions from the family to the media and education are implicated in carrying out this process.

Socialization theory is a powerful antidote to suggestions that gender difference are biologically inherent. It documents in detail a series of social and social-psychological processes through which girls and boys acquire a gendered subjectivity. However, there are a lot of issues which socialization theory does not deal with adequately.

Firstly, despite its obvious anti-essentialist thrust, socialization theory operates with a very static and unitary conception of gender differences. While differences of some kind universally exist between masculinity and femininity, these are significantly variable. Few socialization theorists take sufficient account of the variety of masculinities and femininities, especially within different social classes, ethnic groups, generations, societies or historical periods.

Secondly, there is an ambiguity as to whether femininity and masculinity are merely mirror opposites, in which each sex is restricted, but in equal and opposite ways, or whether masculinity is the mode of the oppressor and femininity that of the oppressed. This is a dilemma which surfaces especially clearly in work which focuses on masculinity (Brod, 1987; Connell, 1987; Fasteau, 1975; Hearn, 1987; Tolson, 1977). Insofar as these analyses slide into the role differentiation type, parallel to that of Parsons, they are problematic in failing to recognize the power which is part of the masculine position. But not all are subject to this error; in particular, Connell and Hearn note the relationship between masculinity and power.

A third problem is that people are assumed to be relatively passive in their acquisition of gender identity, in many, though not all, varieties of this theory. Indeed it tends to assume that women have false consciousness, and this is an account of how they acquire it. Yet people are not 'cultural dopes'. They are more actively involved than this type of theory usually gives space for. Even the meaning of a cultural artefact is not immediately given but is constructed only in a social context, in which the audience has an active role.

A fourth problem is that socialization theory, while providing an account of how individuals become masculine or feminine, does not explain where the content of these notions comes from. This is the most serious shortcoming of this perspective. Socialization theory is a theory of the acquisition of gender, not of its construction. It has little to say on why gender should be dichotomous and why masculinities and femininities have specific contents. Why should contemporary masculinity contain more elements of aggression than femininity does?

Fifthly, this approach assumes that there are specialized times and places on which we can focus in order to understand gender ideology, rather than realizing that all aspects of social life involve gendered cultural notions. This problem is related to most of the four difficulties just mentioned. Gendered culture is actively constructed in all areas of social life, not just families, media and school. Discourses of masculinities and femininities are struggled over in the paid workplace and the state, as well as learnt by individuals.

PSYCHOANALYTIC APPROACHES

While many people would agree that Freud's original position was hopelessly biologistic and mysogynist in relation to women, there have been various attempts to rescue certain aspects of his work. There are two main versions of this in relation to gender. One is the work of object relations theorists, such as Chodorow (1978), the other that of the post-Lacanians who reinterpreted Freud with a focus on the symbolic level, such as Mitchell (1975).

Chodorow

Chodorow (1978) draws upon object relations theory, developing a theory of gender relations which focuses heavily on early childhood experiences. She examines the reproduction of mothering, rather than gender identity *per se*, since she thinks this is the key to understanding both gender differentiation and the oppression of women. Women are brought up to mother as a result of early childhood experiences in a way that men are not. Mothering is a rich experience, but simultaneously traps women into a different adult role from that of men, one which is not as well rewarded in contemporary society. The cause of the difference between the genders is that while girl children continue their gender identification with their mother, boy children have to make a serious break with her and identify with their more distant father, in order to become masculine. This is a wrench for the boys, and gives rise to a different type of personality which is less nurturing. The process is embedded in the unconscious and not amenable to simple conscious resolution. As a consequence girls grow up into nurturing adults, who mother children, while boys do not.

Chodorow values mothering highly. Indeed Hester Eisenstein (1984) considers that she has a woman-centred analysis. The problem is that it is not highly rewarded in our society and that it is done nearly exclusively by women. Indeed Chodorow's solution to gender inequality is for men to mother, or parent, as well as women – in effect, for men to be more like women.

Chodorow's analysis is refreshing in its consideration of the inequality between men and women, its positive rather than negative evaluation of women within a social-psychological perspective, and its suggestion that social changes could change the organization of the psyche. Its strength is its recognition of social processes. Its weakness stems from her failure to analyse the social processes which provide such low rewards for motherhood. Her solution to gender inequality, for men to parent, ignores the wider social issues which devalue women in society.

Lacanian Freudians/dual-systems theory

Mitchell (1975) argues that we cannot understand women's oppression without an analysis of the unconscious. Economic processes do not encompass the whole or even the main part of the ways by which patriarchal relations are reproduced. Her analysis is in part a reaction to some of the more economistic accounts of women's oppression provided by some Marxists. Neither are many accounts of ideology sufficient, since this alone does not enable us to grasp the deeply entrenched nature of ideas about appropriate gender behaviour. She is responding to the difficulties feminists have found in securing change in both society and their own lives.

Mitchell turns to Freud's work in order to develop the conceptual apparatus she considers necessary to provide a full explanation of gender relations. While aware of feminist criticisms of Freud by Firestone, Friedan and others, she argues that the mysogynist elements of his thought are superficial, and that he has some crucial concepts to offer feminist analysis. Mitchell follows the Lacanian development of Freud's work in her attempt to rescue Freud from feminist criticisms and emphasizes the cultural rather than the biological aspects of his theory. She argues that these criticisms do not constitute a sufficient rejection of Freud because they do not deal with his central contribution – a theory of the unconscious. Mitchell argues that we cannot understand the oppression of women without a theory of the unconscious, since such a concept is necessary to theorize the deeply entrenched patriarchal ideology in peoples' psyches. Patriarchal practices are continued because of the way our minds are ordered from generation to generation. She suggests that Freud's sexist statements are peripheral baggage which can be rejected while embracing the central part of his work, rather than being used to dismiss him as an ignorant, sexist bigot.

Emphasis is placed on the almost linguistic form of analysis of the processes of transformation of meanings and symbols in the unconscious, such as condensation and repression. In this study of Freud, references to anatomy are read as symbolic, for instance, 'penis' becomes 'phallus' in an effort to eliminate biologism.

Mitchell has a dualist approach to the analysis of gender inequality in that she sees capitalist relations to be rooted in the economy, while patriarchy is based in culture and the unconscious. The overthrow of patriarchy necessitates dealing with patriarchal ideology on its own terms, not seeing it as derivative from capitalism and hence disappearing after the revolution.

Mitchell draws on the work of the anthropologist Levi-Straus to suggest that women are essential as objects of exchange in a civilized society, and that this exchange of socially significant objects is central to the psychic structures of the human mind. She argues that the relationship between patriarchy and capitalism is undergoing major changes. The development of commodity exchange means tha' there is no longer the same need to treat women as exchange objects, since commodities can now fulfill this function.

However, while Mitchell is undoubtedly right to point to the relevance of ideology and the concept of the unconscious for a full feminist analysis of women's oppression, it is not clear that she manages to refute the criticisms of Freud or to construct an alternative analysis. Freud's account of women's sexuality is still wrong. Further, her attempt to restrict patriarchy to the cultural level and capitalism to the economic is misplaced. There are, as we have seen, patriarchal relations in the economic level, both in paid work and the household. The contemporary rise of 'enterprise culture' should caution against any notion that capitalist relations are restricted to the economic sphere alone. Finally it is not clear that the Lacanian re-reading can rescue Freud from his essentialism and biologism. An analysis in which the phallus is the primary signifyer may take only a small step back from simple biologism, since the phallus only has meaning in relation to that anatomical object, the penis.

Nonetheless Mitchell has been important within psychoanalytic theory in problematizing the previous simplistic equation between penis and phallus. This is now a central question in feminist psychoanalytic work (e.g., Rose, 1983).

The new French feminism

A school of French feminists have attempted, like Mitchell, to critique and develop Freudian thought via a Lacanian interpretation (Cixous, 1981; Irigaray, 1985a; 1985b; Kristeva, 1986; Marks and de Courtivron, 1981). Irigaray, for instance, embraces the Freudian notion that gender identity and sexual identity are intimately bound up. She suggests that there is an essential femininity which is repressed by patriarchal society. She argues, unlike Freud, that women have a multiplicity of sexual organs, not just a vagina, nor even two lips touching, but all parts of her body. The patriarchal symbolic order, represented by the phallus, is a rational one, whereas that of women is different. Women, then, must completely reject patriarchal rationality, or they will be caught up in a world which is not theirs. Women's experience of the world is necessarily different from that of men. Femininity is seen to have positive virtues and women are not considered, as they were by Freud, as inferior to men. Masculine rationality, while dominant, is not a preferable way of being.

In moving beyond the Freudian notion of women as incomplete men, Irigaray preserves the notion of a clear distinction between the genders rooted in biology. This retains problems of essentialism, universalism and ahistoricism. As Brown and Adams (1979) argue, Irigaray and other French feminists, notably Kristeva, face problems because of such essentialism, even though it involves a glorification of things to do with women. Psychoanalytic theory of even feminist variants shares common problems in having difficulty with social variability in the content of masculinity and femininity and with social change. However, these writers do importantly disturb the previous patriarchal closure in psychoanalytic theory and pose the questions of the significance of the unconscious level for a feminist analysis.

DISCOURSE ANALYSIS

While psychoanalytic theory is stuck with a dichotomous division between masculinity and feminity, this is challenged by post-structuralists, whose analysis concentrates on difference and discourse. The project for many feminist post-structuralists is to explore the variety of forms of femininity and masculinity. The substantive focus is usually an investigation of the forms of representation of gender in cultural texts such as film, literature, magazines and pictures. Such writers try to catch the nuances of different forms of femininity, and indeed whether this is a sufficiently cohesive notion to be able to identify it as a unity.

Following Derrida (1976) and Foucault (1981, 1987), these writers make a break with the restrictions of the Freudian tradition and its deep structures of the psyche. As with the Lacanian tradition, though, there is a focus on language and subjectivity. There are two main types of analysis, one following Derrida with a focus on 'difference', and one Foucault, with a focus on 'discourse'. Derrida's idea of difference does not allow much conceptual space for power inequalities, while Foucault's notion of discourse has power through knowledge at its heart (Barrett, 1987). Since neither Derrida nor Foucault had much to say about gender relations, the feminist intervention is an attempt at critique and reworking rather than simply adopting these approaches.

The deconstructionist emphasis, common in the journal *m/f*, takes as its project the breaking down of the unitary notion of 'woman' because of the essentialism it sees behind such a concept (e.g., Adams, 1979). The intellectual project is to examine how the category women is constructed (Adams, Coward and Cowie, 1978; Cowie, 1978). Early Coward (1978) pursues this through an investigation of the multiplicity of discourses of femininity which can be found in contemporary women's magazines. There are many different ways in which 'femininity' is represented. In some, such as *Women's Own* and *Good Housekeeping*, femininity is seen in relation to family roles of cooking, cleaning and child care. In others, such as *Cosmopolitan*, the focus is on the sexualization of the body of women in the context of successful careers and sexual and economic independence, and references to family roles are almost non-existent. In *Cosmopolitan* the glamour image is continued through the advertisements for related products such as make-up, soaps and body lotions. The film *Emmanuelle* offers yet another form of femininity, in which female sexuality is presented for the voyeuristic male gaze. Coward suggests that *Cosmopolitan* is a site of competing definitions of female sexuality, while that of *Emmanuelle* is foreclosed.

Adams and Minson (1978) argue that the subject of feminism is not simply women, since this is an essentialist concept. The emphasis on deconstructing femininity implies the rejection of the usefulness of the categories of men and women in a social analysis. Indeed Barrett and Coward (1982) argue that the project amounts to a denial of their existence as categories at all. It is as if only representations can be analysed.

While the deconstructivist emphasis is on fragmenting the category of women, in drawing attention to differences in the notions of femininity, the discourse tradition examines the implications of such dialogues for gender inequality. For instance, Coward's later work (1984), and that in McRobbie and Nava (1984), explores the way new discourses of femininity are restrictive or represent forms of resistance. Written texts and pictures are analysed for the messages to women contained within them. For instance, Coward (1984) argues that the new trend towards non-smiling models on the front pages of women's magazines is not a positive response to feminist criticism of the simpering, smiling, eager-to-please models of before, but rather a statement that women are sexually available even when not actively inviting male attention by smiling. Winship (1985), less pessimistically, sees subversion and resistance in some of the new portrayals of femininity, even though she admits they might be seen by 'older' feminists merely as soft porn. She describes an advertisement of young women wearing a combination of glamorous underwear and overcoats and heavy shoes against a street scene with rubbish and dustbins. The street-wise consciousness of young women is, she suggests, able to play with these notions of femininity in a way which empowers them. Winship discovers resistance to male dominance within new forms of femininity. However, she notes that not all feminists would read this image as a progressive one.

One of the problems with analyses of representations such as these is that we do not actually know whether the author's surmise as to the meaning of these texts for their intended audience is in fact correct. Indeed the notion of 'authorship' in relation to an advertisement is complex, and certainly not constituted by one person. Further, it is not clear that there is only one meaning in each text. It is more appropriate to consider that there are a number of possible readings to be constructed in the relationship between the text and its viewer (Coward, 1982; Kuhn, 1982). Different audiences bring a range of experiences to the viewing and thus interpret the images and text differently, producing various meanings.

A further problem is that the power relations under which representations are constructed and deployed are rarely a focus of attention in textual analysis; thus the net effect is to ignore them. However, while this is a common feature of these analyses it is not a universal flaw. Kuhn (1982), in her analysis of film, examines not only the content of the images and stories and their different readings, but also the context of their production. She critically notes that some forms of textual analysis, by concentrating on the internal operations of films as texts, tend to bracket the social context which produced that text. Kuhn argues that the economic and social institution of the Hollywood film industry is important to understanding the types of film which were produced there. A change in the institution could lead to a change in the product, though she cautions against any simple notion that increasing the number of women will have a necessarily progressive impact. Kuhn points to the importance of the distinction between 'feminine' and 'feminist' and explores the question of what would be a feminist film. She goes on to examine the way 'woman' operates as a sign in a variety of cinematic texts. For instance, the classic story in which a woman, by breaking out of a conventional heterosexual practice, sets a narrative in motion, which is resolved when the woman is restored to the fold or killed.

Hudson (1984) moves from text to a social setting to explore the cross-cutting and contradictory discourses of femininity and adolescence, and seeks to identify the actual meanings held by different social groups of teenage girls, teachers and social workers. She examines these in the context of who has the power to define conduct as acceptable. More recently there have been some analyses of cultural industries as forms of production, partly as a response to recent interventions of radical local authorities into assisting progressive arts (Lury, 1990).

Winship's article raises the question of whether, in their efforts for personal survival, women's accommodation to and engagement with patriarchal relations is to be described by the label 'femininity', albeit with resistance, or 'feminism', albeit of a new form. The traditional dichotomy between the two terms is such that femininity excludes the notion of resistance, hence the problem. This is a problem which surfaces in debates around what I shall call radical feminist discourse analysis.

Radical feminists and discourse analysis

I think that there are important similarities among the works of some of these discourse analysts and some radical feminist analyses, especially those of Daly (1973, 1978, 1984, 1985), Spender (1980, 1983) and MacKinnon (1982). They share the assumption that the question to be asked is how patriarchal discourses are created and maintained, rather than a focus upon how individuals become socialized.

Spender (1980) argues that language is patriarchally structured, that is, made by and for men. She examines the use of words which cover up women's existence, for instance, the use of male terms such as 'he' and 'man', which supposedly include women; and the active speaking patterns of language in which women use less authoritative forms. Spender maintains that this is both a result of male power and a contribution to it. It promotes male imagery and a masculine view of the world at the expense of women. It makes it more difficult for women to think outside a patriarchal world view. Further, the way that language is organized in conversation is to women's disadvantage, since men are much more likely to interrupt women than vice versa. A study by Zimmerman and West (1975) found that men made 98 per cent of the interruptions in mixed-sex conversation. In later works Spender develops this analysis of men's control over women's ideas and the difficulties men place in their way when women try to write (1983). Women do write subversive feminist texts, but in the face of male opposition. For instance, men attack the sexual integrity of women writers and otherwise abuse them (Wollstonecraft was dubbed a 'hyena in petticoats' by her male critics). Male publishers let significant feminist texts go out of print.

Daly (1978) has a conception of a system of patriarchy which is critically mediated through language and beliefs. It is a world-wide system, and takes slightly varying forms in different countries and times, but is essentially the same. Patriarchal beliefs and practices are at the core of all the world religions, including the contemporary Western world's equivalent of medical science. In all these ideological systems, or discourses, there is a tradition of domination of women by men. In all, there are practices of sado-rituals against women which are authoritatively justified within that system of thought as good for the woman, so that she might marry, be healthy or pure. In many, women are used as token torturers to carry out these mutilations. The practices include: foot-binding in ancient China; suttee, or widow burning, in India; clitoridectomy, or removal of the clitoris, in Africa; witch burning in medieval Europe; gynaecologically unnecessary practices of mastectomy, or breast removal (instead of other equally successful treatments of breast cancer), and psychiatrist practices involving a 'the-rapist', in the contemporary West. In each case Daly explores how the dominant belief system justifies these acts as necessary and good within its own terms. For instance, clitoridectomy is needed to make a young woman marriageable, and hence materially supported. She also shows how contemporary patriarchal scholarship has condoned and covered up the extent of the patriarchal violence, for instance, suggesting that high-caste Indian widows went willingly to their husbands' funeral pyres, rather than often being drugged and held on with sticks. She has a critique of language as a vehicle for patriarchal misconceptions. Religions have usually been the dominant belief systems which have authorized such practices, but modern medical science, as the contemporary authoritative belief system which justifies the mutilation of women, has a similar place in her scheme.

Daly's solution is to uncover the truth by building a non-patriarchal language and a woman's culture. Her books contain examples of how to reclaim words to women which had been distorted from their original meaning. For instance, words which currently have a negative content to women, such as hag and crone, are reappropriated as terms for women who resist patriarchy and are strong and wonderful as a consequence. In order to build an effective opposition women need to create their separate cultural spaces from men, so that they might spin and weave alternatives. This is conceived as a process of journeying, of the creation and uncovering of female strengths and values hidden under patriarchy. Daly thus advocates a separatist strategy which, while including sexual autonomy from men, does not concentrate on lesbianism as a central feature of her analysis.

Daly has provided a powerful account of women's oppressions and a positive vision of women and their potential. Her coverage of world history is striking. Her analysis of the role of religion as an authoritative source of justification of the subordination of women links her into the discourse tradition, even though she makes no reference to it.

The weaknesses of the account stem from the same place as its strengths, its global character. It has been criticised for being too sweeping and overgeneral, without sufficient regard to specific circumstances. Lorde (1981) finds fault with her for not giving an account of the resistance of women of colour to their oppression, only that of contemporary white Western women. Segal (1987) and Grimshaw (1988) consider that she is an essentialist whose separatism is a dangerous political mistake for women. Hester Eisenstein (1984) likewise regards her as a woman-centred analyst whose separatism is a political dead-end. In short she is roundly condemned as essentialist and separatist.

These criticisms are often ferocious and, I think, overstated. In outline they have a point, but they fail to deal with the rich nuances of the work. Firstly, the accusation of essentialism exaggerates the stasis in the account. Daly does not like most women as they are, nor does she want them to stay that way. Rather, she wants to send them all voyaging, discovering and changing. This is hardly embracing essential womanhood. It is true that she thinks women have a potential. It is also true that she does not say that men share this potential, but neither does she say that they do not. The silence on men is a problem, and it is this that I think is the most serious problem in her work. Secondly, the accusation of separatism is overstated, since almost all feminists utilize and defend the use of separatist tactics on occasion, whether as a caucus within a trade union or a women's committee on a local council. The issue should be not whether this is wrong in principle, but whether Daly argues for more forms of separatism than are appropriate. For instance, Daly's criticism of feminists who try to engage with patriarchal professions can be considered to push the separatist case too strongly.

The main problems in the work are its insufficient differentiation of the contexts of women's lives, of the variety of ways in which men engage in gender relations, and its neglect of the material level of the economy.

Sexuality is the key to the definition of women in the work of several radical feminists, for instance, MacKinnon (1982, 1987), Dworkin (1981) and Rich (1980). MacKinnon (1982) considers that sexuality is the basis; women are defined as sexual objects by men in all aspects of life. This is not only in arenas such as the family but also paid work, as her analysis of sexual harassment of women in paid work suggests (MacKinnon, 1979). Like those following the psychoanalytic tradition, these writers see gender and sexuality as inseparably entwined. MacKinnon even goes as far as to interdefine them, though Rich draws back from this. These accounts are limited by their one-sidedness insofar as they purport to be complete analyses of gender relations, but provocative nonetheless. They will be considered in more detail in the following chapter on sexuality.

Review of theories

The socialization theorists made an effective argument against notions that femininity and masculinity were biologically given attributes. But they were limited to accounts of how people became feminine or masculine, and could not account for the content of these ideas. Further, they were typically unable to deal with the variation in the content of gender identity between classes, ethnic groups, or cultures, or with social change.

The psychoanalytic theories argued that unseen processes in the unconscious during early childhood were important in the construction of gender identity. However, these suffered from similar difficulties of essentialism and ahistoricism, ignoring the social mediation of the notions of femininity and masculinity.

Discourse analysis provides the theoretical means to overcome the problems of essentialism and ahistoricism. In shifting the conceptual tools away from the individual to the social level, it enables us to explore the shifting content and relations between femininities and masculinities. However, some versions of it, especially those attuned to Derrida's deconstructionism, lost sight both of the social context of the power relations between the sexes and, in their focus on breaking down essentialist notions of femininity, of any common experiences of woman-hood. But this was not universal, especially when analyses of discourse were related to the circumstances of production of those discourses as well as to their content.

Some radical feminist theorists implicitly utilize some aspects of a discourse approach, albeit one which has a very strong sense of fixed power relations (which is not to be found in Foucault's work). These theorists bring us back to a femininist version of the dominant ideology thesis, in that they see the ideological constructs of patriarchy as critical to women's continued subordination. They have provided some provocative accounts of language and religion as patriarchal discourse. The limit of their analyses is an underestimation of the significance of economic and political institutions and an overstatement of the importance of ideas.

In my account of gendered subjectivity, then, I want to draw upon the theoretical tools of discourse analysis, strengthened with a firmer account of patriarchal power, but tempered with a more thorough interconnection with economic relations both in the household and paid work, with the state, violence and sexuality.

I shall argue that gendered subjectivity is created everywhere, that there is no privileged site, neither early childhood, nor sexuality. Indeed changing gender relations in all sites provide bases for the generation of new norms of femininities and masculinities. Further, struggles over these definitions are crucial to understanding the changes.

CHANGES IN FEMININITIES AND MASCULINITIES

The question which concerns me here is to what extent there have been significant differences in the forms and relationships between femininities and masculinities. I think that there have been major changes, but that a dichotomy is still part of popular cultural practice. The keys to the patriarchal relations in culture are the differentiation of the discourses of femininities and masculinities, and the valuation of masculinity above those of femininity. Having argued that femininities and masculinities are not rooted merely in one base, such as sexuality, I shall examine the variety of sites which are of significance. Overall I think there has been a shift from femininity being located and defined primarily within the private or domestic sphere towards a wider range of arenas.

The changing place of the domestic within notions of femininity has produced important differences over the last 150 years or so. Domestication has usually been seen as a feminine virtue, but to an extent which varies by class, age and ethnicity, as well as by historical period. Among middle-class women in the Victorian period domesticity was key to the feminine ideal (Cott, 1978; Davidoff, 1973; Davidoff and Hall, 1987; Gilman, 1966; Hamilton, 1909; Hayden, 1981; Pinchbeck, 1930). The discourse of femininity defined women as being contained within the family, whether married or not, although marriage was a central ambition. The feminine ideal of the middle-class ladies was one of selflessness, fragility and dependence on a husband or father. This involved the absence of work outside the home for money. Philanthropy, which might appear as work outside the house, did not transgress the feminine ideal because it did not involve payment. Similarly, wives often did a lot of housework which, since unpaid, did not transgress the ideal. However, domesticity was less central, though still important, to notions of feminine virtue among working-class women (Walkowitz, 1980; John, 1980).

Masculinity involved an orientation to the outside world, beyond the family and household. A financially dependent wife was central to the discourse of masculinity. It was necessary to be able to bring home a 'family wage' to achieve full masculinity.

Victorian feminists faced a dilemma over the stigmatizing consequences if they entered activities in the 'male' or 'public' sphere. Some, such as the suffragettes, pursued this despite the slurs it cast upon their 'femininity' and status as ladies. Others sought to work within an expanded notion of 'women's private' sphere. The latter effectively stretched the notion of respectable feminine activities without challenging a dichotomy between it and the masculine. This group included feminists such as Catherine Beecher, who argued that the education of girls was properly women's business and set up schools for them (Sklar, 1973). The efficient care of the sick was declared to be within women's province by Florence Nightingale and other nurses, as was the care of the poor and inadequate by early women social workers such as Octavia Hill. In fact Victorian women created a series of all-female communities in which they lived and worked with each other, in activities which pushed at the limits of respectable femininity. As Vicinus (1985) argues, these institutions were restricted by the class as well as the gender position of the women; nonetheless, women used them as part of an active re-creation of the boundaries of acceptable femininity, rather than being their passive victims. The friendships generated in an all-female context were important in sustaining these activities.

In contemporary Britain domesticity is a less central feature of femininity and, further, is less restricted by class than by age and ethnicity. The class differences have narrowed as have the age differences in participation in paid work. While a Victorian middle-class woman could not take waged work without much loss of esteem as a 'lady', the same is not true today. Today age is more important in distinguishing the centrality of the domestic to the form of femininity, as Coward's (1978) comparison of notions of femininity between women's magazines such as *Cosmopolitan*, on the one hand, and *Woman's Own* and *Good Housekeeping*, on the other, illustrates.

Motherhood remains an important component of the discourse of femininity. While in the nineteenth century this was firmly bound up with domestication, today it is a little more independent. Its significance has been shown in the debates around the new reproductive technologies and around other forms of fertility control, especially abortion. Inability to conceive is regarded by many women as a severe threat to their ideas of their womanhood (see Stanworth, 1987). This is a major area where contemporary notions of gender are still rooted naturalistically.

The place of fatherhood in the discourse of masculinity has been undergoing some significant changes. In the nineteenth century it was bound up with the notion of head of household, which was central to adult masculinity. As Ehrenreich has documented (1983), there has been something of a flight from fatherhood among men in the post-war period, and the notion of man as provider is less important to its contemporary construction. However, there is a significant restructuring of what properly constitutes fatherhood away from economic provider towards emotional nurturer, though this is replete with contradictions. The spate of films on divorcing men and fatherhood, for instance, *Kramer vs Kramer*, illuminates these shifts. In this film, Kramer's adequacy as a 'new man' depends upon his adequacy as a nurturing father rather than economic provider, but its achievement cross-cuts his high-powered masculine job.

Masculinity is today less determined by the possession of a dependent wife. However, the ability to bring in a decent wage is still part of the masculine ideal. Recent studies on unemployment have shown the difficulty of maintaining a masculine identity in the absence of this (Morris, 1985).

The absence of waged work was an important signifier of superior forms of femininity by the end of the nineteenth century, although this necessarily varied by class. The stigmatization of waged work as unfeminine was temporarily abated during both world wars, when any labour was in short supply, and women were exhorted to help the national war effort (Andrews, 1918; Braybon, 1981; Summerfield, 1984). During the Second World War the rates of mobilization of women into war work were particularly high, and popular images of womanhood shifted with dramatic speed to incorporate this into contemporary femininity. Today paid work in itself is not inconsistent with notions of femininity, though there are still areas of ambiguity surrounding particular sorts of work – if it is highly technical or powerful (Cockburn, 1985). Some areas, such as clerical work, underwent a transformation from masculine to feminine at the turn of the century, with the ideological typification following on rapidly from the changed gender composition

(Davies, 1975). I think the different significance of paid work for femininity is a remarkable shift in the content of femininity and for the boundary of femininity and masculinity. While previously the presence or absence of waged work was a significant marker of masculinity and femininity, especially among the middle classes, today this is not so. There remains only a residual element in that the type of paid work has some pertinence as a gender differentiator.

Waged work has been important as a signifier of masculinity. Particular sorts of work are imbued with more ability to bestow masculinity upon its doer than others. For instance, Cockburn (1983) has shown how the shift from working with heavy metal to light keyboards for print workers created enormous problems for their masculine identities. The changes concerned were not smoothly accomplished but were accompanied by much resistance.

Rather than containment within the domestic circle being the key sign of femininity today, I would suggest that it is sexual attractiveness to men. While the latter was a virtue in the Victorian period (Hamilton, 1909), it was so in a relatively undercover way as compared with today. It is no longer merely the femininity of young single women which is defined in this way, but increasingly that of older women as well. It is precisely on this issue of sexuality that the writers disagree: whether it is a sign of resistance for women to display and exert their sexuality (e.g., Winship, 1985), whether it is merely incorporation into a patriarchal system (e.g., Leeds Revolutionary Feminist Group, 1981), or whether it is both simultaneously (Vance, 1984). This will be explored further in the chapter on sexuality.

While many aspects of popular culture appear to be increasing the range of possibilities for women and reducing the restricted area of femininity, there is one which does not: pornography. It has been argued by some liberals that the availability of sexually explicit materials is an increase in freedom, and this after all was a focus of the anti-censorship battles of the 1950s and 1960s. However, this increase in freedom is for the dominant group in the pornography complex – men. The male gaze, not that of women, is the viewpoint of pornography. The materials themselves often include not merely sexually explicit scenes, but ones of violence towards and humiliation of women (Dworkin, 1981; Kappeler, 1986).

One of the sites of gender training which has undergone some of the most changes towards reducing gender differences is that of formal education. In pre-industrial Britain women were barred from such formal educational provision as existed. Training in literacy was confined largely to boys, and elite institutions such as the universities of Oxford and

Cambridge were closed. This exclusionary closure against women changed during the nineteenth century, such that formal education was one of the first of the public spheres to be fully open to women. Girls were admitted to the secondary schools as soon as they were created, and women fought their way into the universities (Deem, 1978; Lewis, 1983; Strachey, 1928). During the twentieth century, education has been the least patriarchal institution, formally open to women at all levels. In very recent years girls have been gaining more qualifications at the age of 16 than boys, and the gap in the qualifications of 18 year olds is closing, as is the number of degrees. Yet despite this lack of exclusion, we still see high levels of segregation by subjects studied, with boys in the sciences and girls in the arts.

A further general change in the ideologies of femininity and masculinity has been from a justification of difference, through a naturalizing ideology, to a dissimulative approach which denies the extent of the inequality. Once patriarchs openly proclaimed that women were not welcome in certain spheres of life; now they are more likely to deny that any barriers to women exist. The patriarchal ideology shifts from open exclusion of women as 'naturally' different, to one of denying the extent of women's disadvantages and denying that women's slight 'under-achievement' is a result of discrimination.

In short I am arguing that, while variable across class, ethnicity, and age in particular, femininity is consistently differentiated from masculinity over the last century and a half. However, there have been some important changes. Abstinence from paid work is no longer such a central element of femininity. Overall there has been a shift in the discourse of femininity away from private domesticity towards more public aspects of sexual attractiveness to men, outside as well as inside the family.

These changes have followed rather than led the material changes in gender relations. As we have seen, the ideology of specific occupations as masculine or feminine follows on after the economic and political struggles over which gender shall occupy these job slots. After women gained entry to paid work, abstinence from such employment ceased to be part of the feminine discourse.

5

Sexuality

INTRODUCTION

Why are women criticized for forms of sexual conduct for which men are considered positively? Why did the myth of the vaginal orgasm have such popularity? Why do some men sexually abuse their children? Why do some people prefer sexual contact with people of the same sex and some with the other sex?

This chapter will address the question of whether sexuality is a major source of pleasure that we seek throughout our lives (cf., Freud, 1977) or the foundation of men's control over women (cf., MacKinnon, 1982), or if it is peripheral to considerations of social inequality (cf., Marx). Sexuality is either irrelevant or central to most analyses of social relations. Class analysis does not even defend its omission, while in Freudian thought and some radical feminist analyses sexuality is the main determinant of social life.

There is a major divide between those who consider sexuality to be an instinct or drive which is biologically inherent in all human beings, and those who consider it to be socially constructed in all its aspects of interest to social science. The former typically adopt a Freudian perspective, the latter more usually either symbolic interactionism, discourse analysis or radical feminism. However, some of the more recent interpretations of Freud have reduced the significance of biology in his texts and increased that of the social and cultural aspects, while some, but certainly not all, of the radical feminist analyses have a conception of an essential female sexuality. Nevertheless, while there is a degree of convergence in specific texts between the Freudians and social constructionists, there is a fundamental discrepancy between the two positions which underlies many of the other differences in the debates on sexuality. A further and related question is that of the significance of sexuality and the degree to which sexual practices are determined or determining of other social relations, together with the related one of the connection to social control.

An issue which runs through all these accounts is that of the reasons for sexual orientation as heterosexual, lesbian or homosexual. It is the central question for radical feminist analysis, since it is through this that the connection between male-dominated forms of sexuality and patriarchy is made. Freud himself considered that all people were originally bisexual, but became heterosexual during the normal path of development. Interactionists, in classic liberal fashion, see sexual orientation as the summation of a series of small-scale interactions, with no overarching significance. Marxists have tended to see the rise of capitalism as responsible for all manner of forms of sexual repression.

PERSPECTIVES

The perspectives which I have been using are less satisfactory as a focus for debate on this topic than some of the others, but they may still be seen. This is partly because Freudian thought has three main variants, each of which has a radically different approach to gender inequality. Firstly, there is the orthodox interpretation of Freud which is explicitly anti-feminist. Secondly, there are syntheses of Marxism and Freudian thought which are radical on class and silent on gender. Thirdly, there are attempts by dual-systems theorists to produce a version of Freud compatible with a feminist analysis. A further problem in the perspectives is that Marxism does not have its own analysis of sexuality but has been synthesized both with Freudian (Marcuse, 1969; Mitchell, 1975; Reich, 1969) and discourse (Weeks, 1981) perspectives. Indeed one of the reasons for the revitalization of Freudian analyses has been a result of Marxists trying to develop an analysis of sexuality, not only of the economy and politics. However, some perspectives are clearly represented, such as liberalism, which is strongly articulated by symbolic interactionism (Gagnon and Simon, 1973; Plummer, 1975), and radical feminist analysis (MacKinnon, 1982; Rich, 1980). Dual-systems theory has so far involved primarily Freudian theory (Mitchell, 1975), and while it could logically involve discourse analysis, this synthesis has not so far been produced.

Freudians

While discussions on class are often debates with the ghost of Marx, those on sexuality are with the ghost of Freud. As in the case of Marxist class analysis, there are an infinite number of variations within Freudian thought, as well as critiques of it. I shall start with a conventional reading of Freud, complete with biological features, then move on, firstly, to attempts to give it a more social and radical aspect by combining it with Marxism, and, secondly, to the reinterpretation by Mitchell and other Lacanians which emphasizes the social and cultural aspects.

In the older, orthodox reading of Freud, sexuality is conceptualized as a drive, as an instinct possessed by all human beings by virtue of their biology. The sexual drive, or libido, as Freud called it, underlay other social constructs as a fundamental powerful force. It exists, shaping behaviour, even when people are unaware of it, and is present from birth, not merely arising at puberty.

Freud considered that the original sexual drive could be directed at any object, but that it was usually channelled in standard ways as children grew up. Thus all people are originally bisexual or, indeed, polymorphously perverse. A person's sexuality passes through stages of fixation upon different zones of the body which became eroticized in turn, moving from the oral, to anal to genital. The last has one stage for boys, but two for girls, first the clitoral and next the vaginal. Repression of sexuality is a universal feature of later childhood.

Girls are differentiated from boys in a number of ways. Freud originally considered that boys were attracted to their mothers and girls to their fathers, but later changed to a view that both sexes are initially attracted to the mother. This attachment is broken in a different manner. Boys loosen the tie when threatened by the father with castration. Girls are considered to suffer from 'penis envy', which is transformed into a desire for a child, and, since only men can provide this, girls break their attachment to their mothers. Thus the essential difference between the sexes is due to anatomy. Further, girls have a different pattern of ego formation, which results in a weaker super ego.

Male homosexuality arises from an overintense fixation on a woman, usually the mother, during a boy's earliest years. As a consequence such boys identify themselves with a woman. They take themselves as their sexual object, that is, they operate on a narcissistic basis. Then as adults they select as a sexual object a man who resembles themselves. Homosexual tendencies may be repressed but, if so, they still remain latent.

This traditional reading of Freud has been subject to a number of criticisms (e.g., Friedan, 1965; Masson, 1984; Millett, 1977). Firstly, the account is essentialist and biologistic. Anatomy is not necessarily destiny for women. Neither is sexuality adequately accounted for as a biological drive. Secondly, it is too universalistic, not recognizing the historical and cultural specificity of the families that were studied among the middle-class Viennese at the turn of the century. On the contrary, sexuality is subject to wide social variations. Thirdly, Freud overstates the importance of infancy, underestimating the potential of humans to change. For instance, Kinsey (1953) showed that, while 37 per cent of men had had a homosexual experience to the point of orgasm at some point in their lives, only 4 per cent become stabilized in a homosexual role, suggesting much greater fluidity and choice in the development of sexual orientation than Freud's theory allows. Fourthly, Freud is wrong in his account of a woman's erotic zone moving from clitoris to vagina on maturity (Koedt, 1973; Masters and Johnson, 1966). Masters and Johnson demonstrated through their clinical research that the centre of a woman's orgasm was never the vagina, but always the clitoris. Koedt (1973) argues that the uptake of Freud's 'myth of the vaginal orgasm' can be explained only in terms of men's vested interests in penetrative sexual intercourse and their fear that, if women knew the truth, they would be less willing to engage in sexual acts which suited men. Fifthly, Freud's analysis is riddled with patriarchal value assumptions, such as that assertiveness was a masculine characteristic and a sign of neurosis in a woman, who should embrace passive femininity in order to be fulfilled as a woman. Sixthly, the methods he used are not scientifically adequate to support his theories. This is based partly on suspicion that a few selected clinical histories are not adequate to provide a universal theory of the unconscious. It is partly a more serious criticism that Freud discounted the words of his female patients when they said that they had been raped by their fathers, for no reason other than his own prejudice and desire to conform with the patriarchal orthodoxy on this matter (Masson, 1984).

A variety of attempts has been made to rectify some of these problems in Freud's analysis, firstly by a synthesis with Marx, secondly, by a reading which emphasizes the cultural rather than the biological aspects of his thought.

Early Marxist-Freudians

The problems in Freud's writings of ahistoric analysis devoid of sufficient account of power in social relations are tackled by a set of Marxist writers who sought to combine Freudian analysis with that of Marx (Marcuse, 1969; Reich, 1969). Marxist analysis is traditionally strong on power and historical change, yet weak on issues of culture and sexuality, and these writers hoped a synthesis of Marx and Freud would overcome the problems in both theories of society.

Marcuse and Reich argued that the repression of sexuality was not necessary for civilization, as Freud had argued, but only for exploitative social structures such as that of capitalism. Reich asserted that the repression of sexuality led to a rigid, authoritarian personality, which itself led to repressive authoritarian states, such as that of Nazi Germany. A release of sexual tension would lead to a freer society. Marcuse qualified this advocacy of sexual liberationism by suggesting that desublimation, or expressing repressed sexual desires, under capitalism may merely implicate one more deeply in oppressive capitalist relations. Commercialized forms of sexual expression are not liberating.

Neither Reich nor Marcuse paid much attention to gender relations, let alone the oppression of women, so did not address the problems outlined above.

Lacanian Freudians/dual-systems theory

The interpretation of Freud so far has been within a conception of sexuality as a drive or instinct. Indeed Reich narrowed Freud's concept of libido to little more than genital sex. Lacan (1977) and later writers have argued that Freud may be read differently, so that we can see the cultural aspects of his theory more clearly (Burniston, Mort and Weedon, 1978; Weedon, 1987).

Mitchell (1975) follows a Lacanian interpretation in her attempt to rescue Freud from feminist criticisms. She argues that these judgements do not constitute a sufficient rejection of Freud because they do not deal with his central contribution -- a theory of the unconscious. A fuller account of this is to be found in the previous chapter on culture. As was seen, Mitchell is able to support her argument that the unconscious is a useful concept, but has little to say about sexual practices.

Symbolic interactionism/liberalism

Symbolic interactionist writers on sexuality take issue with many of the fundamentals of Freudian analysis. Most particularly they argue that sexuality should be analysed as a social construct rather than as an instinctual drive (Gagnon and Simon, 1973; Jackson, 1978a; Plummer, 1975). This perspective emphasizes the social rather than biological or psychological processes, contending that it does not help to view biology or unconscious processes as the basis of sexuality. Sexuality is a 'capacity' which every human being possesses. It is a potential which can be developed, but need not be. It is socially shaped, rather than a drive which shapes society. There is no conception of an underlying force, nor of a proper path of normal development here.

Symbolic interactionism as a general theory of society has three basic foci: meaning, process and interaction (Blumer, 1969; Plummer, 1975). In relation to sexuality an analysis of meaning examines the fluidity of interpretations it is possible to attach to an object or practise. For instance, a pornographic book has very different meanings to a newsagent, schoolboy, wife, priest, feminist or male rugby player. Symbolic interactionists are interested in 'process'; there are no fixed meanings, so there are processes of negotiation over meanings. Socialization into a specific set of sexual practices is not a fixed, once and for always, occurrence; rather the process of construction of sexual meanings never ends. The third element, 'interaction', emphasizes the social nature of life, that interaction between the self and others is central to the process of the construction of meaning. Indeed, since interactionists stress the reflexive nature of human beings (in opposition to behaviourist psychologists, who see people responding to stimulus in a mechanical way), there is also the interaction of the self with the self.

The interactionist account of sexuality is, then, one of the process of becoming sexual. It does not involve the unfolding of a pre-ordained path of development, but rather something which is learnt and negotiated in a complex sequence of events. The process of becoming sexual can start only when an individual understands what the concept of sexuality means, usually at adolescence – not birth, as for the Freudians. People build up repertoires of sexual scripts appropriate to different occasions during the course of their sexual career.

Plummer (1975) offers a symbolic interactionist account of male homosexuality which demonstrates the strengths of this perspective. He is concerned with the process of becoming homosexual rather than its origins or determining causes. In stark contrast to Freud, who fixes the causation of homosexuality in a man's childhood relationship with his mother, Plummer focuses on processes from adolescence and the relationship with peers and a wide range of other people. Whereas Freud's notion is that homosexuality is caused by processes outside the control of the individual, Plummer suggests that there is a degree of conscious choice, at least of drifting which is not totally outside his control. Plummer's homosexual is no victim. Plummer proposes that there are four sequential stages on the route to becoming gay. Once started on this career it is possible to stop; there is no inevitable progression to the last stage in the schema. Firstly, the subject will become sensitized to the possibility that he is gay in conscious or semi-conscious moments, but will generally neutralize these ideas. In our culture both gender confusion and erotic thoughts may act as sensitizers: for instance, that his body is inappropriate to cultural definitions of masculinity, or erotic day dreams about another male. Secondly, there is signification, a process of labelling. This may be done by the man himself, or by others such as peers, teachers or parents. Thirdly, there is the process of coming out to others as gay and the exploration of the homosexual community. Fourthly, there is stabilization into a homosexual role. Plummer emphasizes that there is no such thing as a normal path of sexual development. Within a symbolic interactionist framework there are no implicit value judgements.

Symbolic interactionism is a form of analysis which belongs within the liberal perspective. It has a view of society as a summation of small-scale interactions and is devoid of concepts of an overarching social structure. The strength of the analysis is in its critique of the biologism of orthodox Freudian thought and the concepts it introduces for a sensitive social analysis.

Its weakness is that it has difficulty in explaining any large-scale social patterning, large-scale historical change, and systematic power relations. So it cannot deal with systematic gender inequality in sexual relations. Further, it has no account of where the sexual scripts themselves come from. It provides a description of some of the processes involved in learning to become sexual, but not of the content of those sexual meanings. For instance, Plummer's interactionist account of male homosexuality is unable to explain the homophobia which is such an important force structuring the meaning of homosexuality in contemporary society.

Jackson (1978b) has attempted to construct a feminist interactionist account of rape. She utilizes interactionist techniques in her discussion of how men are able to neutralize the negative aspects of their actions. Meanings are considered negotiable rather than absolute and given within this framework, and she suggests that men are able to negotiate the meaning of a situation so as to excuse themselves from illicit conduct. In discussing the power relations between men and women, her analysis introduces the concept of patriarchy in order to capture the way in which relations between men and women are systematically structured to women's disadvantage. However, while this produces a more adequate analysis, 'patriarchy', as a large structural concept, is inadmissible within the symbolic interactionist perspective. Her account succeeds in its analysis of rape precisely as it moves outside a symbolic interactionist frame of reference.

Discourse analysis: Foucault

Foucault's (1981, 1987) analysis of sexuality is a social constructionist one, similar to that of the interactionists, in that he argues against the notion of sexuality as a biological drive. It is different from that of the interactionists in that, by using the concept of discourse, he is able to link into macro-conceptions of society and social change. Foucault sees sexuality as a discourse, as a set of institutionally rooted social practices constructed in relation with other discourses. Sexuality is what is considered to be sexual; it has no intrinsic meaning or boundary. Foucault is concerned with the way that sexuality is deployed, and the various strategies which shape this.

Foucault (1981) uses his analysis to argue against the notion that the Victorian period was one in which sexuality was repressed. Rather he argues that there was a plethora of discourses on sexuality that constituted or incited its existence, even as they were ostensibly aimed at containing sexuality. Sexuality has increasingly been controlled, but not repressed. Foucault examines the continuity between the modern practice of psychoanalysis and that of the Catholic Church's confessional. The confession entailed speaking about sex in the process of confessing it as a sin. In this way sexuality is put into discourse in great detail. Psychoanalysis continues this within a 'scientific' framework. Sex is seen to be the truth of a person, the most fundamental aspect of their being. Foucault goes on to discuss a series of discourses which similarly called sexuality into being: the psychiatrization of perverse pleasure; the socialization of procreative behaviour in population policy; the pedagogization of children's sexuality involving such things as controlling masturbation; and the hysterization of women's bodies, constructing them as centred on their wombs. Later work (Foucault, 1987) continues the theme of the historical specificity of sexual discourse with an examination of sexuality in ancient Greece.

The overall theme, common in fact to much of Foucault's other work (1971, 1979), is that the growth of expert professionals of social life and their 'scientific' bodies of knowledge leads to greater control over people, not to liberalization and greater freedom. In speaking of sexuality within these professional discourses it is controlled as it is produced. Medical, psychiatric, psychotherapeutic and religious professions and discourses are all nodes of power and control. Foucault implies that the only way to speak of sexuality is within these discourses, so verbal exploration of sexual issues becomes not liberating, but restrictive. His view of recent historical change is thus one of profound pessimism.

In opposition to Marxist notions of power Foucault denies that capitalism and class are the means by which power is structured. Rather, power is highly dispersed, although there are still some sites which are more important than others.

Foucault's concept of discourse is of considerable use in developing the theorization of sexuality. It provides a way to conceptualize sexuality within a social constructionist framework which is not limited by the small frame of reference of interactionists, thus enabling analysis of major social changes. However there are some limitations.

Foucault does not discuss the implications of gender inequality for sexual discourses, despite his general concern for power. For instance, women and men often have different orientations to sexuality, even different discourses, but this is not significantly discussed in his work. Here, as elsewhere, Foucault is concerned to debate with Marxist conceptions of social structure, problematizing simple notions that the bourgeoisie benefited from these changes in sexual discourse. But in his concern to refute Marxist notions of significant concentrations of power he misses significant strategies of control in relation to gender. For instance, he discusses whether the bourgeoisie controls or is controlled by the new discourses, without considering that one gender within the bourgeoisie might be using sexuality to control the other (1981: 122–3). We find that only the words of men, not those of women were analysed. He evaluates only texts written by men, as priests, psychoanalysts, etc. This omits the written words of women, who were barred from such professions, but who nevertheless wrote influential novels as well as personal letters. He omits the words of those who were not literate, more often women than men, and most of the working class. That is, his account of the discourses on sexuality is restricted by class and gender. In Foucault's defence it might be argued that he has analysed the most powerful discourses. While this may be true, the question cannot be determined without more evidence. However, Foucault still omits those discourses of resistance, despite the fact that in his other writings, on topics where gender is less central, he considers resistance to be important.

Marxist discourse analysis

Foucault's conceptual schema has been fruitfully combined with a number of other perspectives. Weeks (1981) attempts a synthesis of Foucauldian discourse analysis and Marxism in order to explain changes in the forms of sexuality since the rise of capitalism. His particular interest is in the increasing stigmatization of male homosexuality. Weeks maintains that the development of capitalism led to greater regulation of male homosexual behaviour. He argues against a crude economic reductionism, and suggests rather that both the family and class ideology played crucial roles in mediating this relationship. The word 'homosexual' was itself used little until the 1880s and 1890s, and had only been invented in the 1860s. In 1885 there was a critical legal change in the passing of the Labouchere Amendment, which made male, but not female, homosexuality illegal.

Weeks contends that changes in the family during the rise of capitalism were crucial to the present configuration of homosexuality. He argues that male homosexuality became increasingly stigmatized because it existed in contradiction to a new family ideal. The domestic ideology of monogamous nuclear family with chaste wife was a paradigm of the rising bourgeoisie. The latter used this ideology to differentiate itself from the older ruling class of the aristocracy, to promote its cohesiveness, and to proclaim its moral superiority. Weeks considered that sexuality had a vital symbolic role for the bourgeois class. This new domestic ideology was exported to the working class, where it did not have an indigenous basis. Male homosexuality was stigmatized because it symbolically contradicted the new family ideal the bourgeoisie promulgated to solidify its position *vis à vis* the aristocracy.

Weeks effectively demonstrates that discourse analysis can be linked to a more materialist and structural explanation. His account of the historical specificity of the forms of regulation of sexuality is important. However, it has problems as a result of the limited attention paid to the dynamics of gender relations. As Marshall (1981) notes, it gives insufficient space to the way in which homophobia is directed at controlling men's gender behaviour, and not only their sexuality. But most particularly, Weeks overstates the newness of men's attempts to control the sexuality of their wives. This is not specific to capitalist society, but to patriarchal ones. That is, Weeks's linking of homophobia with capitalism rather than patriarchy is misplaced.

Radical feminism

The link between patriarchy and male-dominated sexuality is central to the analyses of many radical feminist writers (Coveney et al, 1984; Dworkin, 1981; Leeds Revolutionary Feminist Group, 1981; MacKinnon, 1982; Millett, 1977; Rich, 1980). Sexual practices from heterosexuality to pornography have been included within these analyses. Men sexually objectify women, reducing them to mere sexual objects. Male-dominated forms of sexuality reach into many areas, not merely the conventionally sexual. For instance, MacKinnon (1979) points to the role of sexual harassment in the workplace and indeed suggests that 'labour is to Marxism as sexuality is to feminism' (MacKinnon, 1983).

Indeed, while some radical feminists argue that specific forms of sexual domination are important to gender inequality, MacKinnon (1982, 1987) contends that sexuality constitutes gender. The eroticization of dominance and subordination creates gender as we know it. There is no separation between the concepts of gender and sexuality; they are interdefined. However, while MacKinnon makes some powerful arguments as to the importance of sexuality for women's subordination today, I think interdefinition of sexuality and gender is inappropriate, since it dismisses the significance of forms of male power which are not articulated through sexuality in an a priori fashion.

Dworkin (1981) describes the content of pornography, both modern and Sadeian, to show the depths of the violent sexual domination and humiliation of women involved. Pornography is a part of men's power over women; it is used to terrorize and control women. Dworkin argues not only that a narrowly defined pornography is pernicious, but that, more generally, women are pornography to men in the sense that men cannot see women outside a pornographic frame of reference. Men simultaneously sexualize women and dominate them. Sexuality is the terrain or medium through which men dominate women.

A central institution in men's domination over women is heterosexuality. Heterosexuality is seen not as an individual preference, as something into which people either drift or are fixed as a result of psychological processes in childhood, but rather as a socially constructed institution (Millett, 1977). The explanation of heterosexuality is a central question for radical feminist writings on sexuality. This reverses the traditional practice of setting up lesbianism and male homosexuality as unusual and in need of explanation, an approach predicated upon heterosexuality as the norm and hence not in need of explanation.

Radical feminist analyses see intimate relations between women as to be expected, given what women share under male oppression. Women's closest friends are more usually women than men. If sexual partners are chosen on the basis of sharing, liking and loving, as is generally supposed, then one would expect women to have sexual relations with women rather than men. Since, on the contrary, sexual relations between women are the exception and heterosexuality is the commoner practice, the prevalence of heterosexuality is seen to be in need of explanation.

The circumstances under which the boundary between friendship and sexuality is drawn for women are explored in a number of writings (Faderman, 1981; Sheila Jeffreys, 1985; Raymond, 1986; Rich, 1980; Smith-Rosenberg, 1975). Smith-Rosenberg documents the existence of close romantic friendships between women in the nineteenth century. These long-lived relationships involved emotional intensity and physical sensuality, yet, probably not genital sex. They were not an alternative to marriage, but in addition. Faderman (1981) argues that these romantic friendships were tolerated as long as they were not threatening to patriarchal relations. If they, unusually, involved cross-dressing and a woman's usurpation of masculine privileges then they were attacked.

Later, after the successes of first-wave feminism, these forms of female bonding did start to seem threatening. The development of Freudian-influenced ways of thinking about sexuality led to such passionate friendships being newly interpreted as sexual. As sexual relationships, they were stigmatized as deviant because they were between people of the same sex. Thus the development of neo-Freudian sexology is interpreted as a part of a patriarchal backlash against the advances of first-wave feminism. Jeffreys (1985) argues further that the sexualization and hence stigmatization of romantic friendships helped to undermine first-wave feminism. It replaced a positive image of the independent woman with that of a twisted, dried-up spinster, who was neurotic since she was unfulfilled because of her lack of 'normal' sex.

Rich (1980) suggests that all female bonding is a form of resistance against patriarchy. Rather than making a dichotomy between those women who engage in genital sex with other women and those who do not, she argues that women are on a continuum of bonding and hence resistance. She calls this the lesbian continuum.

Underpinning these radical feminist accounts is an analysis of heterosexuality as a patriarchal institution. Some radical feminists argue that it is the most important base of patriarchy (Leeds Revolutionary Feminist Group, 1981). Within heterosexual relations women, emotionally and materially, as well as sexually, service men. Women support men more than men support women. Women are more emotionally responsive to men than vice versa, since men are both unprepared, because of their masculine upbringing, and unwilling, because of their dominant position, to reciprocate fully. Even the form of sexual practice is problematic for women, since, as studies from Kinsey (1953) to Hite (1981) have shown, women are less likely than men to gain pleasure from conventional modes of intercourse. Men also gain from material servicing in the form of the greater burden of housework which falls upon women.

Further, heterosexuality has important political implications in the way that it divides women from each other, reducing their ability and will to resist. Each woman has her own special oppressor. Members of the Leeds Revolutionary Feminist Group (1981) argue that, in order to survive in this situation, women at least partially adopt the viewpoint of their oppressor, and collaborate with the enemy. They suggest that women who are independent from men are more likely to combine politically to resist patriarchy. This is bound up with the perceived need to create a separate culture of women away from men in order to develop non-patriarchal thinking as a prelude to effective action and the rebuilding of society (cf., Daly, 1978, 1984). However, the degree to which heterosexual activity leads women to be incorporated into patriarchy is a source of debate. Rich (1980), for instance, has argued that, rather than a sharp dichotomy, there is a continuum of feminist resistance which includes heterosexually active women. The discussion on the boundary between friendship and sexuality, recounted above, took place within this debate.

Rich also suggests that heterosexuality is compulsory for women in patriarchal societies. The knowledge of the possibility of lesbianism is withheld from women, so many do not even know of it as an option. This silencing on lesbian existence is carried out primarily by men, but also by women. Rich is critical of feminist theorists who are silent on lesbianism. Women's own sexuality is denied and punished through practices such as clitoridectomy (removal of the clitoris). Male sexuality is forced on women through rape, prostitution, pornography and other cultural practices. Women are controlled by force and physically confined by such practices as footbinding. Women's labour is expropriated in marriage, their fertility is controlled, their creativeness is cramped with persecution and knowledge is withheld from them.

While Rich's analysis of heterosexuality as a patriarchal institution is widely accepted among radical feminists, her concept of a lesbian continuum is not. Firstly, there is a question as to whether it is appropriate to include women who are heterosexually active. This, argue Ferguson, Zita and Addelson (1981), is problematic, since it does not recognize the specificity of lesbian genital sexuality. That is, we have the problem as to whether, and if so where, to draw the line between female friendship and resistance on the one hand and lesbian sexuality on the other. This raises the question as to whether there is a list of actions and feelings which are essentially sexual, separable from those which are not. Is this an absolute question, or simply socially defined? The former position is more in keeping with the Freudian tradition, the latter with that of the social constructionists.

Radical feminist analysis has often been criticized for sliding into essentialism, frequently of a biological sort. I think the analyses of sexuality discussed above demonstrate such criticism to be misplaced. These radical feminist analyses of sexuality are historically and socially sensitive. Further, they are more typical of radical feminism than is Firestone's account of reproduction.

In conclusion, then, sexuality, specifically the institution of heterosexuality, is a central institution of patriarchy for many, but not all, radical feminists. I think that they have impressively demonstrated that sexuality is not a private matter to be explained in terms of individual preference or psychological processes fixed in infancy, but rather that it is socially organized and critically structured by gender inequality. While few of the writers make reference to Foucault and his discourse analysis, in practice most of them have independently adopted a similar method of analysis. Sexuality is a discourse which is a social phenomenon that exists outside individuals, as well as being constituted by the actions of individuals. Unlike Foucault, these writers have managed to integrate an appreciation of gender inequality as structuring the forms of sexual practices. I would conclude from their analyses that heterosexuality is a patriarchal structure. On the vexed question as to whether and where a line is drawn between passionate friendship and sexuality, I would argue that we should adopt a non-essentialist solution and follow the feminist discourse analysis in seeing this as a socially and historically constructed distinction. Indeed I shall argue below that the issues surrounding the division are central to understanding the historically variable place of heterosexuality as a patriarchal structure in patriarchy as a whole.

CHANGES

The question of whether there has been increasing sexual liberalization, and whether this has been of benefit to women, is answered very differently by the perspectives I have considered above. Indeed each has a very different way of identifying the main points of change, if any, in sexual relations.

The liberal view is that there has been increasing liberalization and that this is of benefit to women. The conservative view is that there has been greater liberalization but that this is not to women's advantage, since it is only within stable marriage that women are secure. The Marxist view is that capitalism brought with it greater regulation of sexuality. The radical feminist view is that there has been greater liberalization of certain aspects of sexuality and that this has not been of benefit to women.

Liberal opinion is that the repressive prudery of the Victorian period has been rolled back, and that attitudes to sexuality today are more enlightened. Non-marital sexuality is no longer so severely sanctioned. Women who bear children out of wedlock are no longer social pariahs. The double sexual standard has been partially eliminated and woman are no longer treated so much more harshly than men for transgression from a conventional sexual code. Women, and men, are able to leave sexually unsatisfactory relationships, even if they have been sanctified in marriage. With the advent of reliable forms of contraception and the legalization of abortion, sex no longer means children for women, with a resultant increase in the possibility of sex without reproductive consequences. Censorship of sexually explicit materials has been relaxed, facilitating wider sexual knowledge. These changes have occurred during the twentieth century, and with greatest rapidity during the 1960s.

The Marxist view has focused on a different era, that of the rise of capitalism. It is argued that during this period there has been a greater regulation of sexuality. This is linked to the development of the nuclear family form. As a consequence, forms of sexuality outside marriage are negatively sanctioned. Women are expected to be chaste, that is, sexually active only with a husband, and male homosexuality is also sanctioned.

Radical feminists believe that women have been more actively incorporated into oppressive forms of sexuality during the twentieth century. They argue that there was a sexual counter-revolution as a backlash to the successes of first-wave feminism which incorporated women more effectively into patriarchal society. Consequent upon this more thorough incorporation of women into active heterosexuality, sexuality is now more important as a form of social control of women than it used to be. The threat of being deemed neurotic and twisted if not engaging in heterosexual sex is a disincentive to independent, celibate living. The labelling of close female friendships as lesbian may make some women more reserved about them. This sexualizing of a wider range of human relationships occurred as a reaction against feminism.

Dworkin (1983) develops this view by arguing that we are moving from one form of control over women's sexuality and reproductive capacities to another. The old form is analogous to farming, in that there is a stable, long-term relationship, cultivating the object of control. The form of the future is analogous to a brothel, involving temporary arrangements only.

I shall argue here that the Marxists are wrong and the radical feminists half right in the points chosen as indicating major changes. That is, while radical feminists are right to point to the double-edged nature of the sexual liberalization, it is precisely double edged, not an unmitigated retrenchment. I think they are right in their analysis of the backlash and the potential of the new forms of incorporation, but wrong in underestimating the significance of the diminution of certain forms of sexual control over the century.

From private to public control

I want to argue that heterosexuality constitutes a patriarchal structure, but that it has had varying forms within twentieth-century British history. In particular, we have seen a movement from the practice, at least among the middle classes, of rigorous control over women's access to sexual pleasure, to one in which women's sexual pleasure is encouraged, with the consequence of more willing incorporation into other aspects of patriarchal society. In the first patriarchal strategy, women's sexuality is directed to one patriarchal agent for a lifetime and a plethora of practices exist to prevent her sexual interest from wandering, even though one of the side effects of these is to reduce her sexual interest in anything, including marriage. In the second, a woman's sexual interest in men is encouraged by a variety of methods, even though one of the side effects is to reduce the attachment to any one man in particular.

I think we see the first strategy at work in the nineteenth-century middle classes in Britain. A woman's status was crucially affected by her sexual 'purity' and the negative consequences of pre- or extra-marital sex were severe. During the nineteenth century there was an increase in the direct control by husbands and fathers of the middle classes over the sexual conduct of their wives and daughters (Davidoff, 1973; Davidoff and Hall, 1987; Tilly and Scott, 1978). This process was consistent with the generally greater direct control they had over the conduct of their wives and daughters.

I think we see the second strategy developing from the turn of the century. There are increasing practices to facilitate a woman's active sexuality, from birth control which reduces the consequences of her fertility, to the ability to exchange an inadequate husband for a new one, as a result of changes in the divorce law, to a new post-Freudian ideology which legitimated sexual desires as healthy. Enjoyable sex does make intimate relations with men more attractive than when it is more likely to be nasty, brutish and short, even if it places women in materially exploitative relations.

However, the greater significance attached to sexual activity, together with political pressure, has opened up a space for greater tolerance of a wider range of sexual conduct. This includes lesbianism and male homosexuality. The latter was decriminalized in the 1970s for men over 21, in private. The space for lesbianism (never criminalized) has expanded, with important political implications. It has been utilized by lesbian feminists in pushing for some of the more far-reaching feminist demands. Lesbian feminists constituted the core of many of the more radical of the feminist groups, such as the early rape crisis centres.

There has been a change in the pattern of sexual partnerships away from exclusive life-long monogamous relationships with one partner, towards a greater likelihood of multiple partners. Two aspects of this, the increase in the divorce rate and in single motherhood, have already been discussed in the chapter on the household. These have obvious implications for the tendency for women to have a growing number of sexual partners. This tendency is evidenced in two further ways, the rise in extra-marital sex and in pre-marital sex.

The increase in non-marital sexual conduct is demonstrated by Lawson and Samson (1988). In their sample of 579 British respondents, they found that those married more recently were more likely to have engaged in extra-marital sexual relations. Among women marrying before 1960, 75 per cent had remained 'faithful' to their spouse ten years after marriage, as compared to 53 per cent of those marrying in the 1960s and 46 per cent of those marrying since 1970. Among men, the figures were 70 per cent for those marrying before 1960, 57 per cent for those marrying during the 1960s and 48 per cent for those marrying since 1970. Another way of examining this is in terms of the duration of the marriage before an extra-marital liaison took place. Among women who had married before 1960 the mean duration before they had their first liaison was 15 years, as compared to eight for those who married during the 1960s and four for those who had married since 1970. The pattern among the men showed a similar change over time, from a gap of 11 years for those marrying before 1960, to eight years for those marrying during the 1960s and five for those marrying after 1970. Not only has the overall extent of extra-marital sexual relations increased, but the gap between men and women has changed dramatically. In the earlier period men were more likely than women to engage in extra-marital sex, while in the more recent period it appears that the difference between the sexes is very small; indeed it is slightly more likely for women than men to engage in extra-marital liaisons. The nature of the study means that these figures are likely to provide overestimates of the extent of extra-marital sex, since the sample was primarily a volunteer one, but the changes over time are not necessarily affected by this.

So far I have examined these two modes of patriarchal structuring of sexuality from the points of view of men seeking control and of women's resistance to them. There are three further elements: firstly, women's accommodatory strategies towards sexuality within a patriarchal system; secondly, men and the flight from fatherhood; thirdly, the intersection with class and race.

Women are not passive victims of patriarchy. As we saw in the chapter on patriarchal relations of production in the household, some women have actively sought to strengthen the family in order to protect their interests as long-term homemakers, while other women have sought to weaken it. The issues on sexuality and the household are closely related. Some women have supported the form of sexual relations in which sexuality is restricted to marriage for both women and men, because they see a free market in sexual partners to be to their disadvantage. At the turn of the century this was part of Christabel Pankhurst's slogan 'Votes for women, chastity for men'. There were major feminist campaigns to impose on men the standards of sexual morality expected of women. This included issues around prostitution, the sexual double standard, and the sexual abuse of young girls. Further, under circumstances when intercourse with a husband was not likely to result in much physical pleasure for the woman and might have dire consequences in dangerous childbirth and hard labour in child care, some women wishing to resist their husbands' advances found the ideology of pure, passionless womanhood attractive (Butler, 1896; Cott, 1978; Gordon, L., 1979; Jeffreys, S., 1985; Strachey, 1928; Vicinus, 1985).

Thus some women cultivated the model in which sexuality was contained within marriage, if anywhere. This is not a consequence of false consciousness, but of their perception of their own real interests in a patriarchal society not of their making. This is a form of accommodation to patriarchal power. Gordon and Dubois (1983) characterize it as a conservative response. Indeed Dworkin (1983) suggests that similar considerations underlie the reasons why some women are right wing today.

The movement from the first to the second patriarchal strategy was largely a result of the successes of first-wave feminism. But while such as Faderman, Jeffreys and Millett see this primarily as a patriarchal backlash, I think it should be viewed also as a positive result of feminist campaigns on the terrain of sexuality itself. That is, some women as well as some men actively sought sexual liberalisation.

Women's active pursuit of these changes is seen clearly in the campaigns for birth control. This was solicited by those who realized it as beneficial to women in the conditions under which they lived. Married women who did not have the power to say no to their husbands saw it as a means of preventing repeated pregnancies with accompanying detriment to their health and the labour involved in child care (Stopes, 1981; Mark-Lawson, Savage and Warde, 1985). It is women, more often than men, who support the legalization of abortion (Greenwood and Young, 1976). It was women more often than men who sought the ability to dissolve unhappy marriages. The Women's Cooperative Guild even had its funds withdrawn by the male branch because they supported liberalization of divorce against the wishes of the men (Middleton, L., 1978).

So while in the pessimistic account birth control and divorce are merely a means by which men gain greater sexual access to women's bodies, I think it underestimates the involvement of women in these changes and the benefits they brought to many.

However, there are certain aspects of 'liberalization' where the gains have been more problematic, and recognized as such by feminists. For instance, the reduction of censorship has allowed the expansion of pornography, which is now a major industry (Dworkin, 1981). Its incitement to sexual hatred and abuse of women is highly problematic for women. Interestingly, this is one of the few issues on which right-wing women and feminists agree.

There are other issues where the changes in forms of sexual control are problematic for women. Thus while women seeking divorce are pleased that it is an available remedy to a bad marriage, the material poverty into which they are typically plunged is less welcome (Weitzman, 1985). Further, the radical feminists are correct to argue that, in a context in which heterosexual activity is seen not only as desirable but also necessary for a 'normal' healthy life, the pressures on women to marry or cohabit with a man, with all the consequent forms of servicing, are increased.

Finally, not all aspects of male dominance through sexuality have changed. The sexual double standard is still alive and well (Wilson, D., 1978). Young women are still confronted with the 'options' of being either 'slags' or 'drags' (Lees, 1986). Women still get less pleasure out of the dominant forms of sexual contact (Hite, 1981).

My argument, then, is that heterosexuality is an important patriarchal structure. The form of control of women through sexuality has changed, but it is neither a simple reduction in the degree of control, nor merely a substitution of one form of control for another equally pernicious. There has been a move away from the more rigid private form of control of women's sexuality towards one that is freer and more public.

6

Violence

Male violence against women includes rape, sexual assault, wife beating, workplace sexual harassment and child sexual abuse. It is often thought of as the acts of a few men upon a few women. Male violence is widely considered to be individually motivated and with few social consequences, though with trauma caused to a few women. It is the last place to which most people would look as a typical example of social patterning of the relations between men and women.

I shall argue, on the contrary, that male violence against women has all the characteristics one would expect of a social structure, and that it cannot be understood outside an analysis of patriarchal social structures. Durkheim (1952) used the analysis of suicide, ostensibly one of the most individualistic of actions, to argue for a sociological analysis of society. I shall suggest that rape and wife beating, analogously conventionally considered individual acts, are social facts best analysed in terms of patriarchal social structures.[1]

Male violence exists in a myriad of forms, which may be placed on a continuum, with rape and wife beating and child sexual abuse at one end and sexual harassment and wolf whistles at the other (Hanmer and Saunders, 1984; Kelly, L., 1988a; Russell, 1984; Stanko, 1985). I shall focus on the more extreme types, but they are all interrelated and have similar, if not the same, explanations.

The definitions of forms of violence are contentious. The narrowest are usually the legal ones, and these carry a certain authority because of their status. However, they typically omit acts which some women identify as acts of violence. For instance, in Britain there is no such legal entity as rape of a wife by her husband; the woman is deemed to have consented to sexual intercourse on marriage. The exclusion of husband-wife rape from criminalization has recently been reconfirmed by a legal review. However, in many US states and most of Scandinavia sexual intercourse against the will of the wife is legally rape. A survey in the USA found that 14 per cent of married women reported being raped by their husbands at least once (Russell, 1982).

An alternative approach to the definition of violence is to adopt the definition of women themselves (Stanko, 1985). This captures more than any other method the extent of the impact of violence on women. It is also the most radical in that it takes the word and perception of the women who have suffered the violence as our standard, rather than other bodies which claim authority in this area, such as the police.

A mid-way position is carefully to define the acts which are deemed from a social scientist's point of view to constitute violence, whether recognized as such by the state or all women. This is the approach taken by such social scientists as Russell (1982, 1984), who has carried out detailed surveys of the extent of violence. For instance Russell defines an act of intercourse where the man used force as rape, whether or not the woman concerned is prepared to use the emotive word rape.

A further issue is whether the rate of male violence is increasing. According to the police records of rape, it has increased by 143 per cent during the ten years from 1977 to 1987 (*Criminal Statistics, England and Wales, 1987*). Is this a real increase, or is it due to more women reporting this crime?

There are two substantive focuses to the explanation of male violence: firstly, why and how men use violence; secondly, why and how there is so little state action to discourage the violence.

PERSPECTIVES

It is possible to identify three main theoretical approaches to an analysis of male violence to women: those of liberalism, class analysis and radical feminism. The first explains the violence in terms of the psychological derangement of a small number of men; the second in terms of the frustrations of men who are disadvantaged in a class society; the third in terms of male power in a patriarchal society.

Liberalism

The conventional analysis of male violence sees it as the acts of a few wayward, generally psychologically deranged, men. The latter are considered abnormal, distinct from other men, and to be few in number. The explanation focuses on psychological processes rather than social context.

A typical account within this approach is that of West, Roy and Nichols (1978), who argue that rape is an act of individual men who have not developed normally. They suggest that this is a product of bad childhood experiences and a disrupted family background. In evidence for their thesis, West, Roy and Nichols provide the case histories of 12 rapists. All these rapists reported to the interviewing psychiatrist that they had problematic childhoods. They did not have the love, stability and attention children normally have. One or both of their parents had either actively rejected them or shown marked lack of warmth. As a result of their problematic childhoods these men were not able to acquire the normal form of masculinity; family disturbances left them unprepared to deal with the stresses of life, oversensitive and diffident. Their masculinity was impaired. This psychological maldevelopment shows itself in their later adult lives. The men are unable to establish normal relations with women, lacking the confidence to deal with the difficulties of socio-sexual relationships. The 'final outburst' takes place as a result of the combination of defective personality and a specific period of stress. A time of mounting frustration is seen to precede the rape. The men are discontented with their 'sexual outlets' and sexual performance. Their frustration is considered to be a result of sensitization to stress as a result of difficulties in the man's early upbringing, problems in engaging in heterosexual relationships and the struggle to maintain his conception of masculinity. In frustration they rape women. Their 'insecure' or 'impaired' masculinity is seen to be central to the explanation of rape.

This argument has some very serious problems with empirical evidence. Firstly, the notion that all or most rapists have serious psychological problems is contradicted by other, more reliable, empirical evidence. The majority of convicted rapists are not considered to be in need of psychiatric assistance by the courts. In 1978 only 3.5 per cent of rapists were sentenced by the British courts to a hospital order under the Mental Health Act of 1959. That is, the empirical evidence does not support the contention that rapists are psychologically deranged; this is the exception, rather than the rule. Indeed there are serious methodological problems in the study by West, Roy and Nichols. All the men in the sample were incarcerated in a psychiatric unit and were pre-selected as having psychological problems, so the study does not test the question of how typical it is for rapists to have psychological impairment.

Secondly, rape is far more common than this theory would predict. It is not the rare and unusual occurrence that theories of rape as a result of psychological abnormality suggest. Russell (1982) found in a methodologically rigorous survey about the extent of rape that, in a sample of 930 women in the USA, 44 per cent of women had been the subject of rape or attempted rape at least once in their lives. Many more women are raped than is consistent with a theory that the crime's perpetrators are psychologically disturbed.

A similar argument has been applied to wife beating. Pizzey (1974) argues that men who beat their wives do so as a result of disturbing childhood experiences in which they saw their fathers beat their mothers. Boy children who see this become upset and violent. Again we have the theme of psychological abnormality as a result of problems during childhood. In this instance the start of the problem is quite specific, and the result is considered to be a repetition by the male when an adult. This is referred to by Pizzey as the cycle of violence. As evidence for her thesis Pizzey cites examples from among the women who were resident in the refuge that she helped to set up in Chiswick. She provides case histories in which the man who battered a woman had indeed been reared in a violent household. Further support for Pizzey's thesis can be found in the work of Gayford (1975), who did a questionnaire survey of the residents of the Chiswick refuge and came to similar conclusions.

There are problems with this argument that are similar to those about its application to rape. Firstly, the empirical evidence to support it is shaky. Pizzey simply cited the instances which fitted her claims. Gayford's own evidence shows that only nine of the hundred women interviewed had violent fathers (Wilson, E., 1983b: 93). Secondly, the more rigorous study by Gelles (1972) shows that not all men who had battered had come from a violent home, and that not all men who came from a violent home went on to batter their wives. Gelles's work was based upon a comparison of 40 families with domestic violence and 40 without. The addition of this control group was a vital methodological improvement upon previous studies. Thirty per cent of his violent spouses had never witnessed violence between their parents, while 50 per cent had (Gelles, 1972: 173). Thirdly, the extent of the violence against women in their homes is higher than is consistent with such a theory. Between one-quarter and one-third of married women experience serious violence at some point in their lives (MacKinnon, 1987: 24).

While a higher proportion of batterers have the disturbing home backgrounds than is the case for rapists, it is still a correlate in only a proportion of the cases. The generation-to-generation transmission of male violence to women via psychological processes can explain, at best, a small portion of this violence. Male violence against women cannot be explained primarily as a result of the psychological derangement of a few men.

The liberal approach to the state and male violence is to suggest that the state is a little inefficient and faces technical difficulties due to the nature of the offences in bringing violent men to court. These were criticized for instance, by Pizzey, who found fault with the restrictions on the ability of police and court bailiffs to arrest men molesting their wives.

Implicit in this persepctive is the assumption that violence against women is rather rare. Hence the issues relating to the state are considered to be relatively minor ones. This is problematic, since the majority of men who are violent to women escape criminal sanction. The extent of the 'inefficiency' is, rather, sufficient to warrant the tag of structural bias.

Class analysis

Male violence against women does not form a large part of class analysis. However, there are a couple of examples which draw more upon class analysis than on any other framework. The basis of this approach is that men at the bottom of the class hierarchy are violent towards women as a result of the frustration generated by their circumstances. The violence is then attributed to the workings of class society. There are two main variants; firstly, a general model; secondly, a subcultural model.

Elizabeth Wilson (1983b) takes the first position, suggesting that male violence against women is most common in situations of economic stress. For instance, in times of high unemployment or of housing shortage, men at the bottom of the class order undergo acute stress. As a consequence they lash out in frustration against those nearest to them, their wives. The ultimate cause of this violence is then a capitalist society.

This view is supported by Gelles (1972) and by Straus, Gelles and Steinmetz (1980), who state that the rate of violence between husbands and wives is twice as high in blue-collar families than it is in white-collar families. It is reinforced further by evidence on the social class of women who were subjected to extra-marital rape according to the (US) National Commission on Causes and Prevention of Violence, which found that women with a family income under $6,000 in 1967 reported being raped three to five times more frequently than those where the family income was over this amount (Eisenhower, 1969).

The sub-cultural version, as articulated by Amir (1971), follows the features of the general model in locating male violence among men in the lower social strata. However, he adds to this by suggesting that these men develop a different set of values from the main culture as a consequence of alienation from it. When it is impossible to achieve the values of the main culture, people reject them and develop alternative values which are attainable. In these circumstances men at the bottom of the social order attach value to machismo and physical superiority. A deviant sub-culture of violence then develops at the bottom of the social order as a means of coming to terms with that hierarchy. It is this sub-culture which generates rape merely as one more form of violence. Amir supports his argument with evidence on the socio-economic and racial composition of rapists as reported to the police. He finds that they are disproportionately working class and black, that is, drawn from the social groups at the bottom of the US social order.

The work of these writers is important in drawing attention to social conditions which shape men's violence against women. However, there are a number of problems with their accounts.

The work of both Wilson and Amir is predicated upon a notion that men who are violent towards women are disproportionately drawn from the lower social groupings. However, the evidence adduced to support this is shaky. Amir's figures were based upon those rapists reported to the police. But the majority of rapes are not reported to the police, and those which are reported are more likely to be the ones a white police force in a racist society is most likely to believe. In Russell's study, 24 per cent of black (Afro-American) rapists were reported to the police as compared to 5 per cent of the white rapists (Russell, 1984: 98). Pizzey (1974) argues, on the basis of her experience at the Chiswick refuge, that men who batter their wives are drawn from all social strata, not merely the bottom. Russell, in probably the largest and most rigorous survey of women enquiring into the extent of male violence (described more fully below), found that, in the case of marital rape, husbands were drawn evenly from all social classes: 32 per cent were lower class, 32 per cent middle class and 36 per cent upper middle class (Russell, 1982: 129). She also found that the race distribution of husband-rapists was very similar to that of the proportion of ethnic groups in the wider population: 73 per cent were white, slightly higher than the 68 per cent of the sample women who were white; 10 per cent of husband-rapists were Latino, as compared to 7 per cent of the sample; 10 per cent were black, the same as their presence in the sample; while 4 per cent were Asian, significantly lower than the 12 per cent of the sample which was Asian (Russell, 1982: 130). Thus Russell's findings about rape in marriage is that it is evenly distributed through the class and ethnic structure. It is a general experience that the crimes of the lower classes and races are more closely policed than those of the higher groups. I think the evidence on the socio-economic composition of rapists and batterers is then inconclusive.

A further problem is that neither writer explains why men who are frustrated at their class, and possibly race, position avenge themselves on women. They make no attempt to explain why such men do not attack their more obvious class or race enemies instead. It is not even that they attack women of the superordinate class or race, since the data suggest that women are raped and battered by men of the same social class and race (Amir, 1971). And they provide no explanation for what is surely the most crucial aspect of these attacks, their gendered nature.

If it were the case that it is those at the bottom whom are most prone to be violent, then we should expect to find women more violent that men, since they are surely more socially disadvantaged than men. The fact that women are much less violent than men suggests that the thesis that social disadvantage breeds violent behaviour needs rethinking.

One would expect a class analysis of crime to have an account of a class oppressive state. This does not appear to have been developed.

Class-based analysis of men's violence has one good point: that it examines social, not psychological, processes. It makes some interesting points about why some men might be more prone to violence than others, although there is no conclusive evidence that they are. However, its fundamental flaw is that it is unable to deal with the gendered nature of this violence.

Radical feminism

Radical feminist analyses of male violence focus on both its gendered and its social character. They examine the social forces which shape this violence and its implications for the oppression of women. Some radical feminists such as Brownmiller (1976) argue that male violence is the basis of men's control over women.

Within this approach, both violence and sexuality are considered to be socially shaped. Men are brought up to be macho and are accustomed to using violence to settle disputes. Brownmiller describes the content of popular movies and songs, with their heroic acts of violence, in which men's strength is eulogized. Even the issue of rape itself is usually dealt with as a heroic, manly theme. The cultivation of violence among men finds its peak in the army, in which many young men spend a portion of their lives. This all-male grouping built around a glorification of male strength is a factor in varying rates of rape. Brownmiller argues that in periods of militarization and warfare the amount of rape goes up. The link between militarization and patriarchy has been reinforced by a variety of writers such as Enloe (1983) and activists such as the Greenham Common women.

Brownmiller also contends that sexuality is socially constructed and that it is absurd to suggest that men rape out of sexual frustration. She notes that the provision of prostitutes for American soldiers in Vietnam did not eliminate rape, as a theory of rape as a result of sexual frustration would suppose. Rather, she maintains, once women were reduced to such a level of sexual objectification, rape became more, not less, likely.

Brownmiller asserts that rape is a form of social control by men over women. Not all men rape, but the fact that some do is sufficent to intimidate all women. This is the effectiveness of sexual terrorism.

Brownmiller has produced a brilliant, provocative account of rape, showing it to be socially structured and implicated in the subordination of women. However, rather than being an analytic theorization, it has problems as a consequence of under-theorization (most of the book is a long set of descriptions of rape atrocities) and some inconsistencies.

Brownmiller, like many radical feminists, has been criticized for biological essentialism (Edwards, A., 1987). It is true that she suggests that men rape because biologically they can do so, and so exposes herself to such a criticism. However, I think that this is a misreading of the main direction of the book's argument. Brownmiller discusses the social variability of rape in different social and historical contexts, not its constancy. Indeed it is possible to re-read her in Durkheimian terms, as saying that a social fact, militarization, increases the rate of rape, thus contradicting the notion that rape is either a biological inevitability or an individualistic act.

Insensitivity to race and class issues is a further criticism levelled against Brownmiller's radical feminist account. Davis (1981) argues that this is especially a problem in her analysis of cross-race instances and accusations of rape in a racially divided USA. Brownmiller's interpretation of these cases as ones in which the white women really were raped by black men is criticised by Davis who contends that black men were often falsely and easily accused of raping white women. Davis maintained that a racist state would support these accusations by whites against blacks, whatever their merit, against Brownmiller's contention that a patriarchal state would support men from women's accusations, whatever their merit. Davis goes on to argue that rape charges were linked to the lynching of black men in the period immediately following the end of slavery in such a way as to break up a potential alliance between white women fighting sexism and black men and women fighting racism.

Hanmer (1978) and Hanmer and Saunders (1984) apply a radical feminist perspective to other forms of violence against women, especially that of wife beating. Like Brownmiller, they argue that male violence is a form of social control of women. However, they add to this an analysis of the state, as implicated in the perpetuation of this violence. The refusal of the state to intervene effectively to support women is part of the problem. This is on two levels, one of welfare provision and the other of the criminal justice system. Firstly, the welfare state does not provide the resources a woman needs to remain independent from a violent man; she is pushed into economic dependence. Secondly, the refusal of the state to intervene in all but the most extreme cases of violence contributes to the situation. Women, knowing that they are unable to depend on police protection, are thrown back onto the support of the very men who may be violent to them, the men personally known to them.

One of the questions here is whether men are violent to women as a consequence of their power over women, or in order to gain power over them. The account provided by Hanmer tends to emphasize the former: men are not restricted from being violent to women by the criminal justice system, and women cannot escape because of an economic dependence reinforced by the state. However, the work of O'Brien (1975) suggests that the latter may be more important. O'Brien shows that men are more likely to use violence against women in a marriage if they do not have clear economic and educational superiority over their wives. This is not an absolute difference between men (as the class analysts would suggest), but one between men and women. An examination of divorce petitions showed that men's violence was more likely to be cited if the husband was less educated than his wife, if the husband had a lower occupation than the woman's father, if there were disputes over the adequacy of the husband's income, if the husband was dissatisfied with his job, and if the husband had failed to complete high school or college. Thus O'Brien's work may be interpreted as suggesting that men use violence to maintain control over women when the usual forms of power that they have, such as the superiority of the wage packet, are missing.

EXTENT OF MALE VIOLENCE AGAINST WOMEN

Central to all these accounts of male violence against women are ideas about its extent and distribution. The psychological derangement theorists suggest that it is rare, and, insofar as it happens, is restricted to a very particular category of men. The class analysts suggest that it is a little more common, but confined to the lower classes. Radical feminists assume both that it is very widespread and that women are sufficiently aware of it to modify their behaviour.

The evidence on the incidence of male violence has been until very recently highly speculative. The official figures derived from reports to police are widely believed to underestimate its extent, but the magnitude of this underestimate is controversial.

The official British criminal statistics show that the police recorded 2,471 instances of rape and 13,340 of indecent assault on a female in

England and Wales in 1987 (*Criminal Statistics, England and Wales, 1987*: 35).

The statistics record only a small proportion of attacks by men on women for several reasons. Firstly, many instances are not reported to the police because women do not expect to be treated sensitively and seriously by the judicial system, especially when the attacker was known to them (London Rape Crisis Centre, 1984). Thus the official statistics seriously under-record the extent of male violence against women.

Secondly, some forms of male violence against women, such as the rape of a woman by her husband, are not criminal offences under the law. An adequate measure must deal with the conceptual issue of what counts as violence against women and be able to cover all instances. The conceptual issue is itself difficult. For instance, legally rape involves the penetration of a woman's vagina by a man's penis without her consent. The penetration of the vagina by an object other than a penis, such as bottle or hand, merely classifies the attack as sexual assault, as is the case with the penetration of the anus by penis or other object. That is, legal definition of rape is narrower than most women would define such an act to be.

Given the limitations of reports of violence to the police as a measure of its extent, a number of other methods have been developed. One of these is the random sample survey, in which a large number of women, selected at random, are asked about the violent incidents they have experienced. In 1967 a study of 10,000 households in the USA by the National Opinion Research Centre found a rate of rape four times that of the official figures (Russell, 1984: 32). The problems of asking appropriate questions in a sensitive manner on this topic were highlighted by a study carried out for the federal government for the National Crime Survey in San Jose, which found 600 cases of attempted rape in one year in this area of one million people, but none of completed rape. This highly improbable result is a consequence of methodological flaws, including the fact that no questions explicitly refer to rape, and the one that is most open to including this form of attack asks, 'did anyone TRY to attack you in some other way?'

Britain carried out its first official crime survey in the 1980s. This found much higher levels of incidence of rape and indecent assault than was recorded by the police. On the basis of the 1984 survey it was estimated that only 11 per cent of such crimes were recorded in the police statistics (*Criminal Statistics, England and Wales, 1987*: 18). This means that their number should be multiplied by nine to reach a more accurate figure.

The largest and most rigorous of these sample surveys was carried out by Russell in 1978 in San Francisco, when a random sample of 930 women were interviewed in depth as to the violent incidents in their lives. In this survey the 33 female interviewers were each trained for 65 hours before going out into the field with a carefully piloted questionnaire. The study asked questions about all the violence a woman had suffered throughout her life and carefully distinguished between degrees of coercion (Russell, 1982, 1984).

Russell's survey found that 44 per cent of the women had been the subject of a rape or an attempted rape during their lives. Completed rape was reported by 24 per cent of women and attempted rape by 31 per cent. The definition of rape used was that legally enshrined in California at that time: 'forced intercourse (i.e., penile-vaginal penetration), or intercourse obtained by threat of force, or intercourse completed when the woman was drugged, unconscious, asleep, or otherwise totally helpless and hence unable to consent' (Russell, 1984: 35). These figures include rape within marriage. If this is excluded, so as to make the definition parallel to British law, then the percentage of women who have suffered rape is 19, and attempted rape 31, making a total of 40 per cent for attempted and completed rape (Russell, 1984: 36). Among women who had ever been married, 14 per cent had been the victims of rape or attempted rape by their husbands; of these, 85 per cent reported completed penile-vaginal rapes (Russell, 1982: 57).

The rapist is much more likely to be known to the woman than to be a stranger. The question of the relationship between rapist and woman can be looked at either in terms of the percentages of women having different attackers, or in terms of the percentage of incidents being by different sorts of men. The figures are different because multiple attacks are commonest by husbands. When the focus is on women, 8 per cent of the 930 women in the sample had been the subject either of completed or attempted rape by a husband or ex-husband;[2] 14 per cent by an acquaintance; 12 per cent by a date; 11 per cent by a stranger; 6 per cent by a lover or ex-lover; 6 per cent by a friend of the respondent; 6 per cent by an authority figure; 3 per cent by a boyfriend; 3 per cent by a relative; 2 per cent by a friend of the family. Among the total of 2,588 incidents of rape and attempted rape reported by the 930 women to the interviewers, 38 per cent were by the husband or ex-husband; 13 per cent by a lover or ex-lover; 9 per cent by an acquaintance; 8 per cent by a relative; 8 per cent by a date; 7 per cent by an authority figure; 6 per cent by a boyfriend; 6 per cent by a stranger; 4 per cent by a friend of the respondent; 1 per cent by a friend of the family (Russell, 1982: 67).

Russell's survey also investigated other forms of violence against women. She found that 21 per cent of women who had ever been married had been beaten by their husbands at some time. This catgeory overlaps to some extent with those who were raped, but not entirely. Of women who had ever been married, 10 per cent had been both raped and beaten, while 4 per cent had been raped 'only', and 12 per cent beaten 'only' (Russell, 1982: 89–90).[3] That is, among wives, 26 per cent had been subjected to violence sufficiently extreme to be counted as either rape or beating.

The Russell survey also asked about the incidence of child sexual abuse and incest. It found that 16 per cent of the women reported incestuous abuse before the age of 18 and 12 per cent sexual abuse by a relative before the age of 14. Incestuous child abuse was defined as 'any type of exploitative sexual contact or attempted sexual contact, that occurred between relatives' (Russell, 1984: 181). When the focus is extra-familial abuse before 18, 31 per cent of women reported such experiences; when this was restricted to under 14, the figure was 20 per cent. Extra-familial child abuse was defined as 'unwanted sexual experiences with persons unrelated by blood or marriage, ranging from attempted petting (touching of breasts or genitals or attempts at such touching) to rape, before the victim turned 14, and completed or attempted rape experiences from the ages of 14 to 17' (Russell, 1984: 180). When these two categories are combined, 38 per cent of women reported sexual abuse before 18 and 28 per cent before 14 (Russell, 1984: 183). The perpetrators of the abuse were overwhelmingly male – 96 per cent.

Studies on male attitudes to violence against women show parallel results. Malamuth set up a study which asked men whether they would rape a woman in certain circumstances. Male college students read a short story about a rape and were asked if they would be likely (on a scale from 1 to 5) to act as the rapist did. On average, 35 per cent indicated some likelihood of doing so (Malamuth, 1981).

We do not know whether these figures for the USA reflect the incidence of male violence in Britain and in other countries. (Funds have not been made available for such studies in Britain.) In the absence of such data they might be considered to constitute the best estimate of the extent of men's violence to women in Britain. However, it might be argued that violent crime is generally higher in the USA than in Britain and hence that male violence against women would also be lower. There are three interrelated reasons why the rate of rape might be higher in the USA than in Britain. Firstly, the overall rate of violence is higher. Secondly, it is a more unequal society. Thirdly, it is a more sexualized society, in the sense that gender relations are more highly eroticized. These three factors combined would, on the basis of the previous analysis, be likely to lead to a higher rate of rape. Such qualifications should not be overstated, however, since one of the reasons for differences in rates of violent crime, the greater availability of guns in the USA, is not of much significance in the case of men's violence against women, where guns are not often used.

So far I have discussed actual levels of violence. However, the effect of violence on women's behaviour is mediated by women's fear of violence as well as the actuality of it. While word of mouth is an important means of communication about violence, and women not infrequently discuss their safety precautions with each other, the role of the mass media also needs consideration.

Contemporary newspaper reports of rape are highly selective. They not only focus upon those rapes which are processed by the courts, which are themselves a narrow selection of instances, but they often include warnings to women about the behaviours that the largely male lawyers, judges, police, journalists and newspaper editors consider inappropriate and dangerous for women. Thus the reports will often mention conduct, such as accepting lifts and having a drink with strange men and walking unaccompanied in public places, that these men disapprove of in chaste women. By selective mentioning of the circumstances of a restricted sample of rapes, such reports create a mythology about rape, and the conduct by a woman which may correlate with rape, which is totally spurious in terms of its dangerousness (Walby, Hay and Soothill, 1983; Soothill and Walby, 1990). That is, the public discourse on rape is a form of control over women in its own right.

VIOLENCE AND THE STATE

Given the extent and seriousness of violence against women it might be considered surprising that so few men are convicted of such crimes. In Britain, 2 per cent of rapists are convicted, according to my calculations taken from official estimates. This is based on the number of men convicted of rape in 1987 being 453, which is 18 per cent of the 2,471 rapes recorded by the police during that year; these reported rapes are officially estimated to be 11 per cent of those committed (*Criminal Statistics, England and Wales, 1987*). This is likely to be an underestimate. Kelly suggests that on a conservative estimate one in 250 rapists is convicted, and that the figure may be as low as one in 2,500. This is based on US figures that less than 15 per cent of recorded rapes reach trial, only 1 per cent of recorded rapes result in convictions, and the proportion of rapes being reported is between 4 per cent and 40 per cent (Kelly, L., 1988a: 51–2).

There are many points in the judicial system at which rapists, wife beaters and child abusers escape. The first is that very few such crimes are reported, as described above. The second is that the police are reluctant to take complaints of such violence seriously. An official study by the Scottish Office, investigating the procedures used by the police to deal with complaints of rape, found that the police disregarded 22 per cent of recorded complaints as 'no crime' (Chambers and Millar, 1983). Over half the raped women (55 per cent) were critical of the way they were interviewed by the CID officers. The researchers quote an article by a detective sergeant in the *Police Review* to illustrate the attitudes to which they are referring:

Women and children complainants in sexual matters are notorious for embroidery or complete fabrications of complaints.

It should be borne in mind that except in the case of a very young child, the offence of rape is extremely unlikely to have been committed against a woman who does not immediately show signs of extreme violence. If a woman walks into a police station and complains of rape with no such signs of violence she must be closely interrogated. Allow her to make her statement to a policewoman and drive a horse and cart through it. It is always advisable if there is any doubt of the truthfulness of her allegations to call her an outright liar. (A. Firth, 'Interrogation', in *Police Review*, 28 (November 1975), cited in Chalmers and Millar, 1983: 83)

Chalmers and Millar suggest that the police have unrealistic expectations of the appropriate behaviour of a raped woman which, if she does not conform to it, is used to discredit her complaint. They also utilize higher standards of evidence than are required by the law, such as resisting to the last and bearing the marks of violence. Further, they have a conception of situational logic where the issue of a woman's active consent to intercourse has no place. This is compounded by a conception of male sexuality as having overriding needs. The official report concludes that 'there is considerable scope for the development of police interviewing skills in relation to sexual assault complaints' (Chalmers and Millar, 1983: 95).

Indeed very recently there have been some changes in police procedure as a result of feminist criticisms. These have included the provision of specialized 'rape suites', where raped women can be questioned and examined outside the normal police station. It is too early to evaluate the significance of these changes.

A third stage where rapists escape is in their processing by the courts. There is circumstantial evidence of plea bargaining in which a man pleads guilty, not to rape, but to a lesser charge such as sexual assault. The evidence for this is that the number of rape charges drops between the committal proceedings in the magistrates courts and appearance in the crown court, while those of sexual assault increase. There is a higher rate of acquittals than for many other crimes. The structure of the court and the types of evidence which are deemed admissible all structure the situation against the woman. Evidence about the raped woman's previous sexual history is likely to bias a jury towards the man if she is 'unchaste' and, although this is supposed to be excluded, it is frequently allowed at the judge's discretion (Adler, 1987; Feild and Bienen, 1980).

In short, given the ways that women are treated by the legal system, it is not surprising that so few rapists are convicted. While ostensibly condemning rape, child sexual abuse and wife beating, the practice of the state is to condone such violence except in exceptional and extreme circumstances.

Review of theories

Psychological theories are inadequate to grasp the social nature of men's violence against women. The psychological profile of rapists appears normal. Even if a slightly higher proportion of batterers come from violent homes than the average man, the psychological perspective does not assist us in explaining why women have so few material alternatives that they stay with such men.

Class analysis is an improvement over theories of pyschological derangement in shifting the level of analysis to that of social structure. However, like the psychological accounts, the focus of the explanation on why some men rather than others are violent to women leads it similarly to fail to grasp fully the gendered nature of the violence, its degree of impact on women, and why the state does not intervene to protect women. Further, the evidence for a class distribution of violence to women is inconclusive.

Radical feminist accounts contribute a social structural analysis of male violence against women as a gendered phenomenon in a way no other perspective succeeds in doing. It is able to provide an integrated account of men's actions, women's responses, and the lack of action by the state. However, it is flawed by neglect of the significance of class and race relations, especially as they affect the differential uptake of rape complaints by the state. The judicial system has a structural bias not only against women, but against blacks and the working class as well, so that white and/or middle-class men are less likely to have rape complaints made against them.

The radical feminist account needs to be synthesized with an examination of a class and racist state before a full analysis can be obtained.

An analysis of male violence demands not only an account of why some men are violent, but also why the state does not act to protect women from criminal attack. Most investigations have approached only the first part of the explanation, but the second is equally as important.

Male violence against women is sufficiently common and repetitive, with routinized consequences for women and routinized modes of processing by judicial agencies to constitute a social structure. Women's fear of male violence is realistic, though the expectation that strangers, rather than men they know, are more likely to be the perpetrators is misplaced. Male violence is thus a form of power over women in its own right. It is, however, importantly shaped as a result of patriarchal control over women in other areas. For this reason it is not appropriate to see male violence as the basis of other forms of men's control over women. It cannot be understood outside a context in which the state does not intervene to support a woman's apparent right to name such violence as criminal, and in which access to the material means to escape violence in the home is restricted.

CHANGES

An analysis of changes in the incidence of male violence towards women is extremely difficult given the difficulty of producing adequate measures of its extent today, let alone in the past. However, there have been some attempts to approach this question. The response of the state to men's violence against women is a little easier to track over time.

The official crime figures of male violence to women which is reported to the police has been increasing over recent years. As has been stated, the number of rapes recorded by the police has increased by 143 per cent between 1977 and 1987 (*Criminal Statistics, England and Wales, 1987*). However, given their unreliability, these figures are open to several interpretations. On the one hand, it might mean that the rate of such acts of violence has increased. On the other hand it might mean that the rate of reporting of these acts has increased, but not the actual rate. An increase in the reporting rate might be explained in terms of a decrease in the stigmatization of the rape victim, so she is more willing to come forward.

A curious feature of the figures is that while the rate of recorded rape has increased by 143 per cent over the last decade, that of convicted rapists has increased by only 39 per cent. In 1977, 1,015 cases of rape were recorded by the police, rising to 2,471 in 1987. Yet the increase in the number of men found guilty of rape only rose from 325 in 1977 to

453 in 1987 (*Criminal Statistics, England and Wales, 1987*).

The figures on indecent assault show a small but significant escalation in the number of cases recorded, while the number of men convicted has stayed static over the same period. In 1977, 11,048 instances of indecent sexual assault on a female were recorded by the police, rising to 13,340 in 1987, an increase of 21 per cent. In 1977, 3,466 men were convicted of indecent assault on a female, while in 1987 this was 3,529, a negligible rise of 2 per cent (*Criminal Statistics, England and Wales, 1987*: 107).

The figures on incest show a gain in the number recorded, from 295 in 1977 to 511 in 1987, that is of 73 per cent, while those convicted rose from 157 in 1977 to 244 in 1987, that is by 55 per cent (*Criminal Statistics, England and Wales, 1987*: 107).

The proportion of cases of reported sex crimes against women which culminated in the conviction of men fell dramatically during the same decade. While for rape this rate of conviction in reported cases in 1977 was 32 per cent, by 1987 it had fallen to 18 per cent. The rate of conviction for sexual assault also shows a decline, though less marked, from 31 per cent in 1977 to 26 per cent in 1987. In the case of incest, the rate of conviction fell from 53 per cent in 1977 to 48 per cent in 1987.

How is this decreasing conviction rate to be understood? That while women are more prepared to say to the police that they have been raped or assaulted, and though, according to official Home Office reports, still only a tiny proportion of such women report to the police, the courts are increasingly refusing to convict the men?

It is here worth remembering that the women who are able to secure convictions are specific types of women in specific types of rape situation. Women were more likely to secure a conviction if they had been virgins, or at least chaste before the attack, if they did not know the attacker, if they suffered extensive physical injury in addition to the rape, and if there was more than one assailant (Adler, 1987). As was noted earlier, these are a tiny minority of the instances of rape. Most women know their rapist and most women are, or have been, sexually active outside marriage.

It may well be that more women are reporting to the police attacks which do not fit this narrow stereotype of rape. The result is the humiliation of increasing numbers of women at the hands of the legal system, which will not convict men for rapes outside this false stereotype. Nevertheless, an increase of 39 per cent in men convicted of rape in a ten year period, 1977–87, is a significant change.

Russell (1984) argues, on the basis of the data she has of women's lifetime experiences of male violence, that the real rate of rape has increased. The analysis is complex, since there is a differential likelihood of rape according to age. The most vulnerable age group is women in their earlier twenties (20–4), followed by the 25–35 group, then the 16–19 group. Russell argues that the rate of rape escalated between 1931 and 1961 (Russell, 1984: 55).

However, there is a drawback with this interpretation of the data which stems from a methodological problem. This longitudinal survey relies upon memory, in a way in which repeated cross-sectional surveys are less dependent. People are more likely to remember recent events than distant ones, an effect that is compounded when these are events which women would rather not hold at the front of their minds. So the survey is likely to overstate the extent of the increase. However, the data was collected in a particularly rigorous way so the results are likely to be our best estimate of the rates.[4]

If this is a real increase, how is it to be explained? I have argued that male violence is one of the causes of women's subordination. This is true at both a structural and an individual level. If this violence was merely the result of women's subordination, then we would expect its extent to have decreased as women have gained access to other forms of power. However, if male violence is considered to be primarily a form of power over women, then one would expect a decline in male power in some spheres to be met by a growing rate of male violence in an attempt to compensate and to restore the previous balance of patriarchal control.

Thus we may cautiously suggest that there has been some increase in the rate of rape as a patriarchal backlash to women's gains in other spheres. This argument is parallel to that advanced about sexuality. That is, that there is an attempt to reintegrate women into patriarchal relations via sexuality, as a response to reducing patriarchal controls elsewhere. However, the hypothesis about rape must remain tentative because of the difficulties over data.

Further, we should be careful not to generalize from rape to all forms of male violence. As I noted above, a significant element in understanding wife beating is the difficulty that women have in leaving their homes. We should expect that, as divorce and separation have become easier for both economic and legal reasons (see the chapter on the household), then we should expect the time span during which a wife is beaten to diminish, simply for the reason that women can more readily leave such situations. But whether this change means that there will be lesser or greater likelihood of any particular husband being violent is difficult to ascertain without further research. However, women have not escaped male violence by leaving violent marriages.

'Individual'

Women who experience male violence have often been called 'victims'. This conceptualization is opposed by many feminists working in the area of assault on women, who prefer to use the term 'survivor'. They argue that the term 'victim' gives a misleading impression of women as passive recipients of male violence, and prefer to stress women's survival and the myriad of ways in which they resist (Kelly, L., 1988a). Women resist verbally and physically, sometimes arguing and fighting back, sometimes side-stepping and deflecting, sometimes simply hanging on to life itself. Bart and O'Brien (1986) discuss the strategies which were most likely to prevent rape successfully. They suggest that struggling and screaming may have significant effects in both deterring would-be rapists and enabling escape. Forms of resistance can be both individual and collective.

Changes in the state and violence

Feminists have made many attempts to prevent male violence and to assist women who are subjected to it. This is not new to second-wave feminism, but was also to be found in the campaigns of earlier generations of feminists.

In first-wave feminism there were two major forms of intervention. The first was to enable women who were beaten by their husbands to escape. This was more difficult in the middle of the nineteenth century than now, since there were no legal ways of ending a marriage or leaving a husband. The second was to campaign against those factors that were associated with wife beating, in particular alcohol. Many women supported the temperance demand for the limitation of alcohol on the grounds that drunk men were more likely to beat 'their' wives.

The campaign for divorce and legal separation in the middle of the nineteenth century was significantly informed by the problems of wife beating. During most of the nineteenth century it was generally held that a husband had a right to beat his wife, so long as the rod was not thicker than a man's thumb, and to confine her in his house even if against her will. Feminist pressure was important in reversing this ruling in a court case in 1891. (This issue was described as wife torture in a famous article by Frances Power Cobbe.) Feminists fought both for divorce and legal separation on the grounds of a husband's violence. The provision of the 1878 Matrimonial Causes Act, which made it possible to obtain a separation and maintenance order from local magistrates for a woman whose husband was convinced of aggravated assault against them, was very important in providing practical legal and financial means of escape for both middle-class and working-class women. Feminist campaigns won the right to divorce in 1857 on grounds of adultery, and in 1937 it become possible to divorce on grounds of cruelty (Holcombe, 1983).

By the end of the first wave of feminism, major victories had been won: the legal right of husbands to beat wives was removed and the legal possibilities of escape had been opened up. This is not to argue that wife beating ceased or even significantly diminished, since neither is there the evidence to establish any changes in the extent of such violence, nor is the absence of legal right sufficient to prevent it. Nevertheless, the legal changes were important, both for some individual women, and in providing the necessary basis for effectively challenging this violence.

The campaign for temperance was also significantly informed by the issue of male violence. It was widely held that excessive drinking was a contributory factor in wife beating. Temperance was an issue taken up by the more conservative of the women's organizations in Britain and the USA (Banks, 1981). In the USA the temperance campaign was successful for a time in the inter-war period, but this was never the case in Britain.

Second-wave feminism has made a series of interventions against male violence, which can be grouped into two forms. (There have also been significant non-feminist interventions by women concerned with male violence.) Firstly, feminists have organized to provide support services for women who have suffered male violence, especially in establishing refuges for battered women to escape to, rape crisis lines for women to find a sympathetic person to talk to about their ordeal, and incest survivors' groups for women who suffered incestuous abuse as children (London Rape Crisis Centre, 1984; Nelson, 1987). These forms of political intervention started as self-help agencies in which feminists drew upon their own resources to establish new feminist institutions, and only later did many of them receive partial funding from the state, often at a local level. Most large towns now have a refuge, a rape line and an incest group, and most large cities have several refuges.

Secondly, there have been attempts to make changes in the way the state responds to women's complaints of violence. In the case of rape, this has focused on a critique of the way the official agencies, from police to courts, process complaints. Some of these have found a popular resonance, especially when it has been a criticism of judges for lenient sentencing of a convicted rapist.

One particular wave of protest led to the passage of the Sexual Offences (Amendment) Act 1976, which was intended, by its parliamentary supporters, to shift the balance of the courtroom away from the man accused of rape towards the women. Its main provisions were anonymity for the woman, and the ruling out of evidence of her previous sexual history, except at the judge's discretion. This was because evidence about earlier sexual activity had previously been used to discredit the woman's claim that she had not given consent to intercourse on that occasion, on the basis of the myth that, once a woman has had intercourse with any man not her husband, she is likely to say yes to any other men. This appears as a minor but significant shift in courtroom power; however, Adler (1987) shows that the judge's discretion is used to allow indirect evidence of a woman's sexuality to be routinely introduced in rape cases. Adler bases her evidence on an examination of 80 rape cases at the Old Bailey during the course of one year.

Male violence is not only on the political agenda of feminist groups but also on that of right-wing women. Campbell (1987) has shown how fear of men's violence underlies the preoccupation of Tory women with law-and-order issues. Tory women are much more concerned than Tory men with the adoption of stronger measures to deal with violent crime. Indeed a standard conflict at Tory Party conferences is between male Home Secretaries and female delegates over the adoption of stricter sanctions for criminal violence. The Tory women's advocacy of harsh measures to deal with men's lawlessness has its roots in a view of themselves as a major target for this aggression. Criminality is highly gendered; most criminals are men. So a concern with this subject is necessarily raising a gendered political issue. Campbell laments the narrowness of the vision in which 'hanging-and-flogging' type approaches dominate their solutions, but understands the gendered nature of the matter which provokes it.

Not all attempts to intervene meet with success, as the Cleveland case illustrates. In this, two doctors who utilized the innovatory anal dilation test for child sexual abuse were met by a storm of protest, led by the local male Labour MP, over whether the children identified were actually abused (Campbell, 1988; Kelly, L., 1988b). Nonetheless, the controversy led to reconsideration of the issue at many levels.

CONCLUSIONS

While it was extremely difficult to decide whether there have been changes in the extent of men's violence against women, it is possible to say that there have been significant changes in responses to this violence. Feminist campaigns in the first wave led to the ending of the official condoning of such violence by the state. They opened up legal routes of escape to women who were beaten by their husbands. However, for lack of evidence, we cannot assess the extent to which this reduced the level of violence. Second-wave feminist campaigns, building on the successes of the first, have provided practical routes of escape via refuges and specialized counselling, and assistance to women suffering violence. Some reform of legal procedures has also been achieved. However, we are again without the evidence to assess their degree of success.

The de-legitimating of private male violence against women has reduced, but not removed, one of the forms of power that men have over women. Husbands are no longer the sole arbiter of the acceptable level of violence, which is now also regulated by the state. The infrequency of state intervention, and the humiliation meted out to those women who seek it, indicates that this is more a shift in the locus of control and legitimation of violence than its elimination.

NOTES

1 However, I am not arguing that they may be explained in terms of anomie. I depart from Durkheim here.

2 The figure of 14 per cent of married women being the subject of rape by a husband or ex-husband is higher than that of all women, since not all women have been married.

3 The apparent discrepancy between 21 per cent and the sum of 10 per cent and 12 per cent is due to rounding of numbers.

4 It should be noted that Russell is referring to an increase in the rate of rape, not male violence in general.

7

State

The state is usually defined either as a specific set of social institutions, for instance, as that body which has the monopoly over legitimate coercion in given territory, or in terms of its function, for instance, that body which maintains social cohesion in a class society. There is a question as to whether either of these definitions, the former belonging to a Weberian tradition, the latter to a Marxist one, is appropriate in an analysis of gender relations, since neither of the traditional theories gives much consideration to this issue. Most accounts contain notions that the state is a centralized set of institutions, that force is available to it as a form of power underpinning it, and that it is a focus for political interests.

The problem with the traditional Weberian definition in relation to gender is the notion that the state has a monopoly over legitimate coercion, when in practice individual men are able to utilize considerable amounts of violence against women with impunity. In practice this violence is legitimated by the state, since it takes no effective measure against it. Does this mean that violent men are part of the state, or does the state not have a monopoly over legitimate coercion? The former solution compromises the notion that the state is a set of centralized institutions, the latter that the state has a monopoly over legitimate coercion. I think the latter compromise is preferable, and that Weber's ideal type of the state is rarely attained in practice.

The Marxist definition is problematic in that it usually asserts that the state mediates only between social classes, omitting gendered and racialized groups. As I shall go on to show, the state is engaged with gendered political forces, its actions have gender-differentiated effects, and its structure is highly gendered. The state is patriarchal as well as capitalist, and those Marxist definitions which define the state in terms of its functions for capital are flawed.

Some examples of the kinds of issues that a full theory of gender and the state would need to be able to explain include: the limiting of women's access to paid work, for example, the Dilution Acts (cf., Andrews, 1918; Braybon, 1981) and 'protective' legislation (cf., Equal Opportunities Commission, 1979); the criminalization of forms of fertility control, for instance, at certain times and places, abortion, contraception (cf., Greenwood and Young, 1976; Gittins, 1982; Gordon, L., 1977, 1979); support for a regulation of the institution of marriage through, for example, the cohabitation rule (Fairbairns, 1979) and discriminatory income maintenance (Land, 1976) and by regulating marriage and divorce law (Barker, 1976; Holcombe, 1983; Smart, 1984); actions against some sexual relations through, for instance, criminalizing male homosexual relations in some periods (Weeks, 1977) and denying custody of children to lesbian mothers; actions against radical dissent, for instance, the coercive response to the suffrage movement (Morrell, 1981); yet, lack of intervention against criminal violence against women by men.

There are four main approaches to the analysis of gender and the state: liberalism, Marxist feminism, radical feminism and dual-systems theory.

Liberalism

Liberal analyses often start by noting the relative absence of women from powerful positions in the state and other central decisional arenas. Women are to be found infrequently among the formal political elites. After the 1987 general election women formed only 6.6 per cent of members of the House of Commons. The under-representation of women in the legislatures of the world is not confined to Britain and the USA, but is a common pattern. The highest representation is to be found in Norway, where the figure is 40 per cent. At local government level in Britain women are slightly better represented, forming 19 per cent of local councillors in 1985.

If the sphere of public politics or central decisional arenas is broadened to include representatives in trade unions and those appointed to public bodies, the picture looks little different. In January 1986 in NUPE, with nearly half a million female members, who composed 67 per cent of the membership, women held only 31 per cent of the seats on the executive; in USDAW, with a female membership of nearly a quarter of a million, which was 61 per cent of the total, women held 19 per cent of the seats on the executive; in the NUT, with over 150,000 female members, making 72 per cent of the total, women formed only 16 per cent of the executive (Equal Opportunities Commission, 1987: 44). In 1985 women

composed only 18.5 per cent of appointments to public bodies, and in
1984 only 7 per cent of representatives on Industrial Tribunals (Equal
Opportunities Commission, 1987: 40, 41).

How is this absence of women to be explained? Kirkpatrick (1974)
suggests that there are four main types of account of the constraints
holding women back from entering politics: physiological, cultural, role
and male conspiracy. On the basis of a study of 46 women who had been
elected to state legislatures in the USA, she argues that role constraints
are the most important. Women are not anatomically incapable of
entering politics, nor do men consciously try to exclude them. Kirkpatrick vigorously denies the claims of Epstein (1970) concerning cultural
constraints, that the core attributes of jobs such as that of politician
require masculine characteristics of aggressiveness, persistence and drive,
on the basis that the women politicians in her sample did not think that
these were masculine characteristics. She concludes that the real barrier is
that of sex roles, especially that of being wife and mother for women in
the contemporary USA, but also that of the restriction of women to
occupational categories which do not conventionally lead on to being a
politician – unlike typical male jobs such as lawyer.

Currell (1974) similarly argues that successful women politicians are
exceptional. She studied 40 women who had been elected to the British
House of Commons (she contacted the total population of living past and
present MPs to get this many!) and all parliamentary candidates in 1964
and 1973 (in 1973 she reached around three-quarters of the 41 such
women). Currell found that these women had succeeded where most
other women had not, because they had specific circumstances which
counteracted the usual difficulties. She found that women MPs were
older and rarely entered Parliament until their childbearing years were
over. She suggested that the problem of lack of appropriate socialization
was negated when women were born into 'political families' in which
girls as well as boys imbibed the activist political culture. The final route
by which the exceptional woman was able to enter politics was as a
substitute for a close male relative, perhaps a husband who had died.

Currell proposes that this is due to the problems women face as the
childbearing sex and the different socialization that girls receive, which
makes them more passive and submissive than boys. She states that the
complex of factors around family and home was often cited by the
women in her study as the reason why women were less successful in
politics than men. She does note, however, that it is the articulation of
this with the nature of political institutions that causes the difficulty, for
instance, in the need for at least partial residence in London for MPs, and
also that some technical issues, such as the nature of the voting system –

single or multi-member constituencies – does make some difference.

The gender of the personnel involved in the state is a major concern of liberal writings on gender and the state. These writings contain the assumption that the policies of the state would be more advantageous for women if there were more women in decision-making posts. It is represented in the policy of the 300 Group, which aims to increase the number of seats held by women MPs to 300 out of the 600 or so available.

However, this assumption is problematic. Firstly, it is clear from contemporary British experience that a female Prime Minister does not necessarily mean that government puts forward pro-women policies. Secondly, as a parallel debate on the class composition of Parliament between Milliband (1969) and Poulantzas (1973) showed, structural pressures are more important than personal background in determining the pattern of decision making by the state.

Not all writers on gender and the state within the liberal approach have focused on personnel issues. Pizzey (1974) examined state policy towards battered women from this perspective. Women who are beaten by their husbands or the men they lived with are given very little assistance either by the criminal justice system or the welfare wing of the state. Police are slow to intervene to protect the woman and very reluctant to prosecute the man for his criminal assault. Even enforcement of injunctions can be difficult. Welfare officials are often unhelpful in providing alternative accommodation or necessary payments. Pizzey suggests that the state's response is inadequate for reasons of technical inefficiency. She does not consider it to be a result of structural bias against women by the state. The agencies are seen to be ill-informed and faced with bureaucratically generated problems to action.

Marxist feminism

Many Marxist accounts of the state have very little to say about gender relations. Their focus is on the relation between capital and labour and that between the bourgeoisie and the proletariat (Gramsci, 1971; Gamble, 1988; Jessop, 1982; Poulantzas, 1973). Nevertheless, many of the issues with which they deal are gendered, even if this is not recognized. For instance, Marx attempted to account for the development of legislation to restrict the number of hours worked in terms of the attempts by the working class to limit the extension of the working day. He conceptualized this in terms of the struggle between capital and labour, bourgeoisie and proletariat. However, as I showed in *Patriarchy at Work* (1986), this ignores the differentiation of the sexes both in the impact of the legislation and in the social and political forces pressing for it. The legislation, and its later developments, sought primarily to restrict the hours of women and children, and it was principally men who fought for it. The early legislation, in Britain, which concentrated on the cotton textiles mills, restricted the best, not the worst, jobs held by women – textile jobs were better paid and involved shorter hours than the alternatives of domestic service, the sweated needle trades, agricultural work and, especially, housewifery.[1]

Marxist accounts of the development of the welfare state have usually focused on the capital–labour relation, albeit in a variety of ways. One school of thought, the capital logic school, argues that the provision of welfare in the form of health, education and social security benefits is necessary for modern capitalism, which needs a healthy, well-educated workforce. Hence the development of the welfare state is considered to be part of the logic of capital. Another, the neo-Gramscian school, criticizes the former for ignoring the significance of struggle, of the battle of the working class to win welfare provision from a reluctant capitalist state (see Urry, 1981). A further school around Castells judges that many of the developments typically considered part of the welfare state, such as health and education, and also issues such as public transport, constitute the evolution of 'collective consumption' from a previously 'individual consumption', as a result both of the needs of capital and the working-class struggle (Castells, 1978, 1983).

However, all these neglect the different interests of men and women in the development of welfare state, for instance that these advances include the socialization of previously privatized labour of women in the home. They further disregard the role of women in struggling for these improvements, both independent from, and in alliance with, men. Castells's account is particularly problematic in his attempt conceptually to conflate women's unpaid domestic labour into a notion of 'consumption', with all its connotations of leisure rather than work.

McIntosh (1978) provides a Marxist analysis which does explicitly take notice of the oppression of women in relation to the state. She interprets the state and the oppression of women in terms of the logic of capitalism. Gender inequality is seen as derived from capitalism, and the actions of the state as stemming from the needs of capital.

McIntosh suggests that the state upholds the oppression of women by supporting a form of household in which women provide unpaid domestic services for a male. She argues that the state should be conceptualized as capitalist, since it is acting to maintain the capitalist mode of production. Capitalism benefits from a particular form of family which ensures the cheap reproduction of labour power and the availability of women as a reserve army of labour. She suggests, however, that the family is not the ideal form for the reproduction of labour power for two reasons. Firstly, the ratio of earner to dependent is widely variable in actual families; thus some families cannot survive on their earned income. The state then steps in to shore up the family structure. Secondly, families by themselves do not necessarily produce the right number of children to meet capitalist requirements for population size, so sometimes explicit population policies are introduced to ensure the maintenance of their members. Thus in McIntosh's account the state's support for the oppression of women is indirect, not direct, since it is through the maintenance of this family form that the state acts to the detriment of women. While McIntosh does point to various contradictions in capitalism and in state policy, her argument nonetheless hinges on the notion that the family is maintained because it is functional for capitalism.

This position is problematic in that it does not take sufficient account of the benefits that men derive from the contemporary family structure (Delphy, 1984) and of the subordination of women in general. Further, the analysis pays little attention to the conflicts that take place on the political level over state policy. Yet there have been considerable struggles over state policy by feminists as well as the organized working class (Banks, 1981; Mark-Lawson, Savage and Warde, 1985; Middleton, L., 1978). This is a limitation in the interpretation similar to that of other capital logic school analyses.

Radical feminism

Radical feminist writers challenge the conventional definition of 'politics' with which I have been dealing so far. They broaden it to the extent of including the personal as political. For instance, Millett does not define the political as that relatively narrow and exclusive world of meetings, chairmen and parties. The term 'politics' shall refer to power-structured relationships, arrangements whereby one group of persons is controlled by another (Millett, 1977: 23).

Hence Millett argues that the relations between the sexes are political. The empirical terrain on which she chooses to argue her case is that of sexuality. She takes three famous male writers, who till then had been considered to be progressive, and argues that, in their characterization of the sexual conduct of men to women, they are part of a sexual counter-revolution. She demonstrates that in the novels of these writers men use the sex act to express their power over and contempt for women; that it is a form of humiliation and control over women. That is, something which is conventionally considered to be the ultimate private and personal act is more properly seen as part of a set of structured power relations, and hence as political.

This theme of the 'personal is political' is a crucial part of radical feminist analysis and practice of politics, and recurs in many forms. It was a central component of early second-wave feminism, which introduced consciousness raising groups in which, by sharing and discussing their experiences, women came to see their problems not as private woes, but as public issues; the personal was political, and there was no individual solution. All aspects of the relations came under scrutiny and were analysed through this perspective. For instance, our very forms of interaction – which sex spoke most in mixed conversation (men), which sex interrupted the other more (men) (see Spender, 1980) – were seen as gendered and as political. In this approach, then, everything is political: sexuality (Millett, 1977), conversation (Spender, 1980), housework (Mainardi, 1970; Malos, 1980), rape (Brownmiller, 1976), motherhood (Luker, 1984), abortion (Petchevsky, 1986).

In its strongest form, this argument implies that nothing is not political. And it is this which raises problems for such an approach to the definition of politics, since if everything is political and nothing is not political then the term does not discriminate between two different states. It becomes merely a sensitizing term, but not one which can be used as an analytic tool. Nevertheless it does have a function in problematizing the conventional boundaries to the area of politics and drawing attention to areas of structured inequality which might otherwise be too readily dismissed.

Within this framework the focus on the state which is so central to other analyses of politics is often absent. This is not merely because radical feminists eschew the reformist politics that involvement in electoral politics usually means, but, more importantly, because it is not seen to be the central political site. However, this is not to say that radical feminists ignore the state – they have clearly engaged in theoretical and practical politics around issues of fertility control such as abortion.

One radical feminist study which, usually, does centre on the state is that of Hanmer and Saunders (1984). These writers concentrate on the relationship between women, male violence and the state. They see men's violence as critical in the maintenance of the oppression of women, and the lack of intervention of the state to prevent it is analysed as being the state's collusion. The absence of protection from the extensive and widespread violence that Hanmer and Saunders find in their community study is part of a vicious circle in which women become dependent for protection from violence upon the very people, men they know, who are the most likely source of violence against them. This cycle of violence, so different from the one postulated by Pizzey, is an important basis of men's control over women.

The collusion of the state in this is more clearly spelt out in an earlier piece by Hanmer alone, 'Violence and the social control of women' (1978), when the lack of intervention of either the criminal justice system or the social welfare branches of the state condemn women to subordination. In this analysis, men's violence against women is seen as an important basis of men's control over women, that is, essentially the basis of the system of patriarchy, although Hanmer does not quite express it in such a fashion. The state is seen as an 'instrument' of patriarchal domination, its non-intervention part of the logic of the patriarchal system.

This view raises the question as to whether it is appropriate to conceptualize the state as 'instrumental' in this way, and as part of a logic of patriarchy. This is parallel to the problem of instrumentality, which is often considered a flaw in the analysis of the capitalist state in the writings of Marxists, because of the extent to which the state itself is seen to behave in response to a variety of different pressures, and the extent to which it is contradictory rather than monolithic.

Dual-systems theory

Eisenstein's work is an interesting and important attempt to meet the objections levelled at those analyses of women's position which underplay the significance of either capitalist or patriarchal relations. Eisenstein maintains that capitalist and patriarchal relations are so intertwined and interdependent that they form a mutually interdependent system of capitalist patriarchy.

Eisenstein (1979) contends that capitalism needs patriarchal relations in order to survive, and vice versa. She considers her analysis to be a synthesis of Marxism (thesis) and a radical feminism (antithesis), and argues not merely for a notion of a symbiotic relationship between patriarchy and capitalism, but for an integrated relationship in which they have become one system. Their effect on each other and need for each other is seen as too great for them to be conceptualized as separate systems. She proposes that each system contributes specific things to the whole. Thus patriarchy contributes especially order and control, while capitalism provides the economic system driven by the pursuit of profit. They are fused at the level of the state, where Zillah Eisenstein (1984) argues that patriarchal interests are represented via capitalists, who are male.

The problem with this is that Eisenstein underestimates the significance of organized patriarchal forces among workers, both in the explanation of the changing participation of women in paid work, and in the patriarchal forces which affect the state. In her theoretical account she suggests that patriarchal interests are represented via male capitalists (1984: 92). This is despite the fact that she is also at pains in the rest of that book to differentiate the various currents of anti-feminist as well as feminist agitation. She sees variations in patriarchal strategy as arising within the bourgeoisie. The form of the state, in particular its separation from the family, is seen overall as patriarchal. Yet this account is flawed by failing to integrate theoretically patriarchal forces from outside the bourgeoisie. Hence, I would suggest, she underestimates conflict between patriarchy and capitalism. Thus the way that Eisenstein tries to combine the two sets of relations in her analysis is rather problematic. She is ambiguous on the extent to which it is still possible to write of separate patriarchal and capitalist systems. Indeed, when she writes of systems needing each other, this logically involves a notion of two analytically distinct systems.

The study by Burstyn (1983) recognizes the analytic independence of masculine dominance from capitalism. Burstyn argues that the state has a distinct generic commitment which is revealed by many of its actions, especially those related to marriage, sexuality and inheritance. Indeed Burstyn is a fully blown dualist, despite her partial disguise in refusing to use the term 'patriarchy' on the grounds that its meaning is controversial. She provides an illuminating account of the diverse ways in which the state is appropriately designated masculinist rather than gender-blind. She details the various mechanisms by which women and especially feminists are barred from access to positions of power within the state apparatuses, ranging from the separation of women into auxiliary sections within the political parties to the catch 22 of needing to be aggressive to get to the top, yet this making the women 'unnatural', hence unacceptable.

Both Eisenstein and Burstyn share a common argument and a common problem in their analysis of the relation between the material level of gender relations and the state. Both assume that there is a close connection between changes in the material position of women and gender politics. Both suggest that it is only recently that the opportunity for really radical feminist demands about issues such as the family has opened up. Both propose that developments in capitalism have led to the increase in women's paid employment in the post-war period, that this is challenging the overall nature of patriarchal relations, and is significant in broadening women's political horizons and views of the possible. For Eisenstein this is important in the development of the radical aspect of liberal feminism.

However, both overestimate the significance of the economic logic of capital in affecting the position of women in work, and underestimate the significance of gender struggle in changing the position of women in paid employment. I do not wish to deny a role for capital in the expansion of paid employment for women. Rather, my point is that this is not new; that employers have long sought to employ women, since it has long been easier to employ them at lower rates of pay than men. The role of capital cannot explain the timing of the increase in women's paid employment in the post-war period.

Further, Burstyn is incorrect to suggest that it is only recently that any alternatives to the unpaid labour of women in households have arisen. There has been a long history of struggle for the socialization of housework, which belies the suggestion that there were no historic alternatives and no technologically feasible solutions until the wonders of modern technology. Since the days of the communitarian socialists (Taylor, B., 1984) there have been attempts to organize housework communally, which is lent support by the simple economies of scale involved in communal cooking and child care. This tradition continued with the materialist feminists of the nineteenth- and early twentieth-century women's movement, which set up hundreds of such experiments, and with the welfare feminism of the inter-war period, in which an alliance of feminists and the labour movement made such demands on the state.

I am arguing that both Eisenstein and Burstyn are too economistic; they place insufficient emphasis on the political level and upon gender relations, and too much emphasis on the capital labour dynamic. Nonetheless their analyses constitute an advance in their introduction of both patriarchal and capitalist structures and both economic and political factors into an analysis of gender and state.

So, in my theory of gender and the state I would argue for a conceptualization of the state as both capitalist and patriarchal. Further, the actions of the state should not simply be read off from the interests or logic of the system; rather, there is a degree of autonomy of the political struggle from the material base of patriarchy and of capitalism. This political struggle is important in determining the state's actions.

Hernes (1984) also argues for an understanding of the state in terms of patriarchy and capitalism. Writing in the context of the Norwegian state, she is concerned with a society which is ostensibly granting women equal rights with men. She asserts that gender equality has not arrived in Norway; rather, that there has been a shift from private to public dependence for women. The state is important both because women have entered the labour market, often as employees of the state, and also because the extension of state services has been necessary for their movement from household to market work. This change has weakened the status of individual men in relation to their wives. However, women have become dependent upon the state as they have reduced their dependence upon husbands.

Hernes asks why the removal of women's dependence on husbands has not led to their liberation. She approaches this question through an analysis of the structure of the state as corporatist. She argues that access to political power in the Norwegian state is via powerful groups, not individuals as electors or political parties. Associations of employers and trade unions are the most important of these organizations. The groups, organizations and professions which have political clout are themselves gendered; they are dominated by men, with few women leaders. Women are, then, clients and employees, policy takers rather than policy makers.

Hernes produces a powerful analysis of the form of the state in Norway. Its limitation is that it is focused on the welfare aspect of the state and does not deal with the issues of force.

Review of theories

The state is systematically structured in a way that makes it appropriate to regard it as patriarchal. Its actions are more often in men's interests than women's. Thus the liberal pluralist and Marxist class models are both incorrect. The state should be considered to be both patriarchal and capitalist.

Many accounts of the state in relation to gender have focused on one aspect of its operations. For instance, Marxists have tended to concentrate on welfare and radical feminists on male violence. A full analysis requires an integrated consideration of all the various aspects.

I am not wanting to argue for a patriarchal logic approach to the state, since this would merely reproduce the errors of the capital logic school. The state is not monolithic, and its actions are the outcome of competing political pressures. Indeed there have been major changes in the way in which the state represents patriarchal interests, as I shall show below.

CHANGES

Changes in the state's policy towards gender have occurred in most areas of its operation. I shall begin with a consideration of the changes in the nature of the state itself, then proceed to an analysis of specific areas.

The most important change for women in the state during the last 150 years was the extension to them of the parliamentary franchise in 1918 and 1928. This formally incorporated women as a political force at state level. In 1918 most women over 30 were granted the vote (so long as they were married to a householder or had a very small amount of property), which was extended to all women in 1928. Today the significance of this victory for women is often underestimated. It was the highlight of a prolonged, multi-faceted, powerful feminist wave between 1850 and 1930 which was responsible, together with the development of capitalism, for the shift from private to public patriarchy. The change in the nature and policies of the state was a crucial part of this.

I shall examine some of the key changes over the last hundred years and then address the question of the extent to which the ten years of the Thatcher government constitute a new turn in gender politics.

The acquisition of formal routes to political power has been partly responsible for major changes in state policy towards gender relations. I shall give accounts of changes in the spheres of employment, divorce, the welfare state, culture, sexuality and violence to support this view.

Employment

Before women won suffrage, the state, on those occasions on which it intervened on issues of gender and employment, did so to restrict women's access. Instances include the 1842 Mines Act, the nineteenth-century Factory Acts and the First World War Munitions Act. The 1842 Mines Act forbade women to work underground in the mines, while the Factory Acts restricted the hours and times of women's employment in the cotton mills and, later, other factories and workshops. The legislation during the First World War was to ensure the exclusion of women from the engineering work which they were 'allowed' to undertake for the duration of the war. (For a fuller discussion, see Walby 1986.)

After women won suffrage the state did not engage in significant attempts to exclude them from paid employment. This was despite attempts by organized men to secure such a ban both during the inter-war depression and the Second World War. In the 1920s and 1930s women agitated against these attempts. During the Second World War similar legislation was passed to exclude women from engineering jobs entered during the war, but it was not effectively implemented after 1945. The failure of patriarchal forces to mobilize the state on their behalf is at least partly due to the enfranchisement of women, though other factors are also important, such as the relative weakness of male trade unions under conditions of high unemployment during the recessions, and the buoyant demand for all labour after the Second World War (Smith, H. L., 1984; Summerfield, 1984).

However, there were limits to the extent of change in state policy to women's unemployment. Attempts to secure equal pay for women at the end of the war in 1946 failed, despite the setting up of a Royal Commission on Equal Pay (Smith, J. L., 1984; Summerfield, 1984). Nevertheless, even the establishment of such a commission constituted a major change of policy.

Changes continued with the granting of equal pay to women civil servants in non-industrial employment in 1952 (implemented over a seven year period). This followed much agitation by women in white collar unions (Ellis, 1981).

In 1970 government support for equal pay and in 1975 for equal opportunity in employment was passed into law. The Equal Pay Act, which was implemented in 1975, made it illegal to pay workers of different sexes unequal wages if they were performing the same work. The Sex Discrimination Act of 1975 made it illegal to discriminate against people on grounds of sex in relation to employment and a range of services such as credit, housing and education (activities of the government were, however, exempt). These Acts were modified and broadened in scope in 1984 and 1986 respectively, the 1984 amendment to the Equal Pay Act to include work of equal value.

One of the reasons for these changes was the political pressure from women, especially women organized in trade unions. However, pressure on the government was not restricted to domestic sources, but included European ones too. The conditions of entry to the European Economic Community required the passage of equal opportunity legislation and the upgrading of this over time. It is, then, not merely the national state which has an impact on gender relations in employment but supranational bodies as well. The Common Market has been an important source of power for equal opportunity legislation in Britain.

Whether or not the acts have had a significant effect upon women's position in employment relative to that of men is not immediately obvious. The percentage of men's earnings obtained by women rose significantly in the period immediately after the implementation of the act, from 63 per cent in 1970 to 76 per cent in 1977, fluctuating around this figure, if slightly beneath it since then (Equal Opportunities Commission, 1986: 38). However, the number of cases being won at the Industrial Tribunals, Employment Appeals Tribunals and Courts of Appeal is small: in 1987, 33 out of 68 of the cases heard which had been supported by the Equal Opportunities Commission were successful (Equal Opportunities Commission, 1988a: 44). Whether or not the decrease in the gap can be attributed to the legislation is also at issue (Weir and McIntosh, 1982). While the gains are smaller than some of the acts protagonists had hoped for, nonetheless the slight closure of the wages gap was a significant change, which must be located as a victory at the political level. However, it has been difficult to use the legislation and few cases are carried through to a successful conclusion. The limitations of the legislation stem from two sources: firstly, its inherent weakness and that of the machinery for its implementation, such as the composition of the tribunals and the lack of support given by ACAS (Gregory, 1982); secondly, it does not attempt to address some important problems women face in relation to paid employment, such as that of their extra burdens of care for children, husbands and elderly relatives.

Divorce

Major changes in the treatment of the household have occurred in two major areas of state policy: firstly, the legal framework of marriage and divorce; secondly, welfare provision. There have also been important changes in policy on contraception and abortion, which I shall examine later in the context of sexuality.

Divorce law sets the exit conditions from marriage and hence is a significant factor in determining the nature of marital relations. Before 1857 divorce was impossible (except by Act of Parliament). At this time a woman had no legal rights as an independent person when married, since the law conceptualized the married couple as one, and that one was represented by the husband. The husband's rights over his wife were extensive. He had the right to insist that she lived with him; runaway wives could be returned by force and legally held in the husband's house against their will. He had the right to beat her. He legally owned all her goods, for instance, any wages she earned or property she inherited. He had the right to the care and custody of the children and to determine their education. He had the right of sexual access to his wife's body. A wife could not engage in any financial or legal transaction except as the agent of her husband.

The nineteenth century saw a series of campaigns to transform the legal conditions of marriage. Feminist campaigns were important in the change in the law in 1857 which made divorce a legal possibility. The Act provided for the possibility of a legal separation on grounds of desertion, and enabled a wife to claim maintenance, except in cases of her adultery. Divorce could be obtained by the husband on the grounds of a wife's adultery alone, but the wife had to prove either adultery plus another offence, such as incest, bigamy, cruelty, or else rape, sodomy or bestiality in the husband (Holcombe, 1983).

Under the 1857 law a woman could not divorce a husband for physical cruelty or for desertion. After 1878 the Matrimonial Causes made it possible for her to gain a legal separation and maintenance, but without a full divorce she could not remarry. (These grounds were added after further campaigning in the Matrimonial Causes Act in 1937.) The amount of proof that was required of the woman in these cases was steadily lowered: a conviction was essential in the 1878 legislation, whereas by 1925 it was necessary simply to satisfy the court. Additional grounds for separation were added during the early twentieth century: habitual drunkenness in 1902, drug addiction and venereal disease in 1925, and adultery in 1937 (Holcombe, 1983; Smart, 1984).

Legal procedures were expensive and divorce was in practice available only to the middle classes, though the separation proceedings which took place in the magistrates' court were more widely accessible. Divorce was made effectively attainable in 1949 by the provision of Legal Aid (Holcombe, 1983).

Further major changes in the divorce law came in 1969 when the Divorce Reform Act added an alternative to proving a matrimonial offence with the notion of irretrievable breakdown. This in practice provided divorce on demand after a period of separation of two years if both spouses consented, and five if one did not. Both principles ran side by side for several years. Since the old grounds led to quicker divorces they tended to be utilized more frequently. Matrimonial offences at this point still affected the financial settlement to an extent, although the Acts of 1970 and 1973 were supposed to remedy this and allow financial settlements to be made on the basis of need and fairness (Holcombe, 1983; Smart, 1984).

Legislation in 1984 eliminated the role of matrimonial offences in obtaining divorce. The situation in the late 1980s, then, is one in which divorce is available when marriage is deemed to have broken down irretrievably as demonstrated by separation, and financial settlements focus on the needs of children, not of the wife.

With this final round of legislation the notion of marriage as a life-long contract, which has been steadily eroded during the last century or so, has reached the point at which it is no more than a voluntary practice, with a couple of years' notice at best. The legal implications of marriage today are minor, because of the ease with which it is possible to exit from it.

There has been some resistance to these changes, especially from conservative women's organizations and the churches. Interestingly, it is men's groups who are currently most represented among those who push for further erosion of the remaining financial commitments. These men argue for a 'clean break' whereby financial support is made for a considerably reduced period.

In writing of California, where similar legal alterations took place a little earlier, Weitzman (1985) argues that these changes lead to the impoverishment of women, especially middle-aged homemakers, on divorce. She attributes the significant role of women in the rise of the New Right and in anti-feminist campaigns, such as that which led to the defeat of the Equal Rights Amendment, to the impact of legal transformations such as these which enshrine the notion of equality for the sexes at a time when women are economically still vulnerable. However, the women in Weitzman's sample did not regret their divorces, even after their considerable drop in living standards.

In conclusion, the changes since 1857 have led to the transformation of the legal aspects of marriage. Although it is no longer a life-long contract, this is not to imply that husbands do not have rights over wives during marriage. Indeed a woman still cannot press a charge of rape against a husband, and the domestic division of labour is still evident. However, the legal enforcement of the marriage contract has come to an end. Women can leave marriages where husbands are brutal or simply boring; as a consequence a particular form of women's subordination is effectively ended. However, so also has ended such protection as was provided by husbands for wives. Women are differently placed in relation to marriage. Women whose labour market position is weak after many years of homemaking are particularly vulnerable to retrospective alterations in the marriage contract. The implications of these legal changes for women's position in the household, and the extent to which women leave marriage, was discussed in chapter 3.

The welfare state

Conventional accounts of the welfare state, as we have seen earlier in this chapter, have typically focused on the capital–labour relation, ignoring the significance of gender relations. Gender is central to the development of the welfare aspects of the state, both in that this represents significant changes in the sexual division of labour, and in the role of women in their development. The concerns of health care, education and income support have particular importance for gender as well as class relations.

Women have been the gender more concerned with the care of the sick and socializing the young than men, and, in having access to a wage sufficient to support themselves and their children less often than men, they have a very specific interest in non-wage forms of income. The transfer of the care of the sick and the young away from the household to the state in the processes characterized as the welfare state represents a major change in gender relations. Women still do most of the work in health and education, but under very different relations of production.

These changes constitute the socialization of some of the privatized labour of women under patriarchal relations in the household. In consequence individual patriarchs as heads of household lost control over this aspect of women's labour. Instead the state gained effective immediate control. We saw a shift from a private to public form of patriarchal control.

This is not to argue that such changes do not also constitute a shift in class relations. They do represent a real improvement in the conditions of life for the working class. But they are simultaneously a structural shift in gender relations.

The struggle for the improvement of health and education by the provision of state services was campaigned for by women to a greater extent than men. Both women within a working-class labour movement and women within a middle-class philanthropic tradition were central to these successful crusades (Banks, 1981; Mark-Lawson, Savage and Warde, 1985; Middleton, L., 1978; Vicinus, 1985).

Women were active within the labour movement, especially at the local level, but also at the national, pushing for the extension of health, maternity and educational provision. They were grouped independently as well as within mixed organizations. For instance, there was the Women's Cooperative Guild and the Women's Labour League; after the winning of the vote, the Women's Labour League amalgamated with the Labour Party, but has maintained separate sections to the present day. These organizations took the lead in demands for improvements in health, education and welfare. Among many issues, they campaigned for free school meals for children and free health care for pregnant women, mothers and young children (Middleton, L., 1978).

The representation of women in a local labour movement meant that that movement was more likely to push for welfare reforms, such as spending on child and maternity issues. However, it also mattered how women and men were disposed in the labour movement. Where men had especially strong patriarchal forms of organization, then women, even if present in the paid workforce, were less likely to get their views represented. The significance for the labour movement of women taking up these issues can be shown from a comparative analysis of three localities where women were involved at different levels. Mark-Lawson, Savage and Warde (1985) show that spending on maternity and associated provision was higher in towns where women were a large part of the paid workforce and where the men were not in the more extreme forms of patriarchal organization. In a comparison of Lancaster, Preston and Nelson in the inter-war period, Lancaster (which had the lowest levels of women's paid employment and consequently lesser involvement in the labour movement) saw the lowest levels of spending on maternity and associated provisions. In the engineering town of Preston, with its exclusionary patriarchal union practices, the expenditure on maternity was not as high as that in the textile town of Nelson, where some of the unions were open to women as well as men. That is, the gender of the labour movement and the way men and women organized made a difference in the campaigns undertaken and their outcomes. The most welfare spending came where women were best organized within the labour movement.

Women in the labour movement were not the only ones to be engaged in attempts to improve welfare services. Philanthropic efforts had long been the province of middle-class ladies in the establishment of new welfare institutions, both on an individual level and collectively. These went way beyond the image of the patronizing visitor of the sick and included the development of the nursing and social work professions, and the development of schools, especially for girls. Florence Nightingale was only one of several women who effectively transformed the care of the sick into a systematic, hygienic business. Social work developed out of the efforts of women such as Octavia Hill, who sought the methodical relief of the conditions of the poor. Teaching was another area led by women. The women involved in these professions were drawn from the middle classes and many of them were single (Vicinus, 1985).

Conventionally, such 'lady bountifuls' have been seen to reinforce the traditional role of women as unpaid helpers and strictly to maintain the boundaries of women's sphere. Banks (1981) sees the focus on welfare and protection of women in the inter-war period as a dead-end for feminism. To some extent this is true; these women did typically have a very clear idea of their appropriate sphere and adhered to a strict sexual morality. However, some of them, while maintaining theoretical adherence to a division between 'women's sphere' and 'men's sphere', sought to enlarge what was encompassed by women's sphere. Tasks which were performed by women in the household, such as caring for the sick and raising the young, were argued to fall still in women's sphere when carried out in public institutions outside the household, such as schools and hospitals. This claim broadened the range of activities available to respectable ladies. It stretched the notion of separate spheres while not challenging it.

These developments, during the second half of the nineteenth century and the early decades of the twentieth, laid the foundations of the main professions we today associate with the welfare state. They were overwhelmingly led by women.

The establishment of the welfare state in Britain is often dated from the

1945 Labour Government. However, many of the major advances were built upon these earlier schemes: the welfare state was a result of the struggles of women, both of the working class and the middle class. During some periods there was an effective and powerful alliance with the male-led Labour movement, which was the cause of the greater institutionalization of these developments in the form we know today.

The gender composition of the workforce of the welfare institutions is not predominantly female by accident. This is related to the fact that it was principally women who carved out the area of work. The early female workforce here was mainly single and not infrequently lived in associated housing rather than in conventional households (Vicinus, 1985). In this way they escaped direct control by a private patriarch as husband or father. A number of their institutions survived for some time independent of male-dominated organizations.

However, women did not altogether escape patriarchal relations by working within these new establishments. Some of them were always circumscribed within wider male-dominated institutions, for instance, nurses worked with male doctors and within hospitals. Other, previously independent, foundations were brought within patriarchal control when they were incorporated in a national welfare state – schools lost autonomy; directors of social services are usually male. Today the organization of the welfare state is headed principally by men, with a predominantly female workforce. Previously privatized domestic work is carried out under more public forms of patriarchal organization.

Under the Thatcher government welfare services and income support have been cut back. The policy of community care and reduction in residential provision for the mentally ill and handicapped has led to a greater burden upon the unpaid labour of women in the 'community'. Housing and other benefits have been reduced. These changes disproportionately affect women, since they are dependent upon the welfare state to a greater extent than are men.

Culture

Equal access to education was successfully struggled for by first-wave feminists, who won access to universities and other institutions (Deem, 1978; Strachey, 1928).

Another major change is in the arena of censorship, which is much looser than it was in the nineteenth century. While there are still legal controls over some of the most exploitative forms of pornography, such as that involving children, most has now been released from legal sanction. The proliferation of pornography has followed.

Sexuality

Major changes in state policy relating to sexuality have taken place around women's access to contraception and abortion. Again we see a movement from the nineteenth century, when the state legally restricted women's access to forms of fertility control, to a situation today in which the controls are quite light. Changes in availability to contraception occurred first during the early twentieth century. Campaigns by feminists, together with interest from doctors, led to the development of family planning clinics on a local basis during the inter-war period (Gittins, 1982; Stopes, 1981; Banks, 1981). Free contraception was granted in Britain under the National Health Service in the 1970s.

In Britain the 1967 Abortion Act significantly improved women's access to abortion; however, it was not on demand, but conditional on the approval of two doctors and certain criteria of possible damage to the mother's health being met. These discretionary elements led to wide regional variation in the availability of free abortion on the NHS, according to the views of local doctors, and especially the local consultant gynaecologist. The development of non-profit-making organizations which provided abortion up to the legal time limit of 28 weeks led to the availability of abortion on demand if you could pay for it.

This legislation was the outcome of many years' lobbying, much of which took place before second-wave feminism could be considered to have become firmly established in Britain. It was, nonetheless, a major improvement in the possibility of control for individual women over their own fertility.

There have been repeated attempts to amend the Act so as to restrict the availability of abortion. These have met with considerable political opposition, largely organized through the National Abortion Campaign. Massive demonstrations have been mounted, and these, together with the support of many influential organizations, including the TUC and British Medical Association, have ensured that the legislation has remained untouched despite several years of radical right government in Britain under Margaret Thatcher.

There was a government attack upon homosexuality in 1988 with the passage of Clause 28 (later Section 29) of the Local Government Bill, which was intended to make it illegal for local authorities to spend money 'promoting' homosexuality. This was an attack both on the gay and lesbian movement and also upon radical local authorities. A multi-faceted movement to 'Stop the Clause', including not only gay and lesbian activists but also a civil liberties lobby within the arts and broadcasting, failed to produce more than minor amendments. However, it was discovered that the Act had only very limited legal applicability, since sex education in schools, at which it was aimed, was not affected. However, the Section may lead to self-censorship and other restrictions by nervous local officials.

Violence

Violence is an area in which there have been few significant alterations in state policy towards gender relations. There were a few changes under feminist pressure in both the first and second waves, however. The most important during the first wave was that women won the right legally to separate from a husband on the grounds of his violence (Holcombe, 1983). This was especially important before divorce because it was more widely available. Changes during the second wave are more minor.

Court procedure has been modified as a result of protest. For instance, in response to the outcry raised over the Morgan case, when it looked as if the gang which raped a woman would be acquitted because they claimed that they believed the woman had consented despite her protests, Parliament passed the 1976 Sexual Offences Amendment Act, which ostensibly gave a raped woman anonymity and prevented the revelation of her previous sexual history in court (Hay, Soothill and Walby, 1980). However, the impact of the Act appears to be less than hoped for, since barristers and judges found various loopholes in it (Adler, 1987).

A further small change was to the housing legislation, which now ensures a degree of priority for women who are battered by the men they live with. However, this too is riddled with loopholes, often resulting in long delays while a woman acquires 'local connections' (Binney, Harkel and Nixon, 1981).

The state's response to child sexual abuse was the subject of attention in 1987–8 when doctors in Cleveland began to diagnose a higher number of cases than had previously been usual. In the context of a general move to take child sexual abuse more seriously, two Cleveland doctors used a new and controversial diagnostic technique. By increasing the rate of diagnosis they challenged the presumption that child sexual abuse was a very rare occurrence and took concrete steps towards remedial action. This change in policy, towards more state intervention, was challenged by a campaign led by local men such as the Labour MP Stuart Bell, a local vicar and accused fathers. The media took up the story, attacking not the problem of child sexual abuse, but the doctors, who, it was claimed, were hounding innocent 'parents'. The moral panic that ensued focused on the female professional Dr Marietta Higgs, not on the problem of child sexual abuse. Its net outcome has been to stimulate public debate about the issue. The government has ordered more money to be spent on training social workers to deal with it. Yet the doctors at the centre of the crisis have been scapegoated.

Thus we see increasing challenges to the low level of state intervention against male violence. These have recently become major political issues, though rarely along party lines. The net outcome has been a very slight shift towards greater state intervention against male violence.

CONCLUSION

As the accounts above have indicated, there have been many important changes in state policy towards gender relations over the last 150 years, but these also include some very significant limitations. The state is still patriarchal as well as capitalist and racist. Some areas have seen greater changes than others. State policies directed towards confining women to the private sphere of the marital home have been very significantly reduced, enabling women's movement towards the public sphere. Here we see the cessation of legal backing to exclusionary practices in employment; the increased ease of divorce, and financial provision for non-wage earners; the ending of state backing to exclusionary practices in education and the removal of most forms of censorship of pronography; the decriminalization of contraception and abortion under most circumstances; and minor changes in the law making it marginally easier for a woman to leave a violent man.

However, while there are many changes which facilitate women's entry to the public sphere there are not so many which improve the position of women in it. While the equal opportunity legislation might have been thought to improve women's position in this respect, it is widely considered to have had only a marginal impact. Further, women's position as heads of one-parent families is economically perilous, with low levels of state benefits. The relaxation of censorship has permitted increased circulation of pornography. So while there have been undoubted benefits to women from these transformations, what has occurred is as much a change in the kind of patriarchal control as of degree.

Has the Thatcher era changed the state significantly in relation to women? I do not think that there is a clear break in the gender policies of the state in the way that there has been in the handling of class relations. While some aspects of women's position have become worse, especially those which involve welfare services and payments, in others there have been some small gains, such as marginal improvements in the equal opportunity legislation, numbers of women in public office, and ease of divorce, while in many other areas, such as abortion and contraception, there has been little change.

Thatcherism presents itself as rolling back the frontiers of the state in keeping with a neo-liberal strategy. In practice this applies only to certain sectors of the state, since others, especially those to do with its military and policing functions, are being strengthened. The question here is which strategy is being applied to gender relations. Interestingly, right-wing morality has not been given the backing of the state – for instance, access to abortion and contraception has not been reduced; they have been considered arenas for the neo-liberal strategy. However, women have suffered disproportionately from the rolling back of welfare provision.

NOTES

1 The legislation in Britain took a different form from that in the USA, where women were more actively involved in the campaigns and the focus was on the worst, not best, forms of employment for women.

8

From Private to Public Patriarchy

PROGRESS OR REGRESS?

Patriarchy is not a historical constant.[1] Modifications in gender relations over the last century or so have been interpreted variously as progress, regress and involving no overall change. Liberals typically define them as progress, Marxists as regress followed by stasis, and radical feminists as embracing no significant change. There are, of course, exceptions to these correlations of position within a perspective, but nonetheless they are common.

Liberal feminists have usually painted a picture of progress composed of the winning of the vote, entry into education, growth of the number of women in top jobs and the increase in the number of women in public life. Women have won rights and entered jobs and posts previously barred to them. Such advances accumulate and provide the basis of the next reform.

Marxists have typically argued that the development of capitalism led to a worsening of the position of women, with the separation of the home from paid work, but with little change in degree of inequality since then. Capitalism is considered to need the conventional family form, so there is little prospect of further major alteration in gender relations until there have been major changes in capitalism.

Radical feminists have generally concluded that for every victory won by women there has been a patriarchal backlash in another area. Patriarchy is a dynamic system in which men usually give up an activity only when they no longer wish to undertake it.[2] If women do win a victory, then patriarchal forces will regroup and regain control over them in a different way (see for instance Millett's account of the development of new forms of control over women via sexuality after the winning of political citizenship).

International and multicultural perspectives on gender are divided in similar ways on the issue of progress or regress. The traditional view that modernization and Westernization have been progressive for women has been challenged both by those who have argued that these developments have been regressive, leading to the greater exploitation of women's labour by the capitalist West, and those who maintain that cultures are necessarily incomparable. The traditional position tended towards a white Western ethnocentricity which highlighted the disadvantages, but not the advantages, of non-British cultures for women. However, to declare cultures necessarily incomparable would mean that we could never talk of degrees of oppression nor even discuss the effects of imperialism.

In order to deal positively with these issues I think it is important to differentiate between degrees and forms of patriarchy. Degrees of patriarchy refers to the intensity of oppression on a specified dimension, for instance the size of the wages gap between men and women. Forms of patriarchy refers to the overall type of patriarchy, as defined by the specific relations between the different patriarchal structures. It is important not to conflate these two dimensions.

British feminists have won significant reforms which ameliorate a number of the features of patriarchy, but some have eventually resulted in a different form of patriarchy. Further, different ethnic groups may have different forms of patriarchy, without it being appropriate to suggest that one is better for women than another. Recent British history has seen a change in both the degree and form of patriarchy. There have been reductions in some specific aspects of patriarchy, but progressive reforms have been met with patriarchal counter-attack, often on new rather than the same issues. Private patriarchy has given way to public patriarchy.

DISTINGUISHING FORMS OF PATRIARCHY

The conceptual distinction between different aspects of patriarchy has a long history in the analysis of gender relations. Most previous attempts to utilize the differentiation of the private and public have been narrowly restricted to one aspect of patriarchy. A classic early account is that of Rosaldo (1974), who argues that women's subordination is due to their confinement to the private sphere. She states that men's work is always more highly valued than is that of women. She suggests that women's subordination is a universal phenomenon, although it varies in degree, and that it is to be explained by the universal fact that women are confined to the private sphere of the family because they bear and rear children. Women's subordination in the private sphere may be ameliorated when they are able to combine together, rather than be separated from each other. Rosaldo proposes that women's status would be lowest in those societies where there is the clearest split between the public and the private and where women are isolated from one another.

Other accounts have focused upon the spatial and historical variability in the private–public division. Boserup (1970) provides an empirically rich account of the different forms of sexual divisions of labour, especially in agriculture, on a world basis. She suggests that there are two main forms of sexual division in agricultural societies. In the first, found in most of Africa, women do most of the farming; the men have a restricted range of jobs, perhaps land clearing and hunting. In the second, found in places of plough agriculture such as Asia, men do most of the field labour. This can be further differentiated into those forms where the woman is in seclusion and veiled and those where the woman does perform some domestic labour. (There is another variant in which both sexes do a lot of agricultural labour.) Finally there are complex systems in which these different patterns are overlaid, though separated by class, caste or ethnicity. In the latter the wives of the ruling men are domesticated, while lower categories of women engage in public labour. Indeed the possibility of the first group of women to be domesticated may be predicated upon the exploitation of the labour of a subordinated group of women and men. The two groups of women are differentiated by class, caste or ethnicity. Colonial Europeans disrupted these patterns creating further complex systems of sexual division of labour.

As Beneria and Sen (1986) note, Boserup's account is undertheorized, especially in her use of modernization theory, rather than specifying the capitalist forces at work. However, I think it is also underformulated regarding gender relations. Boserup provides empirical support for an argument that there are major patterns in the sexual division of labour, but does not provide us with any theoretical understanding of this. Some of the issues involved in differentiating between forms of patriarchy have been raised by the work of Guillaumin (1981), Dworkin (1983) and Carol Brown (1981).

Guillaumin (1981) makes a distinction between the collective and private appropriation of women, the latter being a restrictive expression of the former. Patriarchal appropriation includes not only that of women's labour, but all aspects of women from their sexuality to psychological care. Juteau and Laurin (1986) develop this conception, pointing out that even if certain categories of women, such as nuns, escape private appropriation, they are, like all women, subject to collective appropriation. These materialist feminists provide a critical insight by making a distinction between different forms of appropriation simultaneously with recognizing that together they form one system of appropriation. The distinction between collective and private forms catches some important differences in the ways the appropriation is performed. This enables a comparison between the position of women in the form of patriarchy to which they are subject, without any necessary implications for the degree of patriarchy. However, the way the distinction is used places certain limitations on its heuristic utility for capturing historical change. This is because the focus is either on specific institutions or the whole. Rather it is better to have distinctions which relate to the different interconnection between the elements of patriarchy, and their relative significance in different eras.

The notion that there are two major historical forms of patriarchy is discussed in the work of Dworkin (1983) and Carol Brown (1981). Dworkin differentiates patriarchal control over women according to the regulation of their sexuality and reproductive capacity. In the first, the farming mode, the relationship involves being kept and exploited for life; in the second, the brothel mode, women ostensibly have more freedom since they are not possessed for life, but they lose support from men when their sexual and reproductive periods are over. This emphasizes the sexual dimension in the differentiation of the two forms of patriarchy. It is related to Dworkin's overall theory, which places sexuality centrally in relation to gender, even to the extent of conflating the two. Thus it is consistent with her theory of gender relations for her typology of forms of patriarchy to use sexuality as the key dimension. Evidence to support Dworkin's claim includes the movement in the main locus of control over women's sexuality from the private to the public sphere. As women are increasingly able to leave husbands and to engage in non-marital sexual relations, then public forms of control (e.g., via pornography) become more and more important. However, following my argument that sexuality is but one site of patriarchal relations, Dworkin's typology of patriarchal forms is limited because of this restriction and her failure to justify its exclusive focus.

Similarly, Brown is concerned only with a restricted area of patriarchy in her theory, that is, labour, and hence has a typology based upon this. As discussed in the chapter on household production, Brown's work produces powerful insights into the changing relationship of children to mothers and fathers, but is limited by this restriction to labour. It is powerful as an account insofar as the relationship between paid work and domestic work is the key to differences in women's position. Indeed today, with the changing form of the family, the labour market is an especially significant base of patriarchy.

Hernes (1984) also makes a distinction between private and public forms of patriarchy. Her explanation is specific to an analysis of the state, in particular the Norwegian state, though it applies, to a lesser degree, to all the Western industrialized nations that have developed a welfare state. She argues that women have reduced their dependence upon their husbands (private patriarchy), but increased their dependence upon the welfare state both as employees of the state and as clients receiving state services (public patriarchy).

I think that the distinction between private and public types of patriarchy does grasp important differences in form, but the accounts of Dworkin, Brown and Hernes are limited by their restriction to specific arenas, sexuality, labour and the state. We need one which takes into account the full range of patriarchal relations.

I would suggest that the different forms are dependent upon the interaction of six key patriarchal structures. These are the patriarchal mode of production; patriarchal relations in paid work; patriarchal relations in the state; male violence; patriarchal relations in sexuality; and patriarchal relations in cultural institutions including religions, media, education. In different times and places some of the structures are more important than others. The elimination of any one does not lead to the demise of the system as a whole. Logically there could be many forms, since I have identified six structures within patriarchy and two other major systems with which it has been in articulation. I am going to suggest that in recent Western history there have been two major forms, one of which can usefully be subdivided into two. The purpose of doing this is to demonstrate that patriarchy is not an ahistoric, universalistic concept. Further, I am arguing that the different aspects of gender inequality are sufficiently interrelated to be understood in terms of a system of patriarchy.

Critics who argue that the concept of patriarchy cannot deal with historical change have been shown to be wrong. It is sometimes argued that unless a theory of a social system comprehends a theory of the motor of change then it does not constitute a social system. However, I would argue that it is not necessary for a social system to have an inbuilt dynamic of change in order to be conceptualized as a social system. Indeed such a suggestion is an unwarranted a priori assumption (see Smith, 1973). It is predicated on evolutionary notions of society. Patriarchy changes but it does not have an intrinsic evolutionary mechanism. This does not mean that it cannot be a social system. However, the understanding of change in patriarchal relations is an important question which should not be reduced to historical accident.

PRIVATE AND PUBLIC PATRIARCHY

I am distinguishing between two forms of patriarchy: private and public. They differ on a variety of levels: firstly, in terms of the relations between the structures and, secondly, in the institutional form of each structure. Further, they are differentiated by the main form of patriarchal strategy: exclusionary in private patriarchy and segregationist in public patriarchy. Private patriarchy is based upon household production, with a patriach controlling women individually and directly in the relatively private sphere of the home. Public patriarchy is based on structures other than the household, although this may still be a significant patriarchal site. Rather, institutions conventionally regarded as part of the public domain are central in the maintenance of patriarchy.

In private patriarchy it is a man in his position as husband or father who is the direct oppressor and beneficiary, individually and directly, of the subordination of women. This does not mean that household production is the sole patriarchal structure. Indeed it is importantly maintained by the active exclusion of women from public arenas by other structures. The exclusion of women from these other spheres could not be perpetuated without patriarchal activity at these levels.

Public patriarchy is a form in which women have access to both public and private arenas. They are not barred from the public arenas, but are nonetheless subordinated within them. The expropriation of women is performed more collectively than by individual patriarchs. The household may remain a site of patriarchal oppression, but it is no longer the main place where women are present.

In each type of patriarchy the six structures are present, but the relationship between them, and their relative significance, is different. For instance, I am not arguing that in private patriarchy the only significant site is that of the household. In the different forms there are different relations between the structures to maintain the system of patriarchy.

In the private system of patriarchy the exploitation of women in the household is maintained by their non-admission to the public sphere. In a sense the term 'private' for this form of patriarchy might be misleading, in that it is the exclusion from the public which is the central causal mechanism. Patriarchal relations outside the household are crucial in shaping patriarchal relations within it. However, the effect is to make women's experience of patriarchy privatized, and the immediate beneficiaries are also located there.

In the public form of patriarchy the exploitation of women takes place at all levels, but women are not formally excluded from any. In each institution women are disadvantaged.

The second aspect of the difference between private and public patriarchy is in the institutional form of each of the structures. This is a movement from an individual to a more collective form of appropriation of women. There has also been a shift in patriarchal strategy from exclusionary to segregationist and subordinating.

I have traced the movement from private to public patriarchy within each of the six patriarchal structures during the course of this book. Within paid work there was a shift from an exclusionary strategy to a segregationist one, which was a movement from attempting to exclude women from paid work to accepting their presence but confining them to jobs which were segregated from and graded lower than those of men. In the household there was a reduction in the confinement of women to this sphere over a lifetime and a shift in the main locus of control over reproduction. The major cultural institutions ceased to exclude women, while subordinating women within them. Sexual controls over women significantly shifted from the specific control of a husband to that of a broader public arena; women were no longer excluded from sexual relations to the same extent, but subordinated within them. Women's exclusion from the state was replaced by their subordination within it.

PRIVATE AND PUBLIC PATRIARCHY IN BRITISH HISTORY

Recent British history has seen a movement towards the private model, and then a movement away to the public form. The height of the private form was to be found in the mid-nineteenth century in the middle classes. Many scholars have argued that there was an intensification in the domestic ideology and the extent to which middle-class women were confined to the private sphere of the home (Davidoff and Hall, 1987; Gilman, 1966; Pinchbeck, 1930; Schreiner, 1918; Tilly and Scott, 1978). There were extremely strong sanctions against non-marital sexuality for such women. They did not work in public, only in their own households, and were excluded from the public sphere of the state, lacking citizenship rights such as suffrage and, if married, ability to own property. Violence against wives by husbands was condoned as legitimate chastisement 'so long as the rod was no thicker than a man's thumb'. Cultural institutions, such as the church, supported the notion that a woman's place was in the home.

There were some limits and contradictions to this private model of patriarchy, but they do not destroy the general case. For instance, it was applied to middle-class women to a much greater extent than working-class women, although there were attempts to extend it (For instance the legislation which banned women from working down the mines and restricted their factory employment).

The contemporary form of patriarchy is of a more public kind, and the trend is still in this direction. Women have entered the public sphere, yet are subordinated there. Most women of all social classes engage in paid work. Simultaneously, there is a considerable wages gap between men and women and extensive occupational segregation. The sanctions on non-marital sexuality, while still present to a greater degree for women than for men, are much less severe. At the same time the circulation of sadistic pornographic images has increased. Marriages can be, and increasingly are, legally dissolved. While women are thereby freed from marriages which are especially oppressive, they still remain responsible for child care after divorce, thus continuing the demands upon their labour started in marriage. This is now done under circumstances of increased poverty. Women have citizenship rights which are formally the same as those of men, but they form only a tiny proportion of the elected representatives, and a tiny proportion of the political agenda is around women's concerns. Violence against wives, while tolerated, is not quite as legitimate as it once was, since it can now be used as grounds for divorce, and minimal welfare provision is available to those who flee; however, few legal penalties await the vast majority of men who are violent against women. Cultural institutions increasingly allow women's active participation, but usually in an inferior way.

Women have entered the public sphere, but not on equal terms. They are now present in the paid workplace, the state and public cultural institutions. But they are subordinated within them. Further, their subordination, in the domestic division of labour, sexual practices, and as receivers of male violence, continues.

The private and public forms of patriarchy constitute a continuum rather than a rigid dichotomy. The trend towards a more public form has been continuing despite the economic recession which some expected to stop the entry of women into paid work, and despite the development of the New Right. We do not yet see its full development. We should expect the movement into paid work to continue, especially given the increase in the number of young women gaining educational qualifications, the reduced expectancy that a husband is for life, and the slow, but steady, removal of barriers to women's participation in paid work. The private form of patriarchy which existed among the middle classes in the nineteenth century did not reach the full limits of that model. We can see its further development in Islamic populations (especially among the upper classes – the lower classes in the countryside could not afford for women not to work outside the home).

Within Britain itself we see different degrees of public and private patriarchy among different ethnic groups. Afro-Caribbeans are closer to the public form, Muslim Asians to the private form, with whites in the middle. Afro-Caribbean women have the highest rates of participation in paid work and the highest rates of female-headed households of the three groups. Muslim Asian women have the lowest rates of paid work, and have the most intense forms of male-headed families (Brown, Colin, 1984). Whites appear to be moving towards the Afro-Caribbean pattern.

The two main forms of patriarchy I have identified are useful for conceptualizing major changes in gender relations in Britain in the last couple of centuries. In order to grasp the major differences in the forms of patriarchy between various countries in the industrialized world it is further necessary to divide the public form of patriarchy into two: one founded on the labour market and the other on the state as the basis of bringing women into the public sphere. At one end of the continuum we have the countries of Eastern Europe, where the state has played a major role in this, at the other we have the USA, in which the market has played an equivalent role. In the middle we have the countries of Western Europe, in which the state, in its capacity especially as a welfare state, has been of intermediate significance.

The development of the typology beyond a simple duality to one where one of the elements is again divided is based on the introduction of the level of the state as a new element. In Eastern Europe, and to a lesser extent in Western Europe, the state has taken on some of the tasks which were previously performed by women privately in the household and organized them collectively (even if they are still largely performed by women). This is the case for care of children, the sick and the old. There is clearly a major difference between Western and Eastern Europe in the extent of state activity, but the differences between Western Europe and the USA are also striking in this regard (although the existence of a massive state education system in the USA should preclude comparative statements of an absolute kind). Thus the contemporary USA may be seen to have a labour-market-based form of public patriarchy, Eastern Europe a state-based form of public patriarchy, and Western Europe a mixed state/labour-market-form of public patriarchy. In each of these areas this represents a change from a previous form of private patriarchy.

The variation is caused by the difference in state policy which itself is an outcome of the various struggles between opposing forces on both gender and class issues. In eastern Europe the seizure of the state by forces which were radical on both class and gender issues is central, even if that radicalism had very significant limits. The development of the welfare state in Western Europe is usually considered to be the outcome of a compromise in the struggle between capital and labour. I think this should rather be regarded also to be the outcome of gendered political forces, since an alliance between feminism and the labour movement was key to the development of such policies.

THE MOVEMENT FROM PUBLIC TO PRIVATE PATRIARCHY

Capitalism has been seen as the major cause of changes in gender relations by some writers. For instance, it has been suggested that the growth of capitalism led to the separation of home and work (Tilly and Scott, 1978; Zaretsky, 1976; Oakley, 1976; Davidoff and Hall, 1987). Against this there is a school of thought which proposes that the sexual division of labour pre-dated capitalism and cannot be considered to be caused by it (Middleton, C., 1981; Hartmann, 1979). I shall argue that patriarchal relations pre-dated capitalism, and that changes in these have been seriously overstated. Nevertheless there were changes. The rise of capitalism did lead to the development of a new form of patriarchy, but not to an alteration in its basic structures. Patriarchal relations of production in the household pre-dated capitalism; they were not created by it.

The dominant account stresses the significance of the changes in gender relations with the rise of capitalism. It is argued that there was a separation of home and work and the creation of the role of the housewife. This is considered to be a result of the development of capitalism, which pulls men away from the household in search of work in the factories, and the growth of a domestic ideology, which locates women as nurturers in the home. Some of the later writings (e.g., Davidoff and Hall, 1987) pay particular attention to the class dynamics of this process, in which the most acute separation develops among the rising middle classes and bourgeoisie, which is then copied by and sometimes imposed on the working class.

I think this account is mistaken for the following reasons. Firstly, it underestimates the significance of the pre-capitalist sexual division of labour. Middleton has shown that in England there was a well-developed sexual division of labour in both feudal and proto-industrial times (Middleton, C., 1981, 1985). Further, agricultural labour, in which the majority of the British population engaged prior to industrialization, necessarily meant that men left the home in order to work long before the advent of capitalist factories; the separation of home and work is not specific to capitalism. Domestic industries were not the only forms of occupation. Secondly, changes in the gender division of labour during the rise of capitalism are overstated. In cotton textiles, the first industry of the industrial revolution, adult men made up only a minority – 18 per cent – of the workforce in 1819 (Hutchins, 1915: 72). Only in later industries were women excluded, and this was significantly a result of patriarchal not capitalist, pressures (see Walby, 1986). Poor women in pre-industrial England engaged in field labour; poor women in industrial England also engaged in work other than household chores for their own families, ranging from cotton weaving, domestic service and needlework to taking in laundry. Thirdly, changes in the household are overstated. The English household had had a nuclear structure long before capitalism. Laslett (1977) finds this pattern in the sixteenth and seventeenth centuries, while McFarland (1978) finds it in the thirteenth century. Indeed Anderson (1971) shows that households became less nuclear during industrialization, with those in the cotton textile mills taking in additional members. Women married to men of the ruling class did not engage in 'work' in either period. As the size of the British empire grew so did the size of its ruling class as a proportion of the population of Britain. Fourthly, the practice of confining women to the domestic sphere, which is supposed to be the symbol of gender relations after the rise of capitalism, is in fact found in its most developed forms in Islamic societies, both pre-capitalist and capitalist. Capitalism is not an exclusive hallmark of such patterns of gender relations; it cannot be treated as their cause.

Nevertheless, I am not wanting to argue that there were no changes in gender relations during the period of industrialization; rather, that they have been both massively overstated and incorrectly explained.

These changes included the progressive loss by women of areas of work which had been deemed women's and the loss of certain legal rights over property that they had previously held (Pinchbeck, 1930; Schreiner, 1918). In looking at the shifting balance of power between women and men it is essential to examine the gains by men as well as the losses by women. There was the one-sided gain by some men of privileged access to new spheres of power. For instance, the benefit of the development of credit, necessary for capitalist entrepreneurs, was restricted to men because of the limitations on the legal personhood of married women. Other examples include the development of formal, bureaucratized political arenas such as Parliament and the state apparatus to which some men, but no women, had access. Essentially in this period we see the development of many new bases of power, most of which might be considered to be in the 'public' sphere and from which women were debarred. The critical changes are not so much a new confinement of women to a private sphere as the growth of the public sphere to which men had nearly exclusive access.

This is not to say that the proportion of English women who embraced a 'domestic ideolgy' did not increase. Neither is it to deny that this discourse became progressively more restrictive for the women living it.

How do we understand these changes? I have argued elsewhere that there is no part of any logic of capitalism which would explain them (Walby, 1986). The benefits capital gains from the production of labour power from the patriarchal nuclear family are contingent, not necessary, and there are significant costs entailed. Is it then part of a logic of patriarchy? I think not, in the sense of inevitable laws of development of patriarchy. But I do think that it is a result in the shift of resources of male power consequent upon the development of capitalism which led to changes in the critical sites of patriarchal power. The development of capitalism opened up new sites of power, and these were colonized by men because they were strategically placed so to do. This was not always achieved without a struggle, however, as the preferential employment of women by capitalists in early cotton textiles indicates. Simultaneously, the transformation of the domestic economy and domestic industries by capitalism contracted the bases of female power.[3]

THE MOVEMENT FROM PRIVATE TO PUBLIC PATRIARCHY

There have been very important changes in gender relations taking place during the twentieth century, as I have been arguing throughout this book. The movement towards a more intense form of private patriarchy was dramatically reversed during the period at the turn of the century. The twentieth century has seen a shift in the form of patriarchy from private to public as well as a reduction in the degree of some specific forms of oppression of women.

This is not merely a statement that there were important changes, but, further, that the very direction of change was reversed. All six patriarchal structures are involved in these changes. There was a struggle by feminists against patriarchal social practices which met with resistance. Their campaigns took place in the context of, and were shaped by, the capitalist demand for labour. The outcome of these battles was a change from one form and a high degree of patriarchy to another form together with some lessening in the degree of patriarchy in specific areas. These had complex interconnected effects on other aspects of patriarchal relations. Capital's demand for increased supplies of labour was in conflict with the private patriarchal strategy of privatizing women in the home. First-wave feminism's victories of political citizenship gave women not only the vote, but education, and hence access to the professions, property ownership and the right to leave marriages. In combination these meant that women eventually gained effective access to paid employment and the ability to leave marriages, which led to significant changes in the notions of appropriate sexual behaviour. To start with first-wave feminism achieved a victory principally at the political level of the state; the eventual changes at the economic level provided the material possibility of the mass of women taking advantage of their legal independence. The two changes, political and economic, had their impact as a result of their specific combination. In the absence of the political victory the increase in women's wage labour would have been merely additional exploitation. It was only because of the citizenship rights that women were able to use the economic changes to broaden further their sphere of operation.

Capitalism and changes in the form of patriarchy

The main basis of the tension between capitalism and patriarchy is over the exploitation of women's labour. On the one hand, capitalists have interests in the recruitment and exploitation of female labour, which is cheaper than that of men because of patriarchal structures. On the other, there is resistance to this by that patriarchal strategy which seeks to maintain the exploitation of women in the household. The first forms of capitalist industrialization saw the successful recruitment of women (and children) into the cotton textile factories in greater numbers than men. Prolonged patriarchal resistance through political pressure on the state to pass the Factory Acts and by craft unions to bar women entry to specific jobs was not able to do more than stabilize the situation in this industry. In other occupations which entered the capitalist factory later, such as skilled manual engineering work, the men's craft organizations were successful in excluding women. Indeed there was often a strong cross-class patriarchal alliance which supported the exclusion of women, even in the absence of strong male unions. However, this cross-class alliance had weaknesses when it cut across the interests of employers to recruit the cheaper labour of women. Conflict would break out, as it did over the question of women entering the munitions factories during the First World War.

An alternative patriarchal strategy developed of allowing women into paid employment, but segregating them from men and paying them less. Clerical work is a good example of this process, where the male workers' organizations were insufficiently strong to defeat employers' insistent attempts to recruit women. The problem was resolved by a compromise in which the employers ceased trying to substitute women directly for men and instead recruited women for new sub-occupations, which were segregated from those of the men, graded lower and paid less, while maintaining the men in the upper reaches of white-collar work (see Walby, 1986). Whether the exclusionary or the segregation strategy was followed depended upon the balance of capitalist and patriarchal forces in a particular industry in a particular locality. The former was based upon a private form of patriarchy in which women were controlled by excluding them from the public sphere, especially from paid work. The latter was based upon a public form of patriarchy in which women were controlled within all spheres. The power of capital precluded the successful maintenance of the exclusionary mode, except in certain small tight pockets of patriarchal power and resistance. (For insta:·ce, the typesetters were able to sustain this until the last decade, as Cockburn (1983) has shown.) The exclusionary form of patriarchy was also under attack by a large powerful feminist movement from the middle of the nineteenth century to the first quarter of the twentieth.

The development of the economic structures of capitalism was not sufficient by itself to cause the shift from private to public patriarchy. This could only occur in the context of a powerful feminist movement in Britain, and indeed most of the West. Where we find capitalism in the absence of a feminist movement, there is no such change in the form of patriarchy. For instance, in some parts of the contemporary Third World young women have been pulled into wage labour for the capitalist factories of foreigners, yet are still subject to the patriarchal control of their fathers (Jayawardena, 1986; Mies, 1986). Wage labour by itself does not provide freedom from patriarchal control. In the case of Western industrialization first-wave feminism created a different balance of forces.

The tension between capital and patriarchy over the exploitation of women's labour is particularly acute when the dominant patriarchal strategy is the private one, and much less intense when it is the public one. In the latter women's labour is more readily available to capital, because there is less pressure by patriarchal forces for women to be kept domesticated. This is the situation by the second half of the twentieth century. After the Second World War there was an unprecedented increase in women's paid employment in Britain (as discussed in chapter 2). This expansion took place initially under conditions of absolute labour shortage, which strengthened the arguments against the reimposition of pre-war restrictions on the paid work of married women. However, since the 1970s this expansion has continued despite the substantial rise in male unemployment. Women are not used merely as a labour reserve when male labour is already fully utilized. While the employers' demand for labour is a necessary factor behind the increase in women's paid work it is not a sufficient condition. We need also to understand why women's labour is preferred over that of men, and why it suddenly becomes available in the post-war period. The preference for female labour is simple to understand, since women are cheaper to employ at the same level of skill because patriarchal practices depress women's wage rates.

The new availability of women's labour is more difficult to explain, but is to be understood in terms of the shift from private to public patriarchy both within the paid workplace and outside it. The reduction of patriarchal exclusionary practices in the workplace and their replacement by a segregationist strategy is the form of the shift from private to public in the workplace. This was reinforced by changes in legislation affecting and opening up possibilities for women's employment. Outisde the paid workplace the shift from private to public patriarchy loosened women's total commitment to domestic labour, releasing their time for paid work.

The utilization of women in this way had implications for capital labour relations. Employers were able to take advantage both of the size of the pool of available labour and the fact that it was internally differentiated in order to depress the conditions of work. Struggles, such as that over flexibilization, are affected by the fact that labour is divided by gender. The new jobs which have been created in the last two decades have been overwhelmingly, and unsurprisingly, for part-time women workers, who are both available and the cheapest to employ. Gender relations affect capital labour relations.

First-wave feminism

The political level of feminist organization, and a system with which patriarchy was in articulation, capitalism, were vital in this change of direction from private to public patriarchy. First-wave feminism was a large powerful movement which won for women citizenship rights and the formal entry to the public sphere. It can be dated as extending from around 1850 (when the Seneca Falls conference was held in the USA and in Britain employment bureaux were set up by women concerned about the lack of access of middle-class ladies to appropriate employment) to 1930 (women between 21 and 30, and women without any property, became enfranchised in Britain only in 1928). Its continuation in the form of welfare feminism, in alliance with the labour movement, was critical in the development of the welfare state. The expansion of the capitalist economy was important in its dynamic restructuring of jobs and its increasing demand for labour, especially that which was cheaper. This combination was key to the significant expansion of women's paid employment.

First-wave feminism is a significantly underrated political movement; its extent, range and impact is rarely appreciated. Mainstream political, sociological and historical texts are quite simply wrong in characterizing movements for women's emancipation and liberation as small, narrow, of limited duration, and recent. First-wave feminism is frequently thought of as primarily a struggle for the vote; rarely are other issues mentioned, with the occasional exception of the reform enabling married women to own property. Thus the women's movement is described as campaigning on a very narrow range of issues. Further, it is often considered to represent the interests of only a narrow range of women: middle- and upper-class women. This latter view is supported in two ways: by reference to the married women's property acts, which are regarded as of interest only to women with inherited property, and by reference to the apparently middle- and upper-class composition of the movements.

Both these contentions are incorrect: the movement embraced a wide range of demands; it represented the interests of all women, not only those of the middle and upper classes.

First-wave feminism was a large, multi-faceted, long-lived and highly effective political phenomenon. It contained a wide range of political positions and involved a large variety of campaigns. At minimum it may be considered to contain: evangelical feminism, socialist feminism, materialist feminism and radical feminism as well as liberal feminism (Banks, 1981; Hayden, 1981; Liddington and Norris, 1978; Schreiner, 1918; Spender, 1983; Strachey, 1928). Campaigns included not only the famous one for suffrage, but also those for the containment of predatory male sexual behaviour (Christabel Pankhurst's slogan was 'Votes for women, chastity for men'), access to employment, training and education, reform of the legal status of married women so they could own property, for divorce and rights to legal separation at the woman's behest as well as that of the husband (Holcombe, 1983), for the collective rather than private organization of meal preparation, among many others (Gilman, 1966; Hayden, 1981).

The campaigns around the containment of men's sexuality probably best illustrate my claim that the breadth and radicalness of first-wave feminism is neglected. In the last quarter of the nineteenth century feminists argued against the sexual double standard and men's sexual exploitation of women in explicit and controversial ways. The attempt to repeal the Contagious Diseases Act was merely one example. In this case the government, worried about the extent to which venereal disease was incapacitating the strength of its navy, sought to curb it by regulation of female prostitutes. The Acts made it possible for women believed to be common prostitutes by the police to be seized, examined and incarcertated until deemed cured. Feminists such as Josephine Butler vigorously protested at the double standard by which women were to be controlled in order to protect men's health, when they saw men as well as women as responsible for the problem of venereal disease. The Acts were finally repealed after a highly controversial campaign in which Butler was threatened as she tried to address public meetings on the subject. Other feminist campaigns around sexual purity sought to raise the age of consent so as to protect young girls from being forced into prostitution. This was also successful, and the age of consent remains at 16 to the present day (Banks, 1981; Butler, 1896; Walkowitz, 1980).

The actions of feminists in the labour movement are another much neglected area of agitation. Organizations such as the National Federation of Women Workers and the Women's Trade Union League set out to coordinate women workers so as to improve their rates of pay and conditions of employment. Most unions in the nineteenth century refused to admit women so, if they were to be unionized, it had to be in newly created women's unions. Women activists in the trade-union movement are often excluded from designation as part of first-wave feminism by definitional fiat. That is, trade unionist women are a priori categorized as part of the labour movement and not part of the feminist movement. Yet, since they were clearly representing the interests of women as women, this is inappropriate. Such women had to deal both with male workers and employers in order to advance the interests of their members (Andrews, 1918; Drake, 1920; Lewenhak, 1977; Soldon, 1978; Strachey, 1928; Walby, 1986).

Women's domestic labour was another major area of political and theoretical activity among first-wave feminists (Hayden, 1981; Gilman, 1966; Schreiner, 1918), who identified the exploitation of women in the privatized context of the home as a major source of problems. This labour was theorized as work, and as subject to particular forms of exploitation. The barriers to women obtaining work outside the household of a type which would adequately support them, and their children if any, was considered to be a major reason forcing women into marriage as a means of economic survival. The isolated and monotonous nature of the work was seen as a further problem. Initiatives to remedy this varied from cooperatives, in which housework was performed collectively, to the development of hot meals services for profit; that is, they varied as to whether they took on all aspects of domestic labour or merely one, and as to whether this was to be organized cooperatively or for profit.

Access to higher education is one of the few campaigns of first-wave feminism which is sometimes noticed. In this women won the right to attend some universities. This was significant not merely in its own right, but also because it gave women access to those professions for which a university-level training was a prerequisite, such as medicine.

The struggle for suffrage is the only campaign of first-wave feminism which is universally acknowledged, yet even here there are problems in the conventional interpretation. It is customarily described as a battle fought largely by middle-class women around a liberal vocabulary of human rights; that is the campaign is represented as that of middle-class liberal feminists. This is misleading. Working-class women were involved, especially the organized women workers of the Lancashire cotton textile mills (see Liddington and Norris, 1978). While one section of the movement, that of the suffragists, did adhere to a liberal political philosophy, others, such as the militant suffragettes, did not. The latter group had an analysis much more in keeping with that of contemporary radical feminists, seeing society as composed of two main social groupings: men and women. Parliament was described as a male club, and the differences between the two parties was seen as of little significance to women. Militant tactics were designed not to win moderate male support, but both to gain greater female support by exposing what they saw as the charade of chivalry by provoking hostile male reactions, and to force the men into conceding the vote. Tactics such as the coordinated smashing of all the windows in fashionable London shopping streets, burning the slogan 'votes for women' on golf courses by acid, setting fire to pillar boxes, defacing paintings, and hunger strikes when imprisoned do not correspond to most people's conception of liberal actions. This campaign for the vote was not restricted to small groups of women; one of the meetings in Hyde Park was of a quarter of a million people (Pankhurst, 1931; Spender, 1983; Strachey, 1928).

In short, first-wave feminism involved numbers of women much greater than conventional accounts suggest; these women were from a wider range of class backgrounds than is usually proposed; the range of issues and campaigns were much more varied and wide ranging than described. First-wave feminism was not the product of a few middle-class liberal women who wanted the vote and a bit of education; it was a cross-class, multi-faceted, powerful political movement.

The significance of first-wave feminism

Most importantly, for the argument here, first-wave feminism made a major impact on the position of women, and the forms of patriarchy. Women won political citizenship. They won access to higher education, and hence to the professions. They won rights to legal personhood such as the right to sit on juries, to own property, whatever their marital status, and hence to have access to credit. They won the right to leave a marriage, both by legal separation and by divorce.

These are a considerable list of gains, which defeated the patriarchal strategy of restricting women to the private sphere of the home. Women had won access to the public sphere and claims to the rights and privileges of citizenship. They could no longer be legally subsumed to their husbands or fathers.

This is not to argue that women won equality with men. But it is to assert the significance of these victories in the public arenas relating to political citizenship and legal personhood. It is true that many things were still closed to women; the material and political conditions to guarantee full access in many areas were lacking. But, nevertheless, the significance of these gains should not be underestimated. They led women's entry into the public sphere and the change in form of patriarchy from private to public. First-wave feminism caused a change in the form of patriarchy as well as in degree.

While the movement constituted a turning point, the consequences of first-wave feminism took some time to work through. Indeed the direction set at that time has yet, I would suggest, to reach its fullest expression. It is only with women's access both to waged labour and state welfare payments in the post-war period that the possibility of full economic as well as political citizenship is realized. The second moment of the turning point from private to public patriarchy is of critical importance. I shall now discuss the changes for which the winning of political citizenship were vital, before moving onto to a consideration of this second moment.

What is the connection between the first moment of the turning point that I have identified and future developments?

A most important factor is the increasing entry of women into waged labour; this could not have occurred without first-wave feminism. The closure to women of the professions such as law and medicine was overturned by their winning access to the universities during this struggle. While numerically this is not particularly significant, it is in terms of women's collective access to the top jobs, which themselves are significant gatekeepers. Further, the state could no longer be used to back up a patriarchal closure strategy by organized male workers to the same extent after women won the vote. During the nineteenth century a series of Acts of Parliament had sought to regulate women's paid employment. This restricted the best work available to women in terms of pay and hours of work, that in the cotton mills and the mines, rather the worst, such as domestic service and field labour, which paid worse for longer hours (see Walby, 1986). During the First World War male unions had been able to call upon the state to back their demands that 'their' jobs be returned to them after the war if they 'let' women take them for the duration of the hostilities (Braybon, 1981). Yet in the next world war, after women had won the vote, despite the fact that the men attempted to follow the same strategy, it was significantly less successful, with the state much more reluctant to intervene in the aftermath of the war to support the men's demands (Braybon, 1981; Summerfield, 1984). Despite the enormous patriarchal pressure to exclude women (and especially married women) from paid work during the inter-war depression, the national state never passed legislation to enforce this. From the 1950s the state has been backing moves towards equality at paid work for men and women. The first groups of women workers to win equal pay were white-collar government employees (teachers, civil servants, etc.).

I am not trying to argue that the state today is anti-patriarchal; rather, that there was a significant change in its policy from acting to enforce closure in employment against women before they won the vote, in legislation such as the series of Factory Acts and the First World War Munitions Act, to a *laissez-faire* policy in the inter-war period, and then to an active, albeit weak, endorsement of women's rights to employment from the 1950s onwards. Such closure that remains, and it is significant, is enforced principally at a more decentralized level, in the structures which constitute occupational segregation. (See Witz (1987) for an argument that occupational segregation is enforced chiefly at the level of the civil society, not the state.) I would contend that women's winning of political citizenship is crucial to these changes.

A further major change crucially affected by state policy is the ability of women both to leave marriages and to live with their children without a man. First-wave feminism won the right of a woman to leave her husband if she so wanted, and in certain circumstances to oblige him to continue to support her. This was secured not only by means of the revisions to the divorce law, but also in those to legal separation, which brought this right within the financial reach of working-class women who could only afford the procedures of the magistrates courts (Holcombe, 1983; Strachey, 1928). This right has been steadily extended ever since, in particular by the 1969 Divorce Reform Act.

While the legal right to divorce was won by first-wave feminism, it was not until the 1970s that divorce became widespread. This was partly due to the further reforms of the 1969 Act, but most especially because of the availability of economic support for women. It was only at this time that paid employment for women who were married became the majority pattern, and the option of supporting oneself and one's children by paid employment became a real possibility (though this employment is extremely restricted in the case of women with pre-school age children, who are less likely to be in paid work than women with husbands (Cohen and Clark, 1988)). Material independence is also partly a result of state policy in the provision of payments to support a lone mother. She is not obliged to seek the support of relatives or stay with an unwanted partner. In short, first-wave feminism won the right to escape an unwanted husband; it has been steadily extended ever since, both in terms of ever more 'liberal' divorce legislation, and the increasing possibility of material support as a lone woman and lone parent.

I am arguing that the entry of women to the state and political citizenship via the vote was a highly significant factor in changes in gender relations. However, there is a second moment to the change from private to public patriarchy; this is the increased access of women to paid employment which took place after the Second World War and is still occurring.

In 1988 the majority of women are in paid employment, and make up 46 per cent of the paid workforce. Women having children in the 1980s take on average only five years out of the labour market (Martin and Roberts, 1984). Class differences are negligible. Ethnic differences are significant, with women of Afro-Caribbean origin being more likely to be in paid work, Moslem Asian women least likely, and white women in between.

This is significantly different from the peak of the private form of patriarchy in the middle of the nineteenth century, when women of the middle and upper classes were less likely to be in paid work than either the working-class women of that time or the white and Afro-Caribbean women of today. Further, working-class women had restricted access to paid employment, with most of the best jobs barred to them on grounds of sex. For instance, all the skilled manual trades which demanded apprenticeships were closed to them. Among those that remained, the most important form of work, domestic service, entailed forms of control which were mid-way between those of paid work and housework, such as the nearly continuous availability, supervision of 'private' life, living in, and not infrequent sexual demands.

While some branches of paid employment were opened up to women in the decades following first wave feminism most retained the marriage bar. This is a curiously neglected aspect of gender relations in employment. Its consequences for women should not be underestimated. Most married women did not have access to formal paid employment until the removal of the marriage bar during the Second World War, despite demands for this by working women's organizations. The expansion of women's paid employment could then only occur after the marriage bar had been abolished.

Conventionally the growth of women's paid employment is seen, by both Marxists and neo-classical economists, as a result of the expansion of the economy into which women get drawn. That is, the explanatory variable is the capitalist economy or market demand for labour. Some view this as a cyclical phenomenon, others as a long-run one, as was indicated in Chapter 2. The problem with these ungendered accounts is that they are unable to deal with the fact that women are continuing to enter the paid workforce while men are leaving it in the current recession. Simple demand for labour is not a sufficient explanation.

The expansion of women's paid employment has often been considered to be a crucial step on the road to women's emancipation. Engels refers to the significance of the introduction of women to public industry. Young and Willmott (1975) see it as an important factor in the development of the 'symmetrical family'. Bergmann (1986) considers the 'economic emergence' of women as key to their social emergence.

Yet this is controversial. Does the entry of women to paid work merely give them a 'double burden'? The experiences of women in Eastern Europe have sometimes been held up as a warning in this respect; there they are said to have paid work with only minimal reduction of their domestic work and without political or social equality.

I want to argue that the entry to paid work is both a different form of patriarchy and a reduction in its degree.

In summary the changes in gender relations between the two centuries might be described as follows. Women's paid employment has grown significantly since the turn of the century. However, most of this increase did not occur till half a century later, after the Second World War. Marriage has been significantly affected, with one in two ending in divorce, and one-quarter of children being born out of wedlock. Women have some minor representation at the level of the state. There is little evidence of change in the relations around male violence, except a very recent increase in the support given to women whose attackers are strangers. There have been significant changes in sexuality, with less stigmatization of non-marital relations combined with greater pressure to be engaged in some sexual activity. Girls and women have gained greater access to formal education.

There are two types of interpretations of these developments. On the one hand, they may be seen as a decline in the degree of patriarchy. This might be done on a set of indices relating to each of the six areas of gender inequality. On the other, they may be considered as a change in the form, not degree. I want to argue that it is both, but that these two dimensions of change need to be identified separately.

In summary women have found access to the public spheres of contemporary society from which they were previously barred. They have entered paid employment in large numbers. Women are able to leave marriages, and increasing numbers do; one in two of new marriages are predicted to end in divorce. The forms of control are significantly less from a personal patriarch (the husband or father) and increasingly from a collective of public patriarchy. For instance, sexuality is increasingly regulated outside the family, for instance, in the proliferation of pornography.

These changes by themselves might appear to constitute a reduction in the degree of patriarchy. I think they do, but that simultaneously they provoked a change in the form of patriarchy.

With the failure of the exclusionary strategy of private patriarchy we see the development of a new strategy of inclusion, but with new forms of control, with the development of public patriarchy.

One of the strongest arguments that we are seeing a change in form comes from an analysis of sexuality and of household labour. This is an assertion against the conventional view that women gained sexual freedom in the period following the Victorian one. Conventionally we note that women who engage in pre-marital sex are no longer rejected by men seeking brides. Unmarried mothers are no longer quite so badly stigmatized. Contraception is available free and on demand from doctors. Abortion is attainable under certain circumstances. While the AIDS crisis has led to some retrenchment in attitudes, there is little evidence of a change in sexual practices among heterosexuals.

The other argument is that there is now considerable pressure for women to engage in heterosexual sex, in a way unknown to nineteenth-century women. Indeed a school of writers including Coveney et al (1984), Faderman (1981), Sheila Jeffreys (1985) and Millett (1977) have argued that women's oppression through sexuality has intensified in the period after first-wave feminism. This is seen as a patriarchal backlash following the victories of that movement. In the nineteenth century, women were not expected to like or want to engage in sex (Cott, 1978). This approach to sexuality, while to modern eyes restrictive, could in fact be a form of women's resistance, given that it was in a context in which the women were unlikely to derive much sexual satisfaction from their husbands. A legitimate and respectable reason to say no to unwanted sexual intercourse could be to women's benefit. Further, women's supposed asexuality meant that they could maintain close and loving relationships with those for whom they did feel real affection, their female friends, without this being regarded as threatening. Faderman (1981) and Smith-Rosenberg (1975) have drawn convincing pictures of the romantic friendships between women in the nineteenth century and of their often life-long loving and indeed sensual nature. Women friends could spend large amounts of time in each other's company, talking and touching.

These relationships were problematized after 1920 or so by the development and popularization of Freudian and neo-Freudian theories of sexuality for two reasons. Firstly, they led to a way of seeing female romantic friendships as sexual, rather than asexual, and, consequently, as perverted, given the negative view attached to lesbianism. This reduced the possibility of such close bonding between women, unless they were prepared to defy the sanctions against lesbianism. Secondly, the neo-Freudian view gave rise to the notion that to be normal a person had to be heterosexually active. Otherwise the person was considered unfulfilled and liable to neurosis. In particular this fed negative images of older single women as leading distorted lives, resulting in bitter and twisted personalities. Jeffreys (1985) sees this as one of the ways in which first-wave feminism was attacked, since this movement entailed strong bonding between women, without men. The growth of such new notions of proper sexual conduct occurs immediately after the successes of first-wave feminism. Millett, Faderman and Jeffreys all consider the new discourse on sexuality to be part of a patriarchal backlash, indeed in Millett's terms a sexual counter-revolution. Millett analyses this new sexual ideology via the novels of writers otherwise considered progressive – D. H. Lawrence, Henry Miller and Norman Mailer. She exposes their eulogies to increased sexual activity as a new form of domination over women, using their own words to capture this. After the victories of first-wave feminism the imperative on women to engage in sex with men was a new way of ensuring women's subordination to men. The weapon was in the new theories of sexuality which marked as perverted women who were not heterosexually active.

These radical feminist writers have focused upon new forms of pressure on women to engage in sexual relations with men. There are further new forms of control through sexuality. While sex was supposed to take place only inside marriage there were restrictions on the public portrayal of sexuality. The gradual removal of these restrictions has opened the way to such things as the widespread availability of pornography. Degrading images of women as objects of male desire are to be found not only in hard-core pornography but are the staple of many forms of advertising. The main site of control over women through sexuality has shifted away from the individual husband or father in the home to more diffuse patriarchal practices in the public sphere.

However, it is important not to push these arguments too far. There clearly were benefits to women in not being hounded if they bore illegitimate children, in being able to have sex with a man to whom they were not married without the dire consequences which might have befallen them in the nineteenth century. Wilson (1983a) and Gordon and Dubois (1983) warn of the traps of glorying in the purity concerns of the nineteenth century women, preferring to risk the 'danger of the battlefield' of sexuality. Nevertheless, the point is that the new discourse on sexuality introduces new forms of regulation of women, as well as removing others.

Changes in household structure and composition form a further area of change indicating a shift in the form of patriarchy as well as one of degree. The ability of women to leave unwanted marriages has so far been presented as a diminution in the degree of patriarchal control. However, it should also be considered as part of a change in the form of patriarchy. While in female-headed households women escape the duties of serving their husbands, they also lose access to the income such a man might have brought. Women without men usually live in poverty. Lone mothers with pre-school children are likely to live on social security payments. Even when in employment many women will not earn much more than a poverty-level wage if they have children. Women typically have custody of children after divorce and in practice look after them during separation. The absence of a husband does not mean that women are freed from the work, responsibilities and cost of child care. They still produce the next generation. While they lose their own individual patriarch, they do not lose their subordination to other patriarchal structures and practices. Indeed they become even more exposed to certain of the more diffused public sets of patriarchal practices. Their income level and standard of living are no longer determined primarily by that of their husband, but instead either by the patriarchal state, if they are dependent upon welfare benefits, or the patriarchally structured labour market. It is the anonymous state and market rather than her private patriarch which determines the life of the lone mother. She substitutes public for private patriarchy.

The focus of this book has been on gender relations, and in particular on understanding changes in these during the twentieth century. I have argued that they cannot be understood outside an analysis of patriarchy, capitalism and racism. The other side of this claim is that the form of class relations cannot be appreciated outside an analysis of patriarchy, and that changes in capitalism cannot be explained without an examination of its intersection with changing patriarchal relations. While the elucidation of changes in capitalism is not central to my theory, it is pertinent to indicate some of the implications of my argument about changing forms of patriarchy for changes in capitalism.

Most writers on changes in capitalism do not consider gender as a determinant variable, treating it as either a constant, or derivative from capitalism, or exogenous and trivial. I shall examine some recent accounts of the 'new times' of capitalism to illustrate this claim, and go on to show that their failure to take gender seriously flaws their argument about the causes of these changes.

The 'new times' writers have maintained variously that capitalism has changed from being organized to disorganized (Lash and Urry, 1987; Offe, 1985); from mass production to flexible specialization (Piore and Sable, 1984); from Fordist to post-Fordist (Murray, 1988). Further, they assert that the labour process has become flexibilized (NEDO, 1986); labour markets become more segmented (Edwards, R., 1979); that there has been a decline in the degree of homogeneity of the working class and working-class organizations (Lash and Urry, 1987); that the main focus of politics has changed from production to consumption (Castells, 1978, 1983); and that culture has changed from modernist to postmodernist (Lyotard, 1978). These have been grouped together to form a composite 'new times' (*Marxism Today*, October 1988). While there are significant differences between the above writers on a number of issues, they do share some important themes. They agree that there has been a disintegration of the mid-twentieth-century bargain between capital and labour which it is considered was the origin of the welfare state. They share a belief in an increasing complexity in political and cultural cleavages, and a movement away from the politics of the capital–labour struggle over production being the most important political conflict.

These writers are ambiguous as to whether 'capitalist' captures the full range of social relations, but in the absence of any serious exploration of others they can be considered to equate them. Gender is absent from many of the accounts, apart from the occasional footnote, though in a few the arrival of women, in the 'feminization of the workforce', is seen to herald the breakup of the corporatist bargain.

This 'feminization' is rarely explained, but appears as a historical contingency. I would argue that the changing gender composition of the workforce is too important both in itself and for its implications for the relations between capital and labour to be treated in so trivial a manner. The increase in the employment of women is important for the changes in capitalism. In particular, flexibility is centrally about a gendered workforce, Women workers make up the largest group of the numerically flexible workforce, since part-time workers are the biggest category of workers not on permanent, direct, full-time contracts (Hakim, 1987; Walby, 1989). It is not possible to explain the phenomenon of flexibility without understanding the changes in gender relations which make women available to be utilized in this way in paid employment. Women have not always been available as part-time workers. Flexibility is not only about the capital–labour relation, but also about the change from private to public forms of patriarchy. Women are constituted as more vulnerable only because the patriarchal strategies followed by many sections of the labour movements have left women part-time workers outside the protection which full-time workers won. (Part-time workers do not have many of the legal protections against unfair dismissal, nor many fringe benefits, such as employer-paid national insurance contributions – see chapter 2.) The bargain that 'labour' struck with capital was only a sectional bargain reflecting a patriarchal hegemony in the labour movement. The entry of women into paid employment in larger numbers can be understood only in terms of the wider changes in gender relations, from private to public patriarchy.

A further point about the 'new times' thesis is that it presumes that the welfare state was created as a result of a corporatist bargain between capital and labour. It is assumed either that labour was ungendered, or that it was led by men on behalf of all labour. However, as I have argued in chapter 7, this account of the development of the welfare state is wrong, since feminists were a significant part of the political struggle out of which the welfare state was won. Women had their own institutions and organizations which had a tactical alliance with those of the labour movement in the campaigns for the extension of welfare institutions. During the years 1918–68 women were partially incorporated as a political force. By 1928 they had won the right to a formal voice in the state, and were successful in many campaigns at state level during this period in which feminism is popularly believed to have died. That is, I am arguing that women constitute a major political force and that changes in the welfare state cannot be understood without an understanding of their struggles as well as those of capital and labour.

The major changes in social relations which the 'new times' writers are attempting to capture with new distinctions between forms of capitalism are more significantly gendered than these writers allow for. That there are new forms of social relations is not in doubt, but these are new forms of patriarchy as much as new forms of capitalism.

CONCLUSION

Patriarchy comes in more than one form; each form can be found to different degrees. British history over the last century or so has seen a shift to a more intense form of private patriarchy and then a dramatic reversal of this with a move towards public patriarchy. This latter shift was a result of the successes of first-wave feminism against the background of an expanding capitalist erconomy. It took its form in the context of the international economy, and various specific forms in different ethnic groups. The British form of public patriarchy involves the market as well as the state, while there is a different sub-type of public patriarchy in Eastern Europe in which the state plays a more central part in comparison with the market.

The major historical changes are different for gender relations from those of capitalist class relations. Gender and class have independent historical dynamics, although of course they do have effects upon each other. The rise of capitalism transformed class relations, changing the very classes which constituted society. This historical shift did not have such dramatic effects upon gender relations: men remained the dominant gender; all six patriarchal structures continued across this period; only a minor shift in the relative significance of public and private sites of patriarchy occurred. The trajectory towards an intensified private form of patriarchy, which can be identified as far back as the seventeenth century (Charles and Duffin, 1985; Clark, 1919), accelerated.

Gender relations are not static, and a developed concept of patriarchy is the best way of theorizing the changes. The idea of patriarchy does not necessarily give rise to fixed, ahistoric analysis.

Women are not passive victims of oppressive structures. They have struggled to change both their immediate circumstances and the wider social structures. First-wave feminism is a much more important historical force than is usually considered. This major feminist push changed the course of history. However, it did not lead to an elimination of all the forms of inequality between men and women which it sought to eradicate. In some ways early feminists won their goals, and their successes were considerable. However, in response, patriarchy changed in form, incorporating some of the hard-won changes into new traps for women.

The form of patriarchy in contemporary Britain is public rather than private. Women are no longer restricted to the domestic hearth, but have the whole society in which to roam and be exploited.

NOTES

1 Earlier versions of some portions of this chapter may be found in *Women's Studies International Forum* (1989) and Helen Corr and Lynn Jamieson (eds.) (1989) *The Politics of Everyday Life* (London: Macmillan).
2 See for instance, the analysis of fathering by Ehrenreich and by Carol Brown, 1981.
3 I am conscious of some parallels with the writing of Engels on the history of the family, in which he argued that the overthrow of matriarchy and its replacement by patriarchy was as a result of the expansion in significance of the male sphere of production, in particular of its growth in productivity, while the female sphere of reproduction did not undergo a parallel growth. It was this shift in the balance of the two material spheres of society, one the base of women, the other of men, which led to the development of the power of men over women. My main differences with Engels are, firstly, in considering the earlier period to be one of matriarchy, and, secondly, that I have not allocated women a sphere so biologistically defined as that of 'reproduction'. Other smaller differences are that I have suggested that women's material power base actually contracted, not merely stood still, and a slightly different account of the way that men's material sphere expanded. The element I have kept is that of the fluctuating balance of power between men and women as a result of changes in the material sites in which they labour.

Bibliography

Abercrombie, Nicholas, Hill, Stephen and Turner, Bryan (1988), *The Dominant Ideology Thesis* (London: Allen and Unwin).

Abercrombie, Nicholas and Urry, John (1983), *Capital, Labour and the Middle Classes* (London: Allen and Unwin).

Abercrombie, Nicholas, Warde, Alan, Soothill, Keith, Urry, John, and Walby, Sylvia (1988), *Contemporary British Society: a new introduction to sociology* (Cambridge: Polity).

Acker, Joan (1973), 'Women and stratification: a case of intellectual sexism', in *Changing Women in a Changing Society*, ed. Joan Huber (Chicago: University of Chicago Press), pp. 174–83.

—— (1980), 'Women and stratification: a review of recent literature', *Contemporary Sociology*, 9, January, pp. 25–39.

Adams, Parveen (1979), 'A note on sexual divisions and sexual differences', *m/f*, 3, pp. 51–9.

Adams, Parveen, Coward, Rosalind, and Cowie, Elizabeth (1978), 'm/f', *m/f*, 1, pp. 3–5.

Adams, Parveen and Minson, Jeff (1978), 'The "subject" of feminism', *m/f*, 2, pp. 43–61.

Adler, Zsuzsanna (1987), *Rape on Trial* (London: Routledge).

Alcoff, Linda (1988), 'Cultural feminism versus post-structuralism: the identity crisis in feminist theory', *Signs*, 13, 3, pp. 405–36.

Allen, Sheila (1982), 'Gender inequality and class formation', in *Social Class and the Division of Labour: essays in honour of Ilya Neustadt*, ed. Anthony Giddens and Gavin Mackenzie (Cambridge: Cambridge University Press).

Althusser, Louis (1971), *Lenin and Philosophy and Other Essays* (London: New Left Books).

Amir, Menachem (1971), *Patterns in Forcible Rape* (Chicago: Chicago University Press).

Amos, Valerie and Parmar, Pratibha (1984), 'Challenging Imperial Feminism', *Feminist Review*, 17, pp. 3–20.

Anderson, Michael (1971), *Family Structure in Nineteenth Century Lancashire* (Cambridge: Cambridge University Press).

Andrews, Irene Osgood (1918), *Economic Effects of the War Upon Women and Children in Great Britain* (New York: Oxford University Press).

Arditti, Rita, Duelli Klein, Renate and Minden, Shelley (1984), *Test-Tube Women: what future for motherhood?* (London: Pandora).

Bagguley, Paul (1989), *Organising the Unemployed: politics, ideology and the experience of unemployment*, Unpublished PhD thesis, University of Sussex.

Bagguley, Paul and Walby, Sylvia (1988), *Women and Local Labour Markets: a comparative analysis of five localities*, Lancaster Regionalism Group Working Paper, University of Lancaster.

Banks, Olive (1981), *Faces of Feminism: a study of feminism as a social movement* (Oxford: Martin Robertson).

Barker, D. Leonard (1976), 'The regulation of marriage', in *Power and the State*, ed. Gary Littlejohn, Barry Smart, John Wakeford and Nira Yuval-Davis (London: Croom Helm).

Barrett, Michele (1980), *Women's Oppression Today: problems in Marxist feminist analysis* (London: Verso).

—— (1987), 'The concept of difference', *Feminist Review*, 26, summer, pp. 29–41.

Barrett, Michele and Coward, Rosalind (1982), 'Letter', *m/f*, 7, pp. 87–9.

Barrett, Michele and McIntosh, Mary (1979), 'Towards a materialist feminism?', *Feminist Review*, 1.

—— (1980), 'The "Family Wage": some problems for feminists and socialists', *Capital and Class*, 11, summer, pp. 51–72.

—— (1982), *The Anti-Social Family* (London: Verso).

—— (1985), 'Ethnocentrism and socialist-feminist theory', *Feminist Review*, 20, summer, pp. 23–48.

Bart, Pauline and O'Brien, Patricia (1986), *Stopping Rape: Successful Survival Strategies* (Oxford: Pergamon).

Becker, Gary (1965), 'A theory of the allocation of time', *The Economic Journal*, September, pp. 493–517.

Beechey, Veronica (1977), 'Some notes on female wage labour in capitalist production', *Capital and Class*, 3, autumn, pp. 45–66.

—— (1978), 'Women and production: a critical analysis of some sociological theories of women's work', in *Feminism and Materialism: women and modes of production*, ed. Annette Kuhn and AnnMarie Wolpe (London: Routledge).

Beechey, Veronica and Perkins, Tessa (1987), *A Matter of Hours: women, part-time work and the labour market* (Cambridge: Polity).

Belotti, Elena Gianini (1975), *Little Girls* (London: Writers and Readers Publication Cooperative).

Beneria, Lourdes and Sen, Gita (1986), 'Accumulation, reproduction and women's role in economic development: Boserup revisited', in *Women's Work: development and the division of labor by gender*, ed. Eleanor Leacock and Helen I. Safa (South Hadley, Mass.: Begin and Garvey).

Bergmann, Barbara R. (1980a), 'Occupational segregation, wages and profits when employers discriminate by race or sex', in *The Economics of Women and Work*, ed. Alice H. Amsden (Harmondsworth: Penguin).

—— (1980b), 'Curing high unemployment rates among blacks and women', in Amsden (op. cit.).

—— (1986), *The Economic Emergence of Women* (New York: Basic Books).

Bernardes, Jon (1986), 'In search of "the family" – analysis of the 1981 United Kingdom Census: a research note', *Sociological Review*, 34, 4, pp. 828–36.

Beteille, Andre (1977), *Inequality Among Men* (Oxford: Blackwell).

Bhaskar, Roy (1979), *The Possibility of Naturalism* (Brighton: Harvester).

Binney, Va, Harkell, Gina, and Nixon, Judy (1981), *Leaving Violent Men: a study of refuges and housing for battered women* (London: Women's Aid Federation, England).

Blackaby, F. (ed.) (1978), *De-Industrialisation* (London: Heinemann).

Blackburn, R. M. and Mann, Michael (1979), *The Working Class in the Labour Market* (London: Macmillan).

Blumer, H. (1969), *Symbolic Interactionism* (Englewood Cliffs, NJ: Prentice Hall).

Bose, Catherine (1979), 'Technology and changes in the division of labour in the American home', *Women's Studies International Quarterly*, 2, pp. 295–304.

Boserup, Ester (1970), *Woman's Role in Economic Development* (London: Allen and Unwin).

Bowers, J. (1970), *The Anatomy of Regional Activity Rates*, National Institute of Economic and Social Research, Regional Papers 1 (Cambridge: Cambridge University Press).

Braverman, Harry (1974), *Labor and Monopoly Capital: the degradation of work in the twentieth century* (New York: Monthly Review Press).

Braybon, Gail (1981), *Women Workers in the First World War: the British experience* (London: Croom Helm).

Brittan, Arthur and Maynard, Mary (1984), *Sexism, Racism and Oppression* (Oxford: Blackwell).

Britten, Nicky and Heath, Anthony (1983), 'Women, men and social class', in *Gender, Class and Work*, ed. Eva Gamarnikov, David Morgan, June Purvis and Daphne Taylorson (London: Heinemann).

Brod, Harry (ed.) (1987), *The Making of Masculinities: the new men's studies* (Boston: Allen and Unwin).

Brown, Beverley and Adams, Parveen (1979), 'The feminine body and feminist politics', *m/f*, 3, pp. 35–50.

Brown, Carol (1981), 'Mothers, fathers, and children: from private to public patriarchy', in *Women and Revolution: the unhappy marriage of Marxism and feminism*, ed. Lydia Sargent (London: Pluto Press).

Brown, Colin (1984), *Black and White Britain: the third PSI survey* (London: Heinemann).

Brownmiller, Susan (1976), *Against Our Will: men, women and rape* (Harmondsworth: Penguin).

Bruegel, Irene (1979), 'Women as a reserve army of labour: a note on recent British experience', *Feminist Review*, 3, pp. 12–23.

—— (1988), 'Sex and race in the labour market', Paper presented to Socialist Feminist Forum, London.

Burniston, Steve, Mort, Frank, and Weedon, Chris (1978), 'Psycho-analysis and the cultural acquisition of sexuality and subjectivity', in Women's Studies

Group, Birmingham Centre for Contemporary Cultural Studies, *Women Take Issue: aspects of women's subordination* (London: Hutchinson).

Burstyn, Varda (1983), 'Masculine dominance and the state', *Socialist Register*, pp. 45–89.

Butler, Josephine (1896), *Personal Reminiscences of a Great Crusade* (London: Horace Marshall and Son).

Cameron, Deborah (1985), *Feminism and Linguistic Theory* (London: Macmillan).

Campbell, Anne (1984), *The Girls in the Gang* (Oxford: Balckwell).

Campbell, Bea and Charlton, Valerie (1978), 'Work to rule', *Red Rag*, 14, November.

Campbell, Beatrix (1987), *The Iron Ladies: why do women vote Tory?* (London: Virago).

—— (1988), *Unofficial Secrets: child sexual abuse – the Cleveland case* (London: Virago).

Carby, Hazel (1982), 'White woman listen! Black feminism and the boundaries of sisterhood', in Centre for Contemporary Cultural Studies, University of Birmingham, *The Empire Strikes Back: race and racism in '70s Britain* (London: Hutchinson).

Castells, Manuel (1978), *City, Class and Power* (London: Macmillan).

—— (1983), *The City and the Grass Roots: a cross-cultural theory of urban social movements* (London: Edward Arnold).

Centre for Contemporary Cultural Studies, University of Birmingham (1982), *The Empire Strikes Back: race and racism in '70s Britain* (London: Hutchinson).

Chambers, Gerry and Millar, Ann (1983), *Investigating Sexual Assault*, A Scottish Office Social Research Study, Scottish Office Central Research Unit (Edinburgh: HMSO).

Charles, Lindsey and Duffin, Lorna (eds.) (1985), *Women and Work in Pre-Industrial England* (London: Croom Helm).

Chodorow, Nancy (1978), *The Reproduction of Mothering: psychoanalysis and the sociology of gender* (Berkeley, University of California Press).

Cixous, Helene (1981), 'Sorties' (from *La Jeune Née*), in *New French Feminisms*, ed. Elaine Marks and Isabelle de Courtivron (Brighton: Harvester), pp. 90–8.

Clark, Alice (1919), *Working Life of Women in the Seventeenth Century* (London: Routledge and Kegan Paul; reprinted 1982).

Cockburn, Cynthia (1983), *Brothers: male dominance and technological change* (London: Pluto Press).

—— (1985), *Machinery of Dominance: women, men and technical know-how* (London: Pluto).

Cohen, Bronwen and Clark, Karen (1988), 'Maternity issues', Paper presented to Women's Studies Open Seminar, University of Lancaster.

Comer, Lee (1974), *Wedlocked Women* (London: Feminist Press).

Connell, R. W. (1987), *Gender and Power: society, the person and sexual politics* (Cambridge: Polity Press).

Corcoran, Mary and Duncan, Gregory J. (1979), 'Work history, labor force attachment, and earnings differences between the races and sexes', *Journal of Human Resources*, 14, winter, pp. 3–20.

Corea, Gena (1985), *The Mother Machine: reproductive technologies from artificial insemination to artificial wombs* (New York: Harper and Row).

Cott, Nancy (1978), 'Passionless: an interpretation of Victorian sexual ideology, 1790–1850', *Signs*, 4, 2, pp. 219–36.

Coulson, Margaret, Magas, Branka, and Wainwright, Hilary (1975), '"The housewife and her labour under capitalism" – a critique', *New Left Review*, 89, pp. 59–71.

Coveney, Lal, Jackson, Margaret, Jeffreys, Sheila, Kay, Lesley and Mahoney, Pat (1984), *The Sexuality Papers: male sexuality and the social control of women* (London: Hutchinson).

Cowan, Ruth Schwartz (1983), *More Work for Mother: the ironies of household technology from the open hearth to the microwave* (New York: Basic Books).

Coward, Rosalind (1978), 'Sexual liberation and the family', *m/f*, 1, pp. 7–24.

—— (1982), 'Sexual violence and sexuality', *Feminist Review*, 11.

—— (1984), *Female Desire* (London: Granada).

Cowie, Elizabeth (1978), '"Woman as Sign"', *m/f*, 1, pp. 49–64.

Criminal Statistics, England and Wales, 1987 (1988), Home Office (London: HMSO).

Currell, Melville E. (1974), *Political Woman* (London: Croom Helm).

Daly, Mary (1973), *Beyond God the Father: toward a philosophy of women's liberation* (Boston: Beacon).

—— (1978), *Gyn/Ecology: the metaethics of radical feminism* (London: Women's Press).

—— (1984), *Pure Lust: elemental feminist philosophy* (London: Women's Press).

—— (1985), *The Church and the Second Sex* (Boston: Beacon).

Davidoff, Leonore (1973), *The Best Circles: society, etiquette and the season* (London: Croom Helm).

Davidoff, Leonore and Hall, Catherine (1987), *Family Fortunes: men and women of the English middle class 1780–1850* (London: Hutchinson).

Davies, M. (1975), 'Woman's place is at the typewriter: the feminisation of the clerical labor force', in *Labor Market Segmentation*, ed. R. C. Edwards, M. Reich and D. M. Gordon (Lexington, Mass.: Lexington Books).

Davis, Angela (1981), *Women, Race and Class* (London: Women's Press).

Deem, Rosemary (1978), *Women and Schooling* (London: Routledge).

—— (1980), *Schooling for Women's Work* (London: Routledge).

Delmar, Rosalind (1976), 'Looking again at Engels' "Origin of the Family, Private Property and the State"', in *The Rights and Wrongs of Women*, ed. Juliet Mitchell and Ann Oakley (Harmondsworth: Penguin).

Delphy, Christine (1984), *Close to Home: a materialist analysis of women's oppression* (London: Hutchinson).

Derrida, Jacques (1976), *Of Grammatology* (Baltimore: John Hopkins University Press).

Dex, Shirley (1983), 'The second generation: West Indian female school leavers', in *One Way Ticket: migration and female labour*, ed. Annie Phizacklea (London: Routledge).

Donnison, Jean (1977), *Midwives and Medical Men: a history of inter-professional rivalries and women's rights* (London: Heinemann).

Drake, Barbara (1920), *Women in Trade Unions* (London: Labour Research Department and Allen and Unwin; reprinted 1984, Virago).

Durkheim, Emile (1952), *Suicide: a study in sociology* (London: Routledge).

Dworkin, Andrea (1981), *Pornography: men possessing women* (London: Women's Press).

—— (1983), *Right Wing Women: the politics of domesticated females* (London: Women's Press).

Edwards, Anne (1987), 'Male violence in feminist theory: an analysis of the changing conceptions of sex/gender violence and male dominance', in *Women, Violence and Social Control*, ed. Jalna Hanmer and Mary Maynard (London: Macmillan), pp. 13–29.

Edwards, Richard (1979), *Contested Terrain: the transformation of the workplace in the twentieth century* (London: Heinemann).

Edwards, Richard C., Gordon, David M. and Reich, Michael (1975), *Labour Market Segmentation* (Lexington, Mass.: Lexington Books).

Ehrenreich, Barbara (1983), *The Hearts of Men: American dreams and the flight from commitment* (London: Pluto).

Ehrenreich, Barbara and English, Deidre (1979), *For Her Own Good: 150 years of the experts' advice to women* (London: Pluto).

Eisenhower, Milton S. (1969), *To Establish Justice, To Ensure Domestic Tranquillity*, Final Report of the National Commission of the Causes and Prevention of Violence (Washington, DC: Government Printing Office).

Eisenstein, Hester (1984), *Contemporary Feminist Thought* (London: Unwin).

Eisenstein, Hester and Jardine, Alice (eds.) (1980), *The Future of Difference* (Boston: G. K. Hall).

Eisenstein, Zillah R. (1979), 'Developing a theory of capitalist patriarchy and socialist feminism', in *Capitalist Patriarchy*, ed. Zillah R. Eisenstein (New York: Monthly Review Press).

—— (1981), *The Radical Future of Liberal Feminism* (New York: Longman).

—— (1984), *Feminism and Sexual Equality: crisis in liberal America* (New York: Monthly Review Press).

Elger, Anthony (1979), 'Valorisation and deskilling – a critique of Braverman', *Capital and Class*, 7, spring, pp. 58–99.

Ellis, Valerie (1981), *The Role of Trade Unions in the Promotion of Equal Opportunities* (London: Equal Opportunities Commission/Social Science Research Council).

Elson, Diane and Pearson, Ruth (1981), '"Nimble fingers make cheap workers": an analysis of women's employment in third world export manufacturing', *Feminist Review*, 7, pp. 87–107.

Engels, Frederick (1940), *The Origin of the Family, Private Property and the State* (London: Lawrence and Wishart).

England, Paula (1982), 'The failure of human capital theory to explain occupa-

tional sex segregation', *Journal of Human Resources*, 17, summer, pp. 358–70.
—— (1984), 'Wage appreciation and depreciation: a test of neoclassical economic explanations of occupational sex segregation', *Social Forces*, 62, pp. 726–49.
Enloe, Cynthia (1983), *Does Khaki Become You? the militarisation of women's lives* (London: Pluto Press).
Equal Opportunities Commission (1979), *Health and Safety Legislation* (Manchester: EOC).
—— (1987), *Women and Men in Britain: a statistical profile, 1986* (Manchester: EOC).
—— (1988a), *Twelfth Annual Report 1987* (London: HMSO).
—— (1988b), *Women and Men in Britain: a research profile* (London: HMSO).
Epstein, Cynthia Fuchs (1970), *Woman's Place: options and limits in professional careers* (Berkeley: University of California Press).
Faderman, Lillian (1981), *Surpassing the Love of Men: romantic friendship and love between women from the renaissance to the present* (London: Junction Books).
Fairbairns, Z. (1979), 'The cohabitation rule', *Women's Studies International Quarterly*, 2, 3, pp. 319–27.
Fasteau, Marc Feigen (1975), *The Male Machine* (New York: Delta).
Feild, Hubert S. and Bienen, Leigh B. (1980), *Jurors and Rape: a study in psychology and law* (Lexington, Mass.: Lexington Books).
Ferguson, Ann, Zita, Jacquelyn and Addelson, Kathryn (1981), 'On "Compulsory heterosexuality and lesbian existence": defining the issues', *Signs*, 7, 1, pp. 158–99.
Fevre, Ralph (1984), *Cheap Labour and Racial Discrimination* (Aldershot: Gower).
Finch, Janet and Groves, Dulcie (eds.) (1983), *A Labour of Love: women, work and caring* (London: Routledge).
Firestone, Shulamith (1974), *The Dialectic of Sex: the case for feminist revolution* (New York: Morrow).
Flax, Jane (1987), 'Postmodernism and gender relations in feminist theory', *Signs*, 12, 4, pp. 621–43.
Fothergill, S. and Gudgin, G. (1982), *Unequal Growth: urban and regional employment change in the UK* (London: Heinemann).
Foucault, Michel (1971), *Madness and Civilisation: a history of insanity in the age of reason* (London: Tavistock).
—— (1979), *Discipline and Punish: the birth of the prison* (Harmondsworth: Penguin).
—— (1981), *The History of Sexuality*, vol. 1: *An Introduction* (Harmondsworth: Pelican).
—— (1987), *The History of Sexuality*, vol. 2: *The Use of Pleasure* (Harmondsworth: Penguin).
Frank, A. Gunder (1967), *Capitalism and Underdevelopment in Latin America* (New York: Monthly Review Press).
Fraser, Nancy and Nicolson, Linda (1988), 'Social criticism without philosophy:

an encounter between feminism and post-modernism', *Theory, Culture and Society*, 5, pp. 373–94.

Freud, Sigmund (1977), *On Sexuality* (Harmondsworth: Penguin).

Friedan, Betty (1965), *The Feminine Mystique* (Harmondsworth: Penguin).

Friedman, Andy (1977), 'Responsible autonomy vesus direct control over the labour process', *Capital and Class*, 1, pp. 43–57.

Froebel, Folker, Heinreichs, Jurgen and Kreye, Otto (1980), *The New International Division of Labour: structural unemployment in industrialised countries and industrialisation in developing countries* (Cambridge: Cambridge University Press).

Gagnon, John and Simon, William (1973), *Sexual Conduct: the social sources of human sexuality* (Chicago: Aldine).

Gamble, Andrew (1988), *The Free Economy and the Strong State: the politics of Thatcherism* (London: Macmillan).

Gardiner, Jean (1975), 'Women's domestic labour', *New Left Review*, 89, pp. 47–58.

Garnsey, Elizabeth (1978), 'Women's work and theories of class stratification', *Sociology*, 17, pp. 223–43.

Gayford, Jasper (1975), 'Wife battering: a preliminary survey of 100 cases', *British Medical Journal*, 25, January.

Gelles, Richard J. (1972), *The Violent Home* (Beverly Hills, Calif.: Sage).

Gershuny, Jay I. (1983a), *Social Innovation and the Division of Labour* (Oxford: Oxford University Press).

Gershuny, Jonathan (1983b), 'Technical change and "social limits"', in *Dilemmas of Liberal Democracies: studies in Fred Hirsch's "Social Limits to Growth"*, ed. Adrian Ellis and Krishan Kumar (London: Tavistock).

Gershuny, Jonathan, Miles, I., Jones, S., Mullings, C., Thomas, G. and Wyatt, S. (1986), 'Time budgets: preliminary analyses of a national survey', *Quarterly Journal of Social Affairs*, 2, 1, pp. 13–39.

Giddens, Anthony (1981), *A Contemporary Critique of Historical Materialism*, vol. 1: *Power, Property and the State* (London: Macmillan).

—— (1984), *The Constitution of Society: outline of the theory of structuration* (Cambridge: Polity).

—— (1985), *A Contemporary Critique of Historical Materialism*, vol. 2: *The Nation State and Violence* (Cambridge, Polity).

Gilman, Charlotte Perkins (1966), *Women and Economics: a study of the economic relation between men and women as a factor in social evolution* (New York: Harper Torchbooks).

Gilroy, Paul (1987), *There Ain't No Black in the Union Jack: the cultural politics of race and nation* (London: Hutchinson).

Gittins, Diane (1982), *Fair Sex* (London: Hutchinson).

Goldthorpe, John (in collaboration with Catriona Llewellyn and Clive Payne) (1980), *Social Mobility and Class Structure in Modern Britain* (Oxford: Clarendon Press).

—— (1983), 'Women and class analysis: a defence of the traditional view', *Sociology*, 17, pp. 465–88.

Goode, William J. (1963), *World Revolution and Family Patterns* (Glencoe: Free Press).

Gordon, David M. (1972), *Theories of Poverty and Underemployment: orthodox, radical and dual labour market perspectives* (Lexington, Mass.: Lexington Books).

—— (1988), 'The global economy: new edifice or crumbling foundations', *New Left Review*, 168, pp. 24–64.

Gordon, Linda (1977), *Woman's Body Woman's Right* (New York: Penguin).

—— (1979), 'The struggle for reproductive freedom', in *Capitalist Patriarchy*, ed. Zillah R. Eisenstein (New York: Monthly Review Press).

Gordon, Linda and Dubois, Ellen (1983), 'Seeking ecstasy on the battlefield: danger and pleasure in nineteenth century feminist sexual thought', *Feminist Review*, 13, spring, pp. 42–55.

Gramsci, Antonio (1971), *Selections from the Prison Notebooks*, ed. and trans. Quinton Hoare and Geoffrey Nowell Smith (London: Lawrence and Wishart).

Greenwood, Victoria and Young, Jock (1976), *Abortion in Demand* (London: Pluto).

Gregory, Jeanne (1982), 'Equal pay and sex discrimination: why women are giving up the fight', *Feminist Review*, 10, pp. 75–90.

—— (1987), *Sex, Race and Law: legislating for equality* (London: Sage).

Grimshaw, Jean (1988), ' "Pure Lust": the elemental feminist philosophy of Mary Daly', *Radical Philosophy*, 49, summer, pp. 24–30.

Gubrium, Jaber F. (1988), 'The family as project', *Sociological Review*, 36, 2, pp. 273–96.

Guillaumin, Colette (1981), 'The practice and power of belief in nature, part I: the appropriation of women', *Feminist Issues*, 1, 2, pp. 3–28.

Hadjifotiou, Nathalie (1983), *Women and Harassment at Work* (London: Pluto).

Hakim, Catherine (1979), *Occupational Segregation: a comparative study of the degree and pattern of the differentiation between men and women's work in Britain, the US and other countries*, Department of Employment Research Paper (London: Department of Employment).

—— (1980), 'Census reports as documentary evidence: the census commentaries 1801–1951', *Sociological Review*, 28, 3, pp. 551–80.

—— (1981), 'Job segregation trends in the 1970s', *Employment Gazette*, December, pp. 521–9.

—— (1987), 'Trends in the flexible workforce', *Employment Gazette*, 95, pp. 549–60.

Hamilton, Cicely (1909), *Marriage as a Trade* (reprinted 1981, London: Women's Press).

Hanmer, Jalna (1978), 'Violence and the social control of women', in *Power and the State*, ed. Gary Littlejohn, Barry Smart, John Wakeford and Nina Yuval-Davis (London: Croom Helm).

Hanmer, Jalna and Saunders, Sheila (1984), *Well-founded Fear: a community study of violence to women* (London: Hutchinson).

Harding, Sandra (1986), *The Science Question in Feminism* (Ithaca: Cornell University Press).

Harrison, Brian (1978), *Separate Spheres: the opposition to women's suffrage in Britain* (London: Croom Helm).

Hartmann, Heidi I. (1979), 'Capitalism, patriarchy and job segregation by sex', in *Capitalist Patriarchy*, ed. Zillah R. Eisenstein (New York: Monthly Review Press).

—— (1981a), 'The family as the locus of gender, class and political struggle: the example of housework', *Signs*, 6, 3, pp. 366–94.

—— (1981b), 'The unhappy marriage of Marxism and Feminism: towards a more progressive union', in *Women and Revolution*, ed. Lydia Sargent (London: Pluto Press).

Haskey, J. (1984), 'Social class and socio-economic differentials in divorce in England and Wales', *Population Studies*, 38, pp. 419–38.

Hay, Alex, Soothill, Keith and Walby, Sylvia (1980), 'Seducing the public by rape reports', *New Society*, pp. 214–15.

Hayden, Dolores (1981), *The Grand Domestic Revolution: a history of feminist designs for American homes, neighbourhoods, and cities* (Cambridge, Mass.: MIT Press).

Hearn, Jeff (1987), *The Gender Of Oppression: men, masculinity and the critique of Marxism* (Brighton: Wheatsheaf).

Hearn, Jeff and Parkin, Wendy (1987), *"Sex" at "Work": the power and paradox of organisation sexuality* (Brighton: Wheatsheaf).

Hernes, Helga Maria (1984), 'Women and the welfare state: the transition from private to public dependence', in *Patriarchy in a Welfare Society*, ed. Harriet Holter (Oslo: Universitetsforlaget), pp. 26–45.

Hite, Shere (1981), *The Hite Report: a nationwide study of female sexuality* (London: Corgi).

Holcombe, Lee (1973), *Victorian Ladies at Work: middle-class working women in England and Wales 1850–1914* (Newton Abbot: David and Charles).

—— (1983), *Wives and Property: reform of the married women's property law in nineteenth century England* (Oxford: Martin Robertson).

Hooks, Bell (1982), *Ain't I a Woman?* (London: Pluto Press).

—— (1984), *Feminist Theory: from margin to center* (Boston: South End Press).

Hudson, Barbara (1984), 'Femininity and adolescence', in *Gender and Generation*, ed. Angela McRobbie and Mica Nava (London: Macmillan).

Humphreys, Betty V. (1958), *Clerical Unions in the Civil Service* (Oxford: Blackwell and Mott).

Humphries, Jane (1977), 'Class struggle and the persistence of the working class family', *Cambridge Journal of Economics*, September.

Hutchins, Barbara L. (1915), *Women in Modern Industry* (London: G. Bell and Sons).

Irigaray, Luce (1985a), *Speculum of the Other Woman*, trans. Gillian Gill (Ithaca: Cornell University Press).

—— (1985b), *This Sex Which is Not One*, trans. Catherine Porter (Ithaca: Cornell University Press).

Jackson, Stevi (1978a), *On the Social Construction of Female Sexuality* (London: Women's Research and Resources Centre).

—— (1978b), 'The social context of rape: sexual scripts and motivation', *Women's Studies International Quarterly*, 1, 1, pp. 27–38.

James, Selma and Dalla Costa, Maria (1973), *The Power of Women and the Subversion of the Community* (Bristol: Falling Wall Press).

Jayawardena, Kumari (ed.) (1986), *Feminism and Nationalism in the Third World* (London: Zed Press).

Jeffreys, J. B. (1945), *The Story of the Engineers, 1800–1945* (reprinted 1970, New York: Johnson Reprint Corporation).

Jeffreys, Sheila (1985), *The Spinster and Her Enemies: feminism and sexuality 1880–1930* (London: Pandora).

Jessop, Bob (1982), *The Capitalist State* (Oxford: Martin Robertson).

John, Angela (1980), *By the Sweat of their Brow: women workers in Victorian coalmines* (London: Croom Helm).

Joseph, Gloria (1981), 'The incompatible menage à trois: Marxism, feminism and racism', in *Women and Revolution: the unhappy marriage of Marxism and feminism*, ed. Lydia Sargent (London: Pluto Press).

Juteau, Danielle and Laurin, Nicole (1986), 'Nuns in the labor force: a neglected contribution', *Feminist Issues*, fall, pp. 75–87.

Kandyoti, Deniz A. (1987), 'Emancipated but unliberated? Reflections on the Turkish case', *Feminist Studies*, 13, 2, summer, pp. 317–38.

Kanter, Rosabeth Moss (1977), *Men and Women of the Corporation* (New York: Basic Books).

Kappeler, Susanne (1986), *The Pornography of Representation* (Cambridge: Polity Press).

Kelly, Joan (1984), *Women, History and Theory: the essays of Joan Kelly* (Chicago: Chicago University Press).

Kelly, Liz (1988a), *Surviving Sexual Violence* (Cambridge: Polity Press).

—— (1988b), 'Talking about a revolution', *Spare Rib*, 193, August, pp. 8–11.

Kimmel, Michael (ed.) (1987), *Changing Men: new directions in researching men and masculinity* (London: Sage).

Kinsey, Alfred C., Pomeroy, Wardell, Martin, Clyde, and Gebhard, Paul (1953), *Sexual Behaviour in the Human Female* (Philadelphia: W. B. Saunders).

Kirkpatrick, Jeanne J. (1974), *Political Woman* (New York: Basic Books).

Koedt, Anne (1973), 'The myth of the vaginal orgasm', in *Radical Feminism*, ed. Anne Koedt, Ellen Levine and Anita Rapone (New York: Quadrangle).

Koonz, Claudia (1987), *Mothers in the Fatherland: women, the family and Nazi politics* (London: Methuen).

Kristeva, Julia (1986), *The Kristeva Reader*, ed. Toril Moi (Oxford: Blackwell).

Kuhn, Annette (1982), *Women's Pictures: feminism and cinema* (London: Routledge).

Lacan, Jacques (1977), *Ecrits: a selection*, trans. Alan Sheridan (London: Tavistock).

Land, H. (1976), 'Women: supporters or supported?', in *Sexual Divisions in Society: process and change*, ed. Sheila Allen and Diana Leonard Barker (London: Tavistock).

Lash, Scott and Urry, John (1987), *The End of Organized Capitalism* (Cambridge: Polity Press).

Laslett, Peter (1977), *Family Life and Illicit Love in Earlier Generations: essays in historical sociology* (Cambridge: Cambridge University Press).

Lawson, Annette and Samson, Colin (1988), 'Age, gender and adultery', *The British Journal of Sociology*, 39, 3, pp. 409–40.

Leacock, Eleanor and Safia, Helen I. (eds.) (1986), *Women's Work: development and the division of labor by gender* (South Hadley, Mass.: Bergin and Garvey).

Leeds Revolutionary Feminist Group (1981), 'Political lesbianism: the case against heterosexuality', in *Love Your Enemy? The debate between heterosexual feminism and political lesbianism* (London: Onlywomen Press).

Leeds TUCRIC (1983), *Sexual Harassment of Women at Work* (Leeds: TUCRIC).

Lees, Sue (1986), *Losing Out: sexuality and adolescent girls* (London: Hutchinson).

Lerner, Gerda (1986), *The Creation of Patriarchy* (New York: Oxford University Press).

Lewenhak, Sheila (1977), *Women and Trade Unions: an outline history of women in the British trade union movement* (London: Ernest Benn).

Lewis, Jane (1980), 'In search of real equality: women between the wars', in *Class, Culture and Social Change: a new view of the 1930s*, ed. Frank Gloversmith (Brighton: Harvester Press).

Lewis, Jane (ed.) (1983), *Women's Welfare, Women's Rights* (London: Croom Helm).

Liddington, Jill and Norris, Jill (1978), *One Hand Tied Behind Us: the rise of the women's suffrage movement* (London: Virago).

Lockwood, David, Goldthorpe, Hohn, Bechofer, Frank and Platt, Jennifer (1969), *The Affluent Worker in the Class Structure* (Cambridge: Cambridge University Press).

London Rape Crisis Centre (1984), *Sexual Violence: the reality for women* (London: Women's Press).

Lorber, Judith (1987), 'Couples experiences of *in vitro* fertilization', Paper presented to Third International Interdisciplinary Congress on Women (Dublin).

Lorde, Audre (1981), 'An Open letter to Mary Daly', in *This Bridge Called my Back: writings by radical women of colour*, ed. Cherrie Moraga and Gloria Azaldua (Watertown, Mass.: Persephone Press).

Luker, Kristin (1975), *Taking Chances: abortion and the decision not to contracept* (Berkeley: University of California Press).

—— (1984), *Abortion and the Politics of Motherhood* (Berkeley: University of California Press).

Lury, Celia (1990), *Cultural Industries: a political economy* (London: Routledge).

Lyotard, Jean-Francois (1978), *The Postmodern Condition: a report on knowledge* (Minneapolis: University of Minnesota Press).

McFarland, Alan (1978), *The Origins of English Individualism* (Oxford: Basil Blackwell).

McIntosh, Mary (1978), 'The state and the oppression of women', in *Feminism and Materialism: women and modes of production*, ed. Annette Kuhn and Anne Marie Wolpe (London: Routledge).

MacKay, D. I., Boddy, D., Brack, J., Diack, J. A. and Jones, N. (1971), *Labour Markets under Different Employment Conditions* (London: Allen and Unwin).

MacKinnon, Catharine (1979), *The Sexual Harassment of Working Women: a case of sex discrimination* (New Haven: Yale University Press).

—— (1982), 'Feminism, Marxism, method and the state: an agenda for theory', *Signs*, 7, 3, pp. 515–44.

—— (1987), *Feminism Unmodified: discourses on life and law* (Cambridge, Mass.: University of Harvard Press).

McLaren, Angus (1978), *Birth Control in Nineteenth Century England* (London: Croom Helm).

McRobbie, Angela and Nava, Mica (eds.) (1984), *Gender and Generation* (London: Macmillan).

Mainardi, Pat (1970), 'The Politics of housework', in *Sisterhood is Powerful: an anthology of writings from the women's liberation movement*, ed. Robin Morgan (New York: Vintage Books), pp. 447–54.

Malamuth, Neil (1981), 'Rape proclivity among males', *Journal of Social Issues*, 37, 4, pp. 138–57.

Malos, Ellen (ed.) (1980), *The Politics of Housework* (London: Allison and Busby).

Mana, Amina (1984), 'Black women, the economic crisis and the British state', *Feminist Review*, 17, pp. 21–35.

Manley, P. and Sawbridge, D. (1980), 'Women at Work', *Lloyds Bank Review*, pp. 29–40.

Mann, Michael (1986), *The Sources of Social Power*, vol. 1: *A History of Power from the Beginning to A.D. 1760* (Cambridge: Cambridge University Press).

Marcuse, Herbert (1969), *Eros and Civilisation* (London: Sphere).

Mark-Lawson, Jane, Savage, Mike and Warde, Alan (1985), 'Gender and local politics: struggles over welfare policies', in Lancaster Regionalism Group, *Localities, Class and Gender* (London: Pion).

Marks, Elaine and de Courtivron, Isabelle (eds.) (1981), *New French Feminisms* (Brighton: Harvester).

Marshall, Gordon, Newby, Howard, Rose, David and Vogler, Carolyn (1988), *Social Class in Modern Britain* (London: Hutchinson).

Marshall, John (1981), 'Pansies, perverts and macho men: changing conceptions of male homosexuality', in *The Making of the Modern Homosexual*, ed. Kenneth Plummer (London: Hutchinson), pp. 133–54.

Martin, Jean and Roberts, Ceridwen (1984), *Women and Employment: a lifetime perspective* (London: HMSO).

Martindale, Hilda (1938), *Women Servants of the State 1870–1938: a history of women in the civil service* (London: Allen and Unwin).

Marwick, Arthur (1968), *Britain in the Century of Total War: war, peace and social change, 1900–1967* (London: Bodley Head).

Marx, Karl (1954), *Capital*, vol. 1 (London: Lawrence and Wishart).

Massey, Doreen (1984), *Spatial Divisions of Labour: social structures and the geography of production* (London: Macmillan).

Massey, Doreen and Meegan, Richard (1982), *The Anatomy of Job Loss: the how, why and where of employment decline* (London: Macmillan).

Masson, Jeffrey M. (1984), *The Assault on Truth: Freud's suppression of the seduction theory* (New York: Penguin).

Masters, W. and Johnson, V. (1966), *Human Sexual Response* (Boston: Little Brown & Co.).

Middleton, Chris (1981), 'Peasants, patriarchy and the feudal mode of production in England', *Sociological Review*, 29, 1, pp. 105–54.

—— (1985), 'Women's labour and the transition to pre-industrial capitalism', in *Women and Work in Pre-Industrial England*, ed. Lindsey Charles and Lorna Duffin (London: Croom Helm).

—— (1988), 'Gender divisions and wage labour in English history', in *Gender Segregation at Work*, ed. Sylvia Walby (Milton Keynes: Open University Press).

Middleton, Lucy (ed.) (1978), *Women in the British Labour Movement* (London: Croom Helm).

Mies, Maria (1986), *Patriarchy and Accumulation on a World Scale: women in the international division of labour* (London: Zed Books).

Miles, Robert and Phizacklea, Annie (1980), *Labour and Racism* (London: Routledge).

Milkman, Ruth (1976), 'Women's work and economic crisis: some lessons of the Great Depression', *Review of Radical Political Economy*, 8, 1, spring.

Milliband, R. (1969), *The State in Capitalist Society* (London: Weidenfeld and Nicolson).

Millett, Kate (1977), *Sexual Politics* (London: Virago).

Mincer, Jacob (1962), 'Labour force participation of married women: a study of labour supply', in National Bureau of Economic Research, *Aspects of Labour Economics* (Princeton: Princeton University Press).

—— (1966), 'Labor-force participation and unemployment: a review of recent evidence', in *Prosperity and Unemployment*, ed. Robert Gordon and Margaret Gordon (New York: John Wiley).

Mincer, Jacob and Polachek, Solomon (1974), 'Family investments in human capital: earnings of women', *Journal of Political Economy*, 82, 2, S76–S108.

Mitchell, Juliet (1971), *Women's Estate* (Harmondsworth: Penguin).

—— (1975), *Psychoanalysis and Feminism* (Harmondsworth: Penguin).

Mitter, Swasti (1986), *Common Fate, Common Bond: women in the global economy* (London: Pluto Press).

Molyneux, Maxine (1979), 'Beyond the domestic labour debate', *New Left Review*, 116, pp. 3–27.

Moraga, Cherrie and Anzaldua, Gloria (eds.) (1981), *This Bridge Called my*

Back: writings by radical women of colour (Watertown, Mass.: Persephone Press).

Morrell, Caroline (1981), *'Black Friday' Violence Against Women in the Suffragette Movement* (London: Women's Research and Resources Centre).

Morris, Lydia (1984), 'Redundancy and patterns of household finance', *Sociological Review*, 32, 2, pp. 492–523.

—— (1985), 'Local social networks and domestic organisation: a study of redundant steelworkers and their wives', *Sociological Review*, 33, 2, pp. 327–42.

Murdock, G. P. (1959), *Social Structure* (New York: Macmillan).

Murgatroyd, Linda (1982), 'Gender and occupational stratification', *Sociological Review*, 30, 4.

Murray, Robin (1988), 'Life after Henry (Ford)', *Marxism Today*, October, pp. 8–13.

Myrdal, A. and Klein, V. (1970), *Women's Two Roles: home and work* (London: Routledge).

NEDO (1986), *Changing Working Patterns: how companies achieve flexibility to meet new needs* (London: NEDO).

Nelson, Sarah (1987), *Incest: fact and myth* (Edinburgh: Stramullion).

Newby, Howard (1982), *The State of Research into Social Stratification* (London: Social Science Research Council).

Oakley, Ann (1972), *Sex, Gender and Society* (London: Temple Smith).

—— (1974), *The Sociology of Housework* (Oxford: Martin Robertson).

—— (1976), *Housewife* (Harmondsworth: Penguin).

—— (1981), *From Here to Maternity: becoming a mother* (Harmondsworth: Penguin).

O'Brien, John E. (1975), 'Violence in divorce-prone families', in *Violence in the Family*, ed. Suzanne Steinmetz and Murray Straus (New York: Dodd, Mead and Co.).

OECD (1976), *The 1974–5 Recession and the Employment of Women* (Paris: Organisation for Economic Co-operation and Production).

Offe, Claus (1985), *Disorganized Capitalism: contemporary transformation of work and politics* (Cambridge: Polity Press).

Pahl, Jan (ed.) (1985), *Private Violence and Public Policy: the needs of battered women and the response of the public services* (London: Routledge).

Pahl, Ray E. (1984), *Divisions of Labour* (Oxford: Blackwell).

Pankhurst, Sylvia (1931), *The Suffragette Movement: an intimate account of persons and ideals* (London: Longman; reprinted 1977, Virago).

Parmar, Pratibha (1982), 'Gender, race and class: Asian women in resistance', in Centre for Contemporary Cultural Studies, University of Birmingham, *The Empire Strikes Back: race and racism in '70s Britain* (London: Hutchinson).

Parsons, Talcott and Bales, R. F. (1956), *Family Socialization and Interaction Process* (London: Routledge).

Pateman, Carole (1988), *The Sexual Contract* (Cambridge: Polity Press).

Perkin, Harold (1969), *The Origins of Modern English Society, 1780–1880* (London: Routledge).

Petchevsky, Rosalind Pollack (1986), *Abortion and Women's Choice: the state, sexuality and reproductive freedom* (London: Verso).

Phillips, Anne and Taylor, Barbara (1980), 'Sex and skill: notes towards a feminist economics', *Feminist Review*, 6, pp. 79–83.

Phizacklea, Annie (ed.) (1983), *One Way Ticket: migration and female labour* (London: Routledge).

Phizacklea, Annie (1988), 'Gender, racism and occupational segregation', in *Gender Segregation at Work*, ed. Sylvia Walby (Milton Keynes: Open University Press).

Phizacklea, Annie and Miles, Robert (1987), 'Racism and British trade unions', in *The Manufacture of Disadvantage*, ed. G. Lee and R. Loveridge (Milton Keynes: Open University Press).

Pinchbeck, Ivy (1930), *Women Workers and the Industrial Revolution, 1750–1850* (reprinted 1981, London: Virago).

Piore, Michael and Sable, Charles (1984), *The Second Industrial Divide: Possibilities for Prosperity* (New York: Basic Books).

Pizzey, Erin (1974), *Scream Quietly or the Neighbours Will Hear* (Harmondsworth: Penguin).

Plummer, Kenneth (1975), *Sexual Stigma: an interactionist account* (London: Routledge).

Plummer, Kenneth (ed.) (1981), *The Making of the Modern Homosexual* (London: Hutchinson).

Pollert, Anna (1987), *The 'Flexible Firm': a model in search of reality (or a policy in search of a practice?)*, Warwick Papers in Industrial Relations Number 19, University of Warwick.

Poulantzas, Nicos (1973), *Political Power and Social Classes* (London: New Left Books).

Randall, Vicky (1982), *Women and Politics* (London: Macmillan).

Raymond, Janice (1986), *A Passion for Friends: toward a philosophy of female affection* (London: Women's Press).

Reich, W. (1969), *The Sexual Revolution* (New York: Farrar, Strauss and Giroux).

Rex, John and Moore, Robert (1967), *Race, Community and Conflict: a study of Sparkbrook* (Oxford: Oxford University Press).

Rex, John and Tomlinson, Sally (1979), *Colonial Immigrants in a British City: a class analysis* (London: Routledge).

Rich, Adrienne (1977), *Of Woman Born: motherhood as experience and institution* (London: Virago).

—— (1980), 'Compulsory heterosexuality and lesbian existence', *Signs*, 5, 4, pp. 631–60.

Robinson, Olive (1988), 'The changing labour market: growth of part-time employment and labour market segmentation in Britain', in *Gender Segregation at Work*, ed. Sylvia Walby (Milton Keynes: Open University Press).

Rogers, Barbara (1981), *The Domestication of Women: discrimination in developing societies* (London: Tavistock).

Rosaldo, Michelle Zimbalist (1974), 'Woman, culture and society: a theoretical overview', in *Woman, Culture and Society*, ed. Michelle Zimbalist Rosaldo and Louise Lamphere (Stanford: Stanford University Press), pp. 17–42.

Rose, Hilary and Hanmer, Jalna (1976), 'Women's liberation, reproduction, and the technological fix', in *Sexual Divisions and Society: process and change*, ed. Sheila Allen and Diana Leonard Barkers (London: Tavistock).

Rose, Jacqueline (1983), 'Femininity and its discontents', *Feminist Review*, 14, pp. 5–21.

Rothman, Barbara Katz (1982), *In Labour: women and power in the workplace* (London: Junction Books).

Rowbotham, Sheila (1981), 'The trouble with "patriarchy"', in *No Turning Back: writings from the women's liberation movement 1975–1980*, ed. Feminist Anthology Collective (London: Women's Press).

Russell, Diana E. H. (1982), *Rape in Marriage* (New York: Macmillan).

—— (1984), *Sexual Exploitation: rape, child sexual abuse, and workplace harassment* (Beverly Hills, Calif.: Sage).

Saifullah-Khan, Verity (1976), '*Purdah* in the British situation', in *Dependence and Exploitation in Work and Marriage*, ed. Diana Leonard Barker and Sheila Allen (London: Longman).

Sayer, Andrew (1984), *Method in Social Science: a realist approach* (London: Hutchinson).

Schreiner, Olive (1918), *Woman and Labour* (London: Fisher Unwin).

Seccombe, Wally (1974), 'The housewife and her labour under capitalism', *New Left Review*, 83, pp. 3–24.

Segal, Lynne (1987), *Is the Future Female? Troubled thoughts on contemporary feminism* (London: Virago).

Sharpe, Sue (1976), '*Just Like a Girl*': how girls learn to be women (Harmondsworth: Penguin).

Shorter, Edward (1975), *The Making of the Modern Family* (New York: Basic Books).

—— (1984), *A History of Women's Bodies* (Harmondsworth: Pelican).

Showalter, Elaine (1978), *A Literature of their Own: British women novelists from Bronte to Lessing* (London: Virago).

Sklar, Kathryn Kish (1973), *Catherine Beecher: a study in American domesticity* (New York: Norton and Co.).

Smart, Carol (1984), *The Ties that Bind: law, marriage and the reproduction of patriarchal relations* (London: Routledge).

Smelser, Neil J. (1959), *Social Change in the Industrial Revolution: an application of theory to the Lancashire cotton industry* (London: Routledge).

Smith, Anthony D. (1973), *The Concept of Social Change: a critique of the functionalist theory of social change* (London: Routledge).

Smith, Dorothy (1988), *The Everyday World as Problematic: a feminist sociology* (Milton Keynes: Open University Press).

Smith, Harold L. (1984), 'The womanpower problem in Britain during the second world war', *The Historical Journal*, 27, 4, pp. 925–45.

Smith-Rosenberg, Carroll (1975), 'The female world of love and ritual: relations between women in 19th century America', *Signs*, 1, 1, pp. 1–29.

Soldon, Norbert (1978), *Women in British Trade Unions 1874–1976* (Dublin: Gill and Macmillan).

Soothill, Keith and Walby, Sylvia (1990), *Sex Crimes and the Media* (London: Routledge).

Spallone, Patricia and Steinberg, Deborah Lynn (eds.) (1987), *Made to Order: the myth of reproductive and genetic progress* (Oxford: Pergamon).

Spender, Dale (1980), *Man Made Language* (London: Routledge).

—— (1983), *Women of Ideas (and what men have done to them)* (London: Ark).

—— (1984), *There's Always Been a Women's Movement This Century* (London: Routledge).

Stanko, Elizabeth (1985), *Intimate Intrusions: women's experience of male violence* (London: Routledge).

—— (1988), 'Keeping women in and out of line: sexual harassment and occupational segregation', in *Gender Segregation at Work*, ed. Sylvia Walby (Milton Keynes: Open University Press).

Stanley, Liz and Wise, Sue (1983), *Breaking Out: feminist consciousness and feminist research* (London: Routledge).

Stanworth, Michelle (1983), *Gender and Schooling: a study of sexual divisions in the classroom* (London: Hutchinson).

—— (1984), 'Women and class analysis: a reply to John Goldthorpe', *Sociology*, 18, 2, pp. 159–70.

Stanworth, Michelle (ed.) (1987), *Reproductive Technologies: gender, motherhood and medicine* (Cambridge: Polity Press).

Stewart, A., Prandy, K. and Blackburn, R. M. (1980), *Social Stratification and Occupations* (London: Macmillan).

Stone, Lawrence (1977), *The Family, Sex and Marriage in England 1500–1800* (London: Weidenfeld).

Stopes, Marie (1981), *Dear Dr Stopes: sex in the 1920s*, ed. Ruth Hall (Harmondsworth: Penguin).

Strachey, Ray (1928), *The Cause: a short history of the women's movement in Great Britain* (London: G. Bell; reprinted 1978, Virago).

Straus, Murray, Gelles, Richard and Steinmetz, Suzanne (1980), *Behind Closed Doors* (New York: Anchor Press).

Summerfield, Penny (1984), *Women Workers in the Second World War* (London: Croom Helm).

Taylor, Barbara (1984), *Eve and the New Jerusalem: socialism and feminism in the nineteenth century* (London: Virago).

Taylor, John G. (1979), *From Modernisation to Modes of Production: a critique of the sociologies of development and underdevelopment* (London: Macmillan).

Tilly, Louise and Scott, Joan (1978), *Women, Work and Family* (New York: Holt, Reinhart and Winston).

Tolson, Andrew (1977), *The Limits of Masculinity* (London: Tavistock).

Treiman, Donald and Hartmann, Heidi (eds.) (1981), *Women, Work, and Wages: equal pay for jobs of equal value*, Committee on Occupational Classification and Analysis, Assembly of Behavioural and Social Sciences, National Research Council (Washington, DC: National Academy Press).

Tuchman, Gaye, Daniels, Arlene Kaplan and Benet, James (eds.) (1978), *Hearth and Home: images of women in the mass media* (New York: Oxford University Press).

Ungerson, Claire (1987), *Policy is Personal: sex, gender, and informal care* (London: Tavistock).

Urry, John (1981), *The Anatomy of Capitalist Societies: the economy, civil society and the state* (London: Macmillan).

Vance, Carole S. (ed.) (1984), *Pleasure and Danger: exploring female sexuality* (Boston: Routledge).

Vanek, Joann (1980), 'Time spent in housework', in *The Economics of Women and Work*, ed. Alice H. Amsden (Harmondsworth: Penguin).

Vicinus, Martha (1985), *Independent Women: work and community for single women, 1850–1920* (London: Virago).

Walby, Sylvia (1983a), 'Patriarchal structures: the case of unemployment', in *Gender, Class and Work*, ed. Eva Gamarnikow, David Morgan, June Purvis and Daphne Taylorson (London: Heinemann).

—— (1983b), 'Women's unemployment, patriarchy and capitalism', *Socialist Economic Review*, pp. 99–114.

—— (1985), 'Spatial and historical variations in women's unemployment', in Lancaster Regionalism Group, *Localities, Class and Gender* (London: Pion).

—— (1986), *Patriarchy at Work: patriarchal and capitalist relations in employment* (Cambridge: Polity Press).

—— (1989), 'Flexibility and the sexual division of labour', in *The Transformation of Work?*, ed. Stephen Wood (London: Unwin Hyman).

Walby, Sylvia, Hay, Alex and Soothill, Keith (1983), 'The social construction of rape', *Theory, Culture and Society*, 2, 1, pp. 86–98.

Walkowitz, Judith R. (1980), *Prostitution and Victorian Society: women, class and the state* (Cambridge: Cambridge University Press).

Wallace, Phyllis A. (1982), *Black Women in the Labor Force* (Cambridge, Mass.: MIT Press).

Wallerstein, Immanuel (1979), *The Capitalist World Economy* (Cambridge: Cambridge University Press).

Weber, Max (1947), *The Theory of Social and Economic Organisation* (New York: Free Press).

Weedon, Chris (1987), *Feminist Practice and Poststructuralist Theory* (Oxford: Blackwell).

Weeks, Jeffrey (1977), *Coming Out* (London: Quadrangle).

—— (1981), *Sex, Politics and Society: the regulation of sexuality since 1880* (London: Longman).

Weir, Angela and McIntosh, Mary (1982), 'Towards a wages strategy for women', *Feminist Review*, 10, pp. 55–72.

Weitzman, Leonore J. (1985), *The Divorce Revolution: the unexpected social and economic consequences for women and children in America* (New York: Free Press).

West, D. J., Roy, C. and Nichols, F. L. (1978), *Understanding Sexual Attacks* (London: Heinemann).

West, Jackie (1978), 'Women, sex and class', in *Feminism and Materialism:*

women and modes of production, ed. Annette Kuhn and AnnMarie Wolpe (London: Routledge).

Westwood, Sallie (1984), *All Day, Every Day: factory and family in the making of women's lives* (London: Pluto Press).

Wilson, Deirdre (1978), 'Sexual codes and conduct: a study of teenage girls', in *Women, Sexuality and Social Control*, ed. Carol Smart and Barry Smart (London: Routledge).

Wilson, Elizabeth (1983a), 'The context of "Between pleasure and danger": the Barnard conference on sexuality', *Feminist Review*, 13, pp. 35–41.

Wilson, Elizabeth (1983b), *What Is to Be Done About Violence Against Women?* (Harmondsworth: Penguin).

Wilson, Gail (1987), *Money in the Family: financial organisation and women's responsibility* (Aldershot: Avebury).

Winship, Janice (1985), '"A girl needs to be street-wise": magazines for the 1980s', *Feminist Review*, 21, pp. 25–46.

Witz, Anne (1987), *'The Spider Legislating for the Fly': patriarchy and occupational closure in the medical division of labour 1858–1940*, Unpublished PhD thesis, Department of Sociology, University of Lancaster.

—— (1988), 'Patriarchal relations and patterns of sex segregation in the medical division of labour', in *Gender Segregation at Work*, ed. Sylvia Walby (Milton Keynes: Open University Press).

Women's Studies International Quarterly (1980) 3, 1: special issue on 'Women and Media', ed. Helen Baehr.

Wood, Stephen (ed.) (1982), *The Degradation of Work? Skill, deskilling and the labour process* (London: Hutchinson).

Young, Iris (1981), 'Beyond the unhappy marriage: a critique of dual systems theory', in *Women and Revolution: the unhappy marriage of Marxism and feminism*, ed. Lydia Sargent (London: Pluto Press).

Young, Michael and Willmott, Peter (1975), *The Symmetrical Family: a study of work and leisure in the London region* (Harmondsworth: Penguin).

Zaretsky, Eli (1976), *Capitalism, the Family and Personal Life* (London: Pluto Press).

Zimmerman, Don and West, Candace (1975), 'Sex roles, interruptions and silences in conversation', in *Language and Sex: difference and dominance*, ed. Barrie Thorne and Nancy Henley (Rowley, Mass.: Newbury House), pp. 105–29.

Index